THE
ACTIVE ASSET
ALLOCATOR

THE
ACTIVE ASSET
ALLOCATOR

HOW ETFS
CAN SUPERCHARGE
YOUR PORTFOLIO

JENNIFER WOODS

PORTFOLIO

PORTFOLIO
Published by the Penguin Group
Penguin Group (USA) Inc., 375 Hudson Street,
New York, New York 10014, U.S.A.
Penguin Group (Canada), 90 Eglinton Avenue East, Suite 700,
Toronto, Ontario, Canada M4P 2Y3
(a division of Pearson Penguin Canada Inc.)
Penguin Books Ltd, 80 Strand, London WC2R 0RL, England
Penguin Ireland, 25 St. Stephen's Green, Dublin 2, Ireland
(a division of Penguin Books Ltd)
Penguin Books Australia Ltd, 250 Camberwell Road, Camberwell,
Victoria 3124, Australia
(a division of Pearson Australia Group Pty Ltd)
Penguin Books India Pvt Ltd, 11 Community Centre, Panchsheel Park,
New Delhi – 110 017, India
Penguin Group (NZ), 67 Apollo Drive, Rosedale, North Shore 0632,
New Zealand (a division of Pearson New Zealand Ltd)
Penguin Books (South Africa) (Pty) Ltd, 24 Sturdee Avenue,
Rosebank, Johannesburg 2196, South Africa

Penguin Books Ltd, Registered Offices:
80 Strand, London WC2R 0RL, England

First published in 2009 by Portfolio,
a member of Penguin Group (USA) Inc.

1   3   5   7   9   10   8   6   4   2

Publisher's Note
This publication is designed to provide accurate and authoritative information in regard to the
subject matter covered. It is sold with the understanding that the publisher is not engaged in
rendering legal, accounting, or other professional services. If you require legal advice or other
expert assistance, you should seek the services of a competent professional.

LIBRARY OF CONGRESS CATALOGING IN PUBLICATION DATA
Woods, Jennifer.
The active asset allocator : how ETFs can supercharge your portfolio / Jennifer Woods.
p. cm.
Includes index.
ISBN 978-1-59184-195-1
1. Exchange traded funds.   2. Asset allocation.   I. Title.
HG6043.W66 2010
332.63'27—dc22   2009031632

Printed in the United States of America
Set in Baskerville
Designed by Pauline Neuwirth

Contents

Introduction

by Bruce Bond,

CEO of Invesco PowerShares Capital Management LLC

Whether you are a money management novice, seasoned investor, or financial professional, over the past few years you've probably heard the buzz about exchange-traded funds (ETFs). Lately, it seems that ETFs are popping up everywhere—while you are watching CNBC, reading *The Wall Street Journal*, talking to your financial adviser, or even in casual conversations with friends. So what's behind the buzz?

ETFs are unique products that combine characteristics of index-based mutual funds and individual stocks. Like index funds, they represent baskets of securities such as stocks and bonds, which means that a single share of an ETF can provide immediate diversification. Like stocks, ETFs trade on an exchange throughout the day, and this provides a variety of benefits that you will learn about in this book.

The first ETF to trade on a U.S. exchange was introduced in 1993. Although they took a few years to gain traction, ETFs are now being used regularly by growing numbers of individual investors, financial advisers, and large institutions. They have several applications that make them attractive to a wide range of investors. For example, ETFs can be used as core portfolio holdings or provide targeted exposure to many attractive asset classes. They also can increase tax efficiency, flexibility, and transparency while reducing investment complexity and costs.

ETFs' appeal to investors continues to grow as the menu of available options keeps expanding. According to the Investment Company Institute, more than seven hundred ETFs currently trade in the United States—hundreds more trade abroad—and they have diverse objectives and investment applications. Some are designed to provide exposure to specialized segments of the stock market while others track asset classes such as bonds, commodities, and currencies. ETFs can be used to create entire portfolios or to fill specific niche needs for additional portfolio diversification.

While choosing the right product can have a major impact on your portfolio, it is only one part of a sound investment-planning process. Anyone who has taken Finance 101 knows that regardless of the products you use, the way that you allocate your investments among asset classes will have a major impact on portfolio performance and risk exposure. That's why a solid asset allocation strategy should be the foundation for any portfolio. This book offers guidelines that can help you determine an appropriate level of risk and then design a diversified program tailored to your risk tolerance. It also discusses the importance of generating incremental returns, and the ways that ETFs can help with this task.

Since the founding of our firm in early 2003 as PowerShares Capital Management LLC, our mission has been to start with the inherent benefits of ETFs, and then to take them to the next level by creating innovations with value for investors. When we first entered the market, ETFs were limited to replicating basic passive indexes, most of which selected index components based on their market capitalization. I am proud to say that our firm, and the ETF industry as a whole, has had an open-minded attitude toward innovations that empower consumers and enable smart investing. In May of 2003, Invesco PowerShares introduced our first two "Intelligent ETFs" based on innovative new Intellidex indexes of the American Stock Exchange. These indexes attempt to outperform industry averages through intelligent security selection and weighting. In this book, you will learn about these innovations and many others that the ETF industry has created in recent years. You also will gain a better understanding of how to use dynamic new ETF concepts in your investment planning.

In 2005, Invesco PowerShares began an aggressive expansion, launching more than thirty new ETFs in that year alone, the most of any sponsor that year. Of course, this contributed to an ongoing expansion in the universe of ETF choices. While the growing number of ETF choices works to investors' advantage, it also creates complexities in evaluating options.

Fortunately, the author of this book, Jennifer Woods, offers methods and advice that I believe are helpful and practical. More important, her insights seek to help you create a sound planning framework that will continue to guide your total investment planning (and specific ETF decisions) over time.

In the years ahead, I believe the entire ETF industry will keep growing and changing. While ETFs based on conventional benchmark indexes will remain a big part of the industry, I expect the idea of adding value through innovative indexing concepts will continue to evolve and be accepted by more investors.

I believe this book will not only put you on a path to a better understanding of how ETFs can enhance your portfolio, but will also motivate you to take advantage of their many benefits. Along with sound professional guidance, a disciplined asset allocation program, and a patient attitude, this book has the potential to help you become a more informed and confident investor.

THE
ACTIVE ASSET
ALLOCATOR

1

Divide and Conquer

When it comes to establishing an investment portfolio, there are few conventions that have stood the test of time. One of the most important, perhaps, is that having a strong asset allocation is among the most essential decisions an investor can make. Asset allocation is the process of diversifying assets among varied types of investments in order to create a portfolio that will deliver the necessary returns while not taking on too much investment risk. Whatever an investor's financial goals are—buying a house, saving for retirement, sending kids to college—developing a sound asset allocation strategy is the most effective way to begin the path to those goals. This chapter will discuss the importance of diversification and varied ways to do it, from creating a portfolio that is broadly distributed among the core asset classes of stocks, bonds, and cash to more advanced asset allocation techniques that include more strategic investments and alternative asset classes.

• DIVERSIFICATION •

One of the most important components of creating a well-allocated portfolio is diversification—the process of dividing assets between different investment categories. Investors also could consider it dividing their eggs into several baskets: Every investment tool, be it stocks, bonds, cash, or alternative assets, carries some level of risk, and putting assets into different investment baskets spreads out that risk. That makes a portfolio less volatile—it will have fewer variations in its investment returns. Over time, lower volatility also can lead to more consistent results. Because of its simplicity and effectiveness, in the financial community diversification is often referred to as "the only free lunch."

The most basic diversified portfolio should, at a minimum, include three broad asset classes: stocks, bonds, and cash. But a well-diversified portfolio should also be varied *within* those asset classes. This means investing in a range of different stocks and bonds. Alternative asset classes—which include real estate, hedge funds, currencies, venture capital, private equity, and commodities—can also increase a portfolio's diversification. Some alternative asset classes aren't necessarily appropriate for all investors, but we'll get into that later on.

• THE CORE ASSET CLASSES •

Stocks, bonds, and cash are considered the core asset classes. Stocks, or equities, represent ownership in a company. When shares of a stock are bought, the purchaser literally becomes an owner of a piece of that company. Bonds are debt investments, like IOUs, that a company or other entity sells to investors when they need to generate capital. The issuer of the bonds (the debtor) promises to repay the bondholder the loan principal plus interest payable periodically at the bond's "coupon rate." While investors who purchase stock in a company become equity owners and are able to share in the future profits of the company, investors who purchase bonds become creditors. This does not entitle them to share in future profits the same way as equity investors; however, it does mean that in the event the company goes bankrupt, bondholders will be reimbursed their investment before stockholders. Cash can mean the obvious—the dollar bills carried in everyone's pockets, perhaps withdrawn from a savings or checking account. But in an investment portfolio, the term includes "cash equivalents," such as money market funds and Treasury Bills. These instruments are considered cash because they are relatively safe, and in a pinch they can be liquidated quickly, easily, and economically.

One of the biggest differences among the three core asset classes is their volatility, or the extent to which their returns have bounced around over time. Investments that have had fairly consistent returns over time, with small fluctuations around their average (or mean) return, are low volatility investments. In such investments, it is assumed that if future price fluctuations remain consistent with the past, then future performance will be relatively easy to predict. These generally appeal to investors with low risk tolerance. Conversely, investments with returns that experience sharp increases and declines over time are exhibiting higher volatility, which makes it more difficult to predict future performance. As a result, these investments are considered riskier and appeal to investors with a greater risk tolerance. One statistical measurement that is often used to measure volatility is standard deviation, which measures the dispersion of returns around the mean. Less-volatile securities have lower standard deviations, while more-volatile securities have higher standard deviations. While investments with lower volatility typically pose less risk, they often produce lower returns than more-volatile, higher-risk investments. In other words, investors who take on more risk (higher volatility) should eventually be compensated with greater returns. This trend can be seen by looking at the historical volatility and returns of each of the core asset classes.

Stocks are generally the most volatile of the three broad asset classes. But over time, they also have demonstrated an ability to produce higher returns. Bonds are generally less volatile than stocks. To compensate, they also tend to have more muted returns than stocks. Cash and cash equivalents are by far the least volatile of the three broad classes. Returns for cash are the steadiest, but also by far the most modest in size. Because it is such a safe investment, cash is often referred to as a risk-free asset, though as the market of 2008 proved—when the Reserve Primary money market fund dipped below $1—that is not always the case.

For most investors, being well diversified does not require a big cash position in a portfolio. In fact, for most investors generally, having about 5 percent to 10 percent of their assets in cash is enough. However, during times where the market is very volatile, investors often increase their cash position to reduce risk exposure. The following figure illustrates the annual variations in both volatility and total returns for the three broad asset classes for the period 1985 through 2007. Note the more dramatic highs and lows that stocks experienced during this period, compared to the more stable returns and lower volatility of bonds, which almost never reach the same levels as stocks on the upside or the downside. The very steady performance of T-Bills can also be seen.

Figure 1.1: Annual Returns: Stocks, Ten-Year Treasury Bonds, and T-Bills

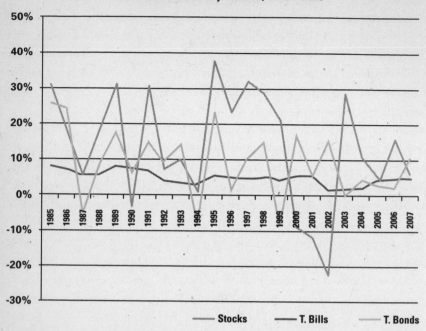

SOURCE: DATA BASED ON FEDERAL RESERVE DATABASE

Because these three core asset classes have varying levels of risk and return potential, they tend to respond differently to economic developments, changes in the political landscape, and other factors that impact the market, such as inflation and corporate earnings. This often creates a seesaw relationship between them, whereby in many cases, when stocks rise, bonds fall, and vice versa. For example, during periods where interest rates are on the rise, bonds (particularly longer-term bonds) generally perform poorly. That's because as interest rates rise, new bonds come to market that carry a higher yield, making older bonds relatively less valuable. During these times, however, stocks often perform well, because rising interest rates are often an indication that the economy is strong. (The Federal Reserve, which controls short-term interest rates, increases rates to cool off strong economic growth.) But not *all* stocks perform well during rising interest rate periods. Some stocks are more sensitive to increases in interest rates and as a result don't tend to do well during these times. Stocks in the financial and utility sectors in particular often fall into this category.

• THE RISK/REWARD TRADE-OFF •

The divergent relationship that occurs between stocks and bonds can be seen by looking at their performance in the period from 1989 to 2007. One way to measure this relationship is by comparing the performance of the S&P 500 Index of stocks to the Lehman Brothers Aggregate Bond Index. The S&P 500 consists of five hundred of the largest stocks in the United States as measured by their market capitalizations (the current market price of shares multiplied by the number of shares outstanding). The Lehman Brothers Aggregate Bond Index measures the performance of a large quantity of investment-grade bonds trading in the United States. It includes liquid issues of government bonds, corporate bonds, and asset-backed securities. The figure below shows the relationship between these two indexes. The performance of the Lehman Aggregate index remained relatively consistent over time, fluctuating between gains of nearly 20 percent and losses of less than 5 percent. Meanwhile, the S&P 500 exhibited substantially higher returns during certain periods and

Figure 1.2: Annual Returns for S&P 500 Index versus the Lehman Brothers Aggregate Bond Index

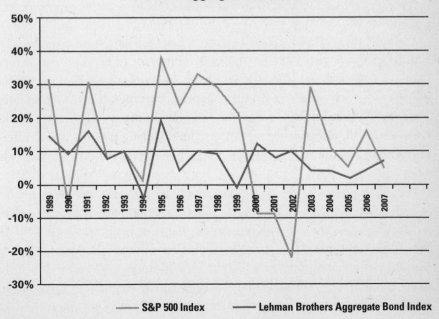

SOURCE: CALLAN ASSOCIATES

substantially greater losses during others, generating returns greater than 35 percent and losses of more than 20 percent depending on the year.

Because this relationship exists between stocks and bonds, it is important to include both in a portfolio to help balance out the risk inherent in each separate asset class. By creating a portfolio with a large allocation to riskier investments, such as stocks, investors may have more potential for long-term returns. But since they are also taking on a lot more risk, they will need to be able to weather major drops in their portfolios. That is why, if the stock market is going through a tough period, having exposure to bonds can often help to soften the blow. On the other hand, if an investor has a portfolio that is more heavily invested in conservative assets such as bonds and cash, which have less return potential, it may not be able to generate enough return to meet his long-term financial objectives. Each investor's asset allocation should depend on the amount of risk he wants to take on in his portfolio, a subject discussed later in this book.

•DIVERSIFYING INVESTMENTS •

In addition to diversifying broadly between stocks, bonds, and cash, it is also important to diversify among varied types of stocks and bonds within a portfolio. For this purpose, the stock market can be segmented in several different ways. For example, stocks can be categorized according to their market capitalization, which is a measure of their size, or market value. Using market cap, stocks can be divided into various categories, including: megacaps, which are generally valued at more than $100 billion; large caps, which are typically between $10 billion and $100 billion (though megacaps are often grouped with large caps); midcaps, which generally include stocks valued between $2 billion and $10 billion; small caps, valued between $300 million and $2 billion; and microcap ETFs, typically valued at less than $300 million.

Stocks also can be grouped together according to their style, which takes into account whether they have more growth or value features, which will be discussed shortly; by geography, which refers to the country or region they represent; or by the economic sector that they provide exposure to, such as finance, technology, or health care. Most well-diversified portfolios are, at a minimum, diversified among the first three categories, thereby including in their portfolios stocks of a variety of sizes, styles, and geographies. Investors with larger portfolios also may wish to diversify by investing in narrower segments of the market, such as those representing different economic sectors. This type of investing can increase risk exposure, so depending on the investor's risk tolerance and total assets, these investments may account for a smaller portion of his or her portfolio.

The bond market also can be divided into varied segments. For instance, bond investments can be allocated among different bond issuers, such as government issues and corporate entities. Bonds also vary by the amount of time remaining until they mature, how they are taxed, and their credit quality.

Diversifying among types of stocks and bonds can help to increase portfolio diversification and spread risk even more, which can result in lower portfolio volatility and smoother returns over time. The reason this works is due largely to the cyclicality of the market. Recall the seesaw relationship between stocks and bonds that caused them to react differently to various catalysts. The same relationship often occurs between different types of investments. This means that at times one segment will generally outperform another, and then the trend will often reverse. Studying the historic performance of large and small cap stocks can be useful for understanding this principle.

Large versus Small

Large cap stocks are generally less risky than small caps because the large cap universe consists of more mature and established companies that are able to weather big swings in the economy. Large cap stocks also tend to be more liquid, which means that it is easier to find investors willing to buy or sell shares at any time. Small cap stocks are more risky because they are generally less established companies and more likely to be affected by downturns in the economy or market. Small caps are also less liquid. That means, if it is necessary to sell a small cap stock quickly, it can be difficult to receive an attractive price because fewer investors stand willing to buy the shares.

Because of these different characteristics, the performances of large caps and small caps are often conflicting. This can be seen in a chart comparing the large cap–focused S&P 500 Index with the Russell 2000 Index, which represents the two thousand smallest stocks in the broad-market Russell 3000 Index. Looking at the performance of these indexes from 1989 through 2007 in Figure 1.3, it can be seen how these two equity asset classes performed in different market cycles. The graph illustrates the annual performances of these indexes. Notice how in both 1992 and again in 2004, small caps had periods of strong outperformance compared with large cap stocks. However, between 1995 and 1998, the performance of large caps was substantially superior to that of small caps.

Figure 1.3: Annual Performance of Small Caps versus Large Caps

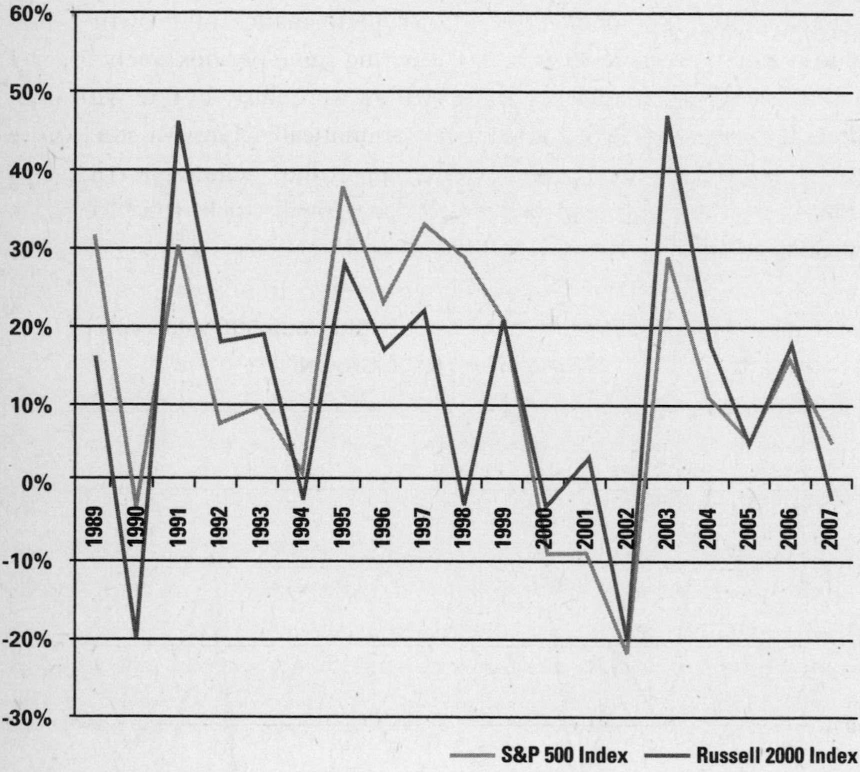

SOURCE: CALLAN ASSOCIATES

Value versus Growth

Value and growth stocks are often impacted by market cycles also. There are no definitive criteria to distinguish between these two styles of investing. Generally, though, value stocks have higher average dividend payouts. They also tend to be less expensive than growth stocks when they are evaluated using metrics such as price-to-earnings ratio (P/E), which is calculated by dividing the current market price of a stock by its annual earnings per share, and price-to-book ratio (P/B), which is a ratio of a company's book value to its market value. Growth stocks, on the other hand, have generally exhibited faster than average gains in earnings over several years and are expected to continue to show high levels of profit growth. Typically, growth stocks are more volatile than value stocks, as they often make little or no dividend payments to shareholders and tend to exhibit a higher price-to-earnings ratio.

The graph below depicts the annual performance of growth versus value stocks between 1989 and 2007. During some periods, such as 1994 to 1997, the performances of these indexes were fairly in line with each other. However, in 1998 that changed dramatically: Growth stocks rose more than 40 percent as value stocks dipped into negative territory. In 2000, there was another trend reversal, as growth stocks tumbled more than 20 percent while value managed to rise 6 percent.

Figure 1.4: Annual Performance of S&P/Citigroup 500 Value versus S&P/Citigroup 500 Growth

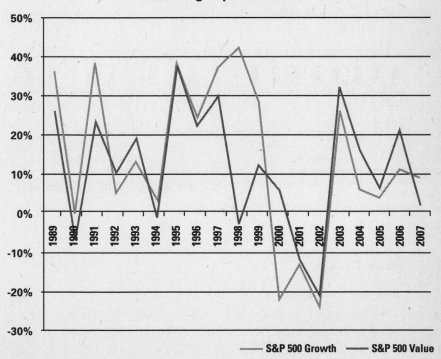

SOURCE: CALLAN ASSOCIATES

• DIVERSIFYING INTERNATIONALLY •

Diversifying a portfolio internationally is also important. Until about a decade ago, portfolios of most U.S. investors were heavily concentrated in domestic securities. By offering access to the world's dominant economy, the United States, and many of its most respected companies, U.S. financial markets met the diverse needs of individual and institutional investors alike. Then, gradually but with great momentum, the global investment revolution of the twenty-first century began, driven by many developments, including the birth of the euro as a powerful new currency. Currently, investors that are well diversified dedicate a sizable portion of their portfolio to non-U.S. investments, particularly international stocks.

The international stock market can be divided broadly into three groups: stocks of companies based in developed countries, which are included in the Morgan Stanley Capital International Europe, Australasia, and Far East (MSCI EAFE) Index; stocks of companies based in the BRIC countries (Brazil, Russia, India, and China); and stocks of companies located in various emerging markets. It can be seen how the different countries are categorized in the list below.

TABLE 1.1: INTERNATIONAL STOCK MARKET

DEVELOPED FOREIGN MARKETS	BRIC EMERGING MARKETS	OTHER SIGNIFICANT EMERGING MARKETS
Australia	Brazil	Argentina
Austria	Russia	Chile
Belgium	India	Colombia
Denmark	China	Czech Republic
Finland		Hungary
France		Indonesia
Germany		Israel
Greece		Jordan
Hong Kong		Malaysia
Ireland		Mexico
Italy		Peru

DEVELOPED FOREIGN MARKETS	BRIC EMERGING MARKETS	OTHER SIGNIFICANT EMERGING MARKETS
Japan		The Philippines
The Netherlands		Poland
New Zealand		South Africa
Norway		South Korea
Portugal		Taiwan
Singapore		Thailand
Spain		Turkey
Sweden		
Switzerland		
UK		

SOURCE: POWERSHARES

Of the three lists, the BRICs clearly represent the fewest countries—just four. Yet they will be a powerful force in driving future growth. According to the United Nations, the four BRIC nations recently had a combined population of 2.8 billion people, representing 42.5 percent of the earth's total population. By 2050, their combined population will have increased to 3.7 billion. In general, the world's population balance is expected to dramatically shift over about the next forty years, as emerging markets grow larger and some developed markets shrink.

India alone will contribute 19 percent of the world's expected population growth through 2050. China, currently the most populous country in the world with 1.3 billion people, will grow modestly in the decades ahead due to government-enforced limits on family size. The UN expects that India will surpass China as the world's most populous country in about 2025.

In terms of economic growth, the BRICs will drive gross domestic product (GDP) output for the next several decades. According to Goldman Sachs's research, at the start of 2000 the BRICs' share of world GDP was just 9 percent, and this share could increase to 30 percent by 2025 and to nearly 50 percent by 2050. As the pace of globalization quickens, it is becoming clearer that U.S. investors who do not participate in international opportunities may be limiting their exposure to the highest rates of future economic growth.

While some investors may believe that investing in only the United

States is more familiar and perhaps safer, investing abroad actually can offer attractive returns while increasing portfolio diversification, which also can reduce risk. This can be seen by evaluating the historic performance of some well-known international indexes. Take the Morgan Stanley Capital International Europe, Australasia, and Far East Index, for example. This index tracks public securities trading in twenty large developed markets outside North America. It can be seen in the chart below that from 1989 to 1992 the MSCI EAFE Index underperformed the S&P 500, followed by a brief reversal in 1993 and 1994. It underperformed almost every year between 1995 and 2001; however, it rebounded in 2002 and continued to outperform through 2007. From 2005 to 2007 it was actually one of the best performing equity categories.

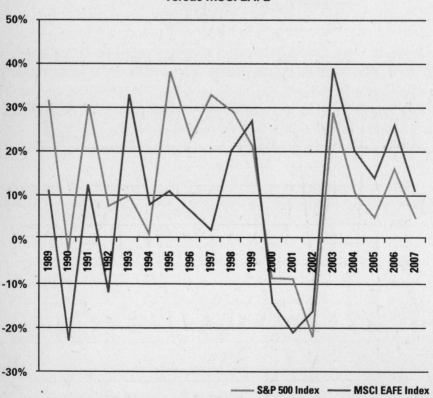

Figure 1.5: Annual Performance of S&P 500 Index versus MSCI EAFE

SOURCE: CALLAN ASSOCIATES

To diversify even more widely around the world, investments in emerging markets, which are excluded from MSCI EAFE, can be included. The MSCI Emerging Markets Free Index tracks the performance of twenty-five emerging markets: Argentina, Brazil, Chile, China, Colombia, the Czech Republic, Egypt, Hungary, India, Indonesia, Israel, Jordan, Korea, Malaysia, Mexico, Morocco, Pakistan, Peru, the Philippines, Poland, Russia, South Africa, Taiwan, Thailand, and Turkey.

Because of the nature of this index, it is significantly more volatile than the MSCI EAFE Index. However, it has also had impressive performance. The graph below shows the annual performance of the index from 1989 to 2007 compared with the S&P 500 Index. Notice the significant outperformance of emerging markets between 1989 and 1993. Between 1994 and

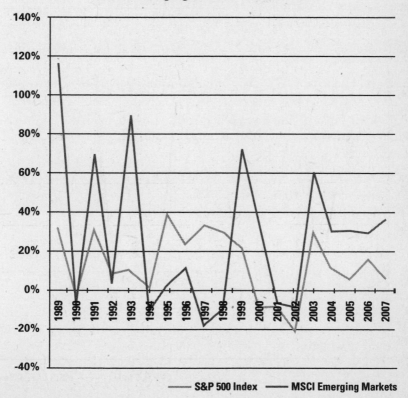

Figure 1.6: Cumulative Performance of the S&P 500 versus MSCI Emerging Markets: 1998 to 2007

S&P 500 Index   MSCI Emerging Markets

SOURCE: CALLAN ASSOCIATES

1998, there was a major reversal, though from 1999 on emerging markets once again continued to outperform.

• SECTORS AND COUNTRIES •

Another way to increase the level of diversification within a portfolio is to invest in smaller segments of the stock market, such as sectors. Standard & Poor's divides the U.S. economy into ten basic economic sectors: consumer discretionary; consumer staples; energy; financials; health care; industrials; materials; information technology; utilities; and telecommunications. Below is a description of each sector, including a description of the type of companies that the sector encompasses, and some examples of companies that fall into each sector. For each sector, I have also included in parentheses its weight in the S&P 500 Index as of September 2008.

► **Consumer Discretionary** (8.5 percent) includes companies that make or sell clothing, restaurants, automobiles, hotels, and leisure companies. Some examples of consumer discretionary stocks are Walt Disney, McDonald's, and Starbucks.

► **Consumer Staples** (12.2 percent) includes companies involved in making nondiscretionary, essential consumer products such as food, beverages, and household products. Some examples of companies in the consumer staples sector are Procter & Gamble, Kraft Foods, and Coca-Cola.

► **Energy** (13.4 percent) includes companies that provide energy or energy-related services. ExxonMobil and Chevron are examples of stocks in the energy sector.

► **Financials** (15.9 percent) includes stocks from varied areas of finance, such as investment management and commercial banking. Companies in this sector include Citigroup and Bank of America.

► **Health Care** (13.1 percent) includes companies that provide health care services, such as pharmaceuticals, health insurance, and medical equipment or supplies. Pfizer and Johnson & Johnson fall into this sector.

► **Industrials** (11.1 percent) includes companies in the aerospace and defense industries and those involved in construction, electrical equipment, and building products, among others. General Electric and Boeing are examples of companies in this sector.

▶ **Materials** (3.4 percent) includes companies involved in areas such as packaging, paper products, metals, mining, and chemicals. Companies in this category include Alcoa and Dow Chemical.

▶ **Information Technology** (16 percent) includes companies that create software, engage in information technology services, or are involved with semiconductors, computers, technology hardware, the Internet, or related areas. Microsoft, Intel, and IBM fit into this sector.

▶ **Utilities** (3.6 percent) includes companies that are involved in water, electricity, and natural gas. Companies such as PG&E and Duke Energy are represented here.

▶ **Telecommunications** (3.1 percent) includes companies that are involved in providing phone and cellular service and telecommunications hardware. Examples include AT&T and Verizon.

Diversifying among different sectors can be a good addition to a portfolio. However, investing in sectors can be more or less risky depending in part on the tools used to get exposure to these investments.

• ALTERNATIVES •

For many investors, it also may make sense to diversify with alternative asset classes, as this is a way to increase exposure to many attractive areas of the global economy. Alternative asset classes include real estate, commodities, currencies, hedge funds, and private equity, to name a few. Investing in alternative asset classes is a way of increasing diversification, which can help lower the volatility of a portfolio. The following are some commonly held alternative investments:

▶ **Private Equity.** This is an investment in a company or entity that is not publicly offered or traded. Most of the holdings of private equity funds consist of equity securities, although some holdings may be debt or convertible instruments. Some private equity firms specialize in new companies that have not yet gone public, while others identify opportunities to take public companies private, often in leveraged buyout (LBO) transactions. A few leading private equity fund managers have listed their own stocks for public consumption, and this has expanded access to this asset class.

- ► **Venture Capital.** This is a type of private equity in which money is often invested in small start-up businesses on the bet that they will have good future growth. Usually the investment provides capital to help the business run in the early stages until it is able to develop a good revenue stream. Many leading technology-related companies, such as Google (Ticker symbol GOOG), began with venture capital support.
- ► **Hedge Funds.** These are funds that use sophisticated investment strategies in the hopes of generating high returns. They generally require very high minimum investments and are only available to a limited number of qualified investors. A common fee structure for hedge funds is "2 and 20." This means that they charge investors an annual management fee of 2 percent and then take an additional 20 percent of investment profits. Most hedge funds are not registered publicly, and therefore they are not allowed to market or advertise to the public.
- ► **Real Estate.** Investments in real estate can include direct investments in residential or commercial properties. They also can participate in real estate investment trusts (REIT), which are trusts that invest in diversified portfolios of real estate through ownership of properties or mortgages. REITs have certain tax advantages for investors.
- ► **Commodities.** This category includes precious metals, base metals, energy products (such as oil and gasoline), as well as livestock and agricultural products. A traditional way to participate in commodities is through an account that lets an investor trade futures contracts. (Futures contracts allow the purchase or sale of a set quantity of a commodity on a future date, at a price determined when the contract is purchased.) Increasingly, though, other products are coming to market that allow investors to trade baskets of commodities or participate in commodity futures contracts without having to open a futures account. This will be covered later in the book.

Not all alternative asset classes are appropriate for all investors, in part because their performance can be volatile or unpredictable. Investors should proceed into alternative assets cautiously. The idea of investing in alternative asset classes has been gaining traction over the last few years. Institutions—particularly pension funds and university endowments—have long been using alternative assets for a portion of their investments, and this part has been increasing lately. The endowments of some major universities such as Yale, Stanford, and Harvard have become visible in the financial media as acknowledged users of alternative assets. Many other universities have been ramping up their use of alternatives also. A study by the National Association of College and University Business Officers (NACUBO) and Teachers Insurance and Annuity Association–College Retirement Equities Fund (TIAA-CREF) found that among college and university endowments, "allocations to traditional asset classes have declined 1 to 2 percentage points a year over the past ten years. Meanwhile the portion of investments in asset classes other than equities and fixed income has more than tripled, rising from 5.4 percent to 17.3 percent of investment portfolios."

The table below shows that the average allocation of university endowments in certain alternative asset classes increased notably between 1997 and 2006. A prominent example is investment in private equity, which increased a whopping 533 percent!

TABLE 1.2: AVERAGE ALLOCATION TO SELECTED ASSET CLASSES FROM 1997 TO 2006

ASSET CLASS	1997 ALLOCATION (%)	2006 ALLOCATION (%)	INCREASE (%)
Private Equity	0.3	1.9	533
Natural Resources	0.3	1.5	400
Hedge Funds	2.2	9.6	336
Real Estate	1.9	3.5	84
Venture Capital	0.7	0.9	29

SOURCE: NACUBO AND TIAA-CREF

Investing in alternative asset classes also can have a meaningful impact on performance. According to the NACUBO study, a diversified investment strategy helped managers of higher education endowment funds earn an average one-year return rate of 10.7 percent for fiscal year 2006.

• CHAPTER SUMMARY •

▶ Diversification entails dividing assets among varied investments. A basic plan of diversification that should be considered divides a portfolio among the broad asset classes: stocks, bonds, and cash.

▶ Stocks tend to have greater risk than bonds or cash, but they also have the potential for generating long-term returns. Bonds are less risky, but they also have more muted return potential. Cash is the safest investment, but it also offers the lowest potential for returns on a historic basis.

▶ Because of market cycles, different types of investments perform better or worse during certain periods. That's why a well-diversified portfolio should also include investments in different types of stocks and bonds.

▶ The stock market can be diced up into many categories, according to the size of the stocks, their growth or value characteristics, or the sector, country, or region that they provide exposure to.

▶ Alternative asset classes also can add another layer of diversification to a portfolio, as they provide exposure to many different trends in the global economy. Alternative asset classes include private equity, venture capital, hedge funds, real estate, and commodities.

2

ETFs: The Blueprint
for Asset Allocation

Understanding how to create a diversified portfolio is essential in creating a successful asset allocation strategy, but that is only part of the battle. It is equally important to construct that portfolio using the right building blocks. One option is to use individual securities such as stocks and bonds. While this may be a good option for some investors or financial advisers, creating a portfolio with enough individual securities to be well diversified can be difficult to research and costly to implement. Mutual funds—managed portfolios consisting of many securities—are another common option for adding greater diversification to a portfolio. While mutual funds can provide a useful way to increase exposure to certain areas of the market, they often have disadvantages of their own. In some cases, they charge high expenses, which can eat into performance. In addition, they may lack important characteristics, such as transparency, tax-efficiency, or trading flexibility. In addition, finding mutual funds that are able to beat their benchmark indexes consistently can be a challenge.

Enter exchange-traded funds. Exchange-traded funds—ETFs—are tools that comprise many of the best features of individual securities and mutual funds. For putting together a diversified portfolio, ETFs can be great tools either to create an entire portfolio or to complement an existing asset allocation that consists of mutual funds, individual securities, and/

or other investment products. Like mutual funds, ETFs hold a variety of securities, which is important in creating a well-diversified portfolio. However, they are structured to trade like stocks, which makes them more flexible and provides them with a range of other advantages. This chapter will discuss the differences and similarities that ETFs have with individual stocks and mutual funds. It will also explain why the ETF structure equips these products with many of the benefits that make them such effective tools inside a portfolio.

• INDIVIDUAL SECURITIES •

Stocks, which represent ownership in companies, trade on stock exchanges, such as the New York Stock Exchange or the American Stock Exchange. Stocks are bought and sold through brokers and can be traded at any time during the trading day, from 9:30 A.M. EST to 4:00 P.M. EST. Investors are able to engage in several strategies with stocks other than just buying and selling. For instance, investors can sell stocks short. That means that they borrow stocks and then sell them on the expectation that the price will fall and they will be able to buy shares back at a lower price and pocket the difference. With stocks, investors can also place stop-loss orders, which instruct a broker to trade a stock once it hits a certain price. In addition to trading in stocks directly, investors can participate through exchange-traded derivatives such as options and futures, which basically allow the purchase or sale of securities at a specific price and a specified date in the future.

The bond market is considerably more difficult to master than the stock market. The bond market consists of a primary market, which is the market in which companies sell new issues of debt to large institutions (similar to an initial public offering of stock), and a secondary market, where those securities can then be traded among investors. While bonds can be traded on exchanges like stocks—in fact the New York Stock Exchange is currently the largest centralized bond market—in the secondary market the majority of bonds are traded over-the-counter (OTC) in trades executed through brokers. Bonds can be much more difficult for investors to trade than stocks, particularly in the OTC market, where bond pricing can be difficult to decipher.

For investors who wish to diversify their portfolios broadly, buying individual securities poses several risks. First and foremost, there are thousands of different securities available and choosing the right ones for a given need is very difficult. History has shown that in many cases even the most gifted financial professionals can have a difficult time picking securities that beat the overall market—but we'll get into this more later.

Second, if an investor is choosing individual securities to diversify, how does he or she know how many stocks or bonds will be needed to be well diversified? There has been a lot of debate surrounding this issue and the jury is still out. When it comes to stocks, some believe that owning fifteen in a portfolio is enough. Others say at least thirty are needed. An article published in the winter 2000 *Journal of Investing* found that neither of those was enough! According to the article:

> Fifteen-stock portfolios, on average, achieve only 75%–80% of available diversification, not the 90%-plus typically believed. Even 60-stock portfolios achieve less than 90% of full diversification. Conscious efforts to diversify can improve these figures, but even optimizations won't achieve the diversification levels that were once believed possible with simple random portfolios. The implications of these findings for both the portfolio manager and the investor are significant. The portfolio manager can no longer rely on a simple rule of thumb to decide on the number of stocks to include in the portfolio. Diversification is more complex than the "30-stock" saw suggests. Similarly, investors should be less sanguine in the achievement of their diversification objectives if their confidence comes from a count of the names they hold in their portfolios.

Because of these issues and various other complexities, picking individual securities should in many cases be left to financial professionals or sophisticated investors with enough time to thoroughly research the multitude of securities and enough money to construct a well-diversified portfolio.

• MUTUAL FUNDS •

Because of the difficulty in selecting individual securities and the challenges involved in knowing how many securities are needed to be well diversified, many investors have turned to mutual funds. Mutual funds represent professionally managed portfolios of securities. Each share of a fund can represent anywhere from dozens to thousands of securities, depending on the fund.

This is an advantage, because it can add substantial diversification to a portfolio. For instance, if an investor wanted exposure to small cap stocks, he or she could simply buy shares in one of the hundreds of small cap funds that invest in different small cap stocks. Mutual funds also provide an easy way to obtain exposure to most broad segments of the equity and fixed-income markets, as well as various alternative asset classes. For instance, there are mutual funds that represent a sampling of the total U.S. stock or bond market and international markets. There are also funds that represent more specific slices of the market, such as a fund of financial stocks or technology stocks, value or growth stocks, municipal bonds or corporate bonds.

Mutual funds work by pooling together money from different investors. That money is then used to acquire a portfolio of stocks, bonds, and/or other assets. Each share of the mutual fund represents pro rata ownership of the whole portfolio. The value of each share is determined by the net asset value, or NAV, of the fund. The NAV is the market value of the securities inside the portfolio divided by the number of shares.

Each mutual fund has a certain investment objective, which determines what types of securities it will own. For instance, one fund's objective may be to own large-cap growth stocks. Another fund's objective might be to own municipal bonds, and yet another fund might be a balanced fund that invests in a combination of stocks and bonds. The research firm Morningstar, which rates mutual funds, divides the universe of funds into about seventy subcategories.

Mutual funds can be managed in one of two ways: active management or use of an index. With actively managed funds, a portfolio manager (or a team of portfolio managers) is at the helm, selecting securities for the portfolio. The idea of these funds is to create a portfolio that outperforms a chosen benchmark on either an absolute or risk-adjusted basis. The benchmark is the target that the manager is aiming to match or outperform, such as the S&P 500 Index.

Index funds do not have an active portfolio manager. Instead, they are designed to track a particular index and often hold the same securities as that index. For example, an S&P 500 index fund would aim to track the same five hundred stocks that are listed in the S&P 500 Index. Some indexes represent the broad stock market, while others are narrower, providing exposure to specific segments. For instance, there are indexes made up of only technology or health care stocks. There are also indexes that hold stocks from certain countries or regions. Some indexes are very well known and have a long history, such as the Dow Jones Industrial Average, which has been published continuously since 1896 and comprises thirty blue-chip stocks. But there are many newer indexes that are gaining visibility and acceptance too.

For many investors, mutual funds can be a better option than choosing individual securities because of the added level of diversification that they offer. However, mutual funds aren't always the answer. Depending on the investor's needs, there are certain elements of mutual funds—both actively managed and index funds—that may not make them appropriate for everyone.

Let's first look at actively managed mutual funds. These funds often charge relatively high management fees and expenses, compared with index funds, much of which is allocated to the portfolio manager and research team charged with picking winning securities for them. The fee can be measured by the expense ratio, which divides annual fees and expenses by average fund assets. The average expense ratio for a mutual fund is 1.44 percent. Fees in international equity funds can be even higher than those for domestic equity funds, due mainly to higher investment research costs. The median and average expense ratios for various types of mutual funds can be seen in the table below.

TABLE 2.1: MEDIAN AND AVERAGE EXPENSE RATIOS

TYPE OF MUTUAL FUND	MEDIAN EXPENSE RATIO	SIMPLE AVG EXPENSE RATIO
U.S. Equity Funds	1.39	1.46
Sector Funds	1.54	1.61
International Equity	1.55	1.61
Hybrid Funds	1.26	1.35
Bond Funds	0.95	1.07

There are also other characteristics of mutual funds to consider. For instance, mutual funds only have to disclose which securities are in their fund on a quarterly basis, which means investors don't always know exactly what is inside the fund. While that may not be a big deal for all investors, if someone wants to know exactly what he or she owns at all times, an actively managed mutual fund probably isn't the answer. Second, mutual fund shares do not trade throughout the day like stocks. Shares can be bought or sold only once a day, and the price that investors receive when they buy or sell shares is the NAV calculated after the close of trading on the same day, less any surrender charges. This means that if an order is placed at 10:00 A.M. to invest $10,000 in shares of a fund with a NAV of $14.50 a share, that wouldn't necessarily end up being the price. Instead, if the fund ended the trading day with a NAV of $15, that would be the price per share received, plus any applicable sales charges. The same thing goes for selling shares. Therefore, investors who require exact pricing or more trading flexibility may not fare well with mutual funds. Another point to consider with actively managed mutual funds held outside retirement plans is their level of tax efficiency. This is particularly true for funds that have a high turnover, which means that the portfolio manager is buying and selling securities frequently.

Another aspect of mutual funds that detracts from their tax efficiency is the annual capital gains distributions. This occurs when the portfolio manager needs to have enough cash to meet redemptions when investors want to sell their shares of a mutual fund. If the rate of redemption is fairly low, the fund may have enough cash sitting on the sidelines that can be used to pay out to the investors. But if redemptions increase, the fund may not have enough cash available. In that case they would have to sell securities to generate cash. When the fund sells securities in the portfolio that have appreciated, it realizes a capital gain, which is then passed on to shareholders in the form of a distribution. Whether an investor has been a shareholder for ten days or ten years, this gain must be included on his or her tax return, regardless of the fund's performance in that same year. These capital gains distributions are not small. The graph on page 25 shows the capital gains distributions of mutual funds between 1998 and 2007. You can see that in 2007 these distributions peaked at almost $415 billion. Preliminary data indicate that in 2008 this number had fallen substantially, to $133 billion— $35 billion of which went to taxable households. During that year 30 percent of stock funds were found to have made a capital gains distribution.

Index funds are generally more cost-efficient and tax-efficient than actively managed mutual funds. Because they track indexes they don't have to worry about beating a benchmark. Also, since they aren't paying a portfolio manager to pick individual securities, the expense ratios that they charge are generally lower than with actively managed mutual funds. They also tend to have lower turnover, which can be helpful in minimizing taxes.

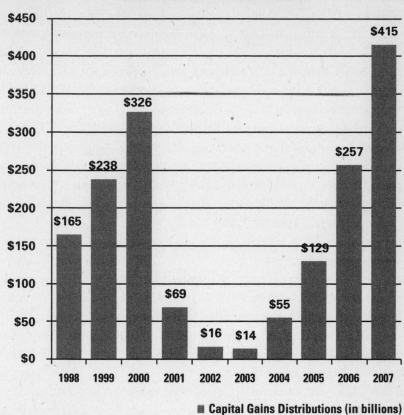

Figure 2.1: Mutual Fund Capital Gains
Distributions from 1998 to 2007

■ Capital Gains Distributions (in billions)

SOURCE: INVESTMENT COMPANY INSTITUTE

However, index funds do share some characteristics with their actively managed cousins that can be drawbacks, such as the lack of trading flexibility.

• EXCHANGE-TRADED FUNDS (ETFS) •

ETFs combine some of the most compelling features of index mutual funds and stocks. Like index funds, most ETFs are baskets of securities that track an index. This means they offer immediate portfolio diversification and, in most cases, do not rely on a portfolio manager to actively select securities. Generally, this allows ETFs to charge lower fees than actively managed mutual funds and to maintain low turnover. Also, investors can identify the specific securities that are held by an ETF on a daily basis, which makes them very transparent. In terms of trading efficiencies, ETFs are more akin to stocks. They are bought and sold through a broker, and shares trade throughout the day on stock exchanges at any time the market is open. This means that if a market order is placed to buy shares of ETFs during the trading day, the investor will get the best price available when his or her order is executed rather than waiting until 4:00 P.M. EST like the mutual funds that get the end-of-day net asset value. (There is also a fairly new breed of ETF that has a more active element to them. These active ETFs are somewhat more akin to actively managed mutual funds, as there is someone at the helm making security selections; however, they generally still function like other ETFs and maintain the majority of advantages, such as low costs and a high level of tax efficiency. These funds will be discussed in greater detail later in the book.)

• ANATOMY OF AN ETF •

ETFs most commonly are structured in one of two ways—as unit investment trusts (UITs) or open-end funds—though as time has passed additional structures have been created. A UIT is essentially a portfolio that is sold to investors with a fixed number of securities inside. Open-end funds, on the other hand, have the ability to continuously create new shares to satisfy investor demand. UIT-based and open-end ETFs must be registered under the Investment Company Act of 1940. This act, generally referred to as the "40 Act," essentially contains the rules that govern how ETFs work. They are the same rules that are used to regulate mutual funds. However, because ETFs are different from mutual funds in many ways— such as being able to trade like stocks—ETFs also need exemptions from some of the rules within this act. ETFs that are structured as UITs and open-end funds cannot come to market without first getting these exemptions from the Securities and Exchange Commission.

Most of the earliest ETFs to launch in the United States were created as UITs. This includes the Standard & Poor's Depositary Receipts (Ticker symbol: SPY), also nicknamed the "Spyder," which was the first ETF on the market, as well as several well-known ETFs that followed, such as the Dow Diamonds (Ticker symbol: DIA), which tracks the Dow Jones Industrial Average, and the PowerShares Trust, nicknamed the "Qs" (Ticker symbol: Q), which tracks the tech-heavy NASDAQ-100 Index. But the UIT, while still used, has not remained the primary ETF structure. Not long after the first ETF came to market, new ones were launched that were instead constructed as open-end funds. Today, this is the form most commonly used when creating ETFs.

While there are many similarities between the UIT and open-end fund configurations, there are some differences that are worth noting, because in some cases these differences can have an impact on the way a particular ETF performs. For instance, a UIT must hold every stock in the index that it tracks. That means an ETF that tracks the S&P 500 must hold each of the five hundred stocks represented in the index. (The 40 Act includes rules for how diversified a fund or trust has to be, which means that on occasion UITs will have to deviate a bit from the exact index holdings to comply with this rule.) Open-end funds, however, do not have to replicate an index exactly but are allowed to use optimization and sampling techniques to weed out certain securities from it. Another difference in the two structures is how they deal with dividends. When dividends are paid out, ETFs configured as UITs don't reinvest them. Instead, they hold them as cash and distribute them to investors quarterly. With open-end funds, dividends may be reinvested in the fund and then paid out quarterly or semiannually. Reinvesting dividends is generally preferred because it eliminates the possibility of "cash drag," which basically means that holding extra cash in a rising market will be a drag on performance, since it isn't participating in the market. Of course, if the market is declining, an ETF that holds dividends as cash instead of reinvesting them will actually benefit from having that extra cash on the sidelines.

Open-end funds are also a little more flexible than UITs. For instance, they allow for the use of derivatives like futures and options, which basically allow securities to be traded for a certain price on a certain day in the future. Also, open-end funds can generate additional income by loaning securities, which is not allowed with UITs. These differences can cause two ETFs to perform differently—though usually only marginally—and have different standard deviations, dividend yields, earnings yields, etc., even if they track a similar or even the same index.

• GRANTOR TRUSTS AND LIMITED PARTNERSHIPS •

There are a few other formats ETF providers have begun to use in order to create products that tap into other areas of the market. One reason these alternatives have emerged is because ETF providers have been looking to expand beyond products that simply track stock and bond indexes, to include assets such as commodities or currencies, which cannot be done in an ETF that is in compliance with the 40 Act rules. One way ETF providers have found to create ETFs that don't comply with the 40 Act is to structure them as grantor trusts and register them under the Securities Act of 1933. These ETFs do not have to replicate exactly, or even closely, an index. For instance, a group of ETFs known as Holdrs, which are grantor trusts, own a select basket of stocks that isn't rebalanced over time. If a stock is removed from the basket—for example, if the company merges with another or goes private—a new stock is not added. ETFs created as grantor trusts do not even need to hold stocks at all. For instance, there are various ETFs that track commodities, such as gold and silver, and currencies that are also grantor trusts. An example of this is State Street Global Advisors SPDR Gold Trust (Ticker symbol: GLD), which physically holds gold bullion in a vault and issues shares according to its value.

Another way to structure ETFs is as partnerships. An example of an ETF that uses this structure is the United States Oil Fund, LP (Ticker symbol: USO). This product is actually a commodity pool that allows investors to buy and sell limited partnership units. Instead of physically holding oil, in the way the gold ETF holds gold bullion, by using this structure the ETF is able to provide more direct exposure to oil by investing in futures contracts—in this case, for light, sweet crude oil and other types of oil futures contracts.

• EXCHANGE-TRADED NOTES •

Other exchange-traded products that have emerged in recent years and have quickly gained acceptance as a viable alternative to ETFs are exchange-traded notes (ETNs). These products, which were first launched by Barclays and labeled iPaths, are registered under the Securities Act of 1933. ETNs offer a cost-effective way to gain exposure to certain areas of the market or to strategies that have previously been difficult for investors, specifically retail investors, to access, such as currencies and commodities. They also allow investors to engage in certain strategies such as trading equity volatility.

ETNs function in ways similar to ETFs, but they are actually a hybrid between a stock and a bond. Like traditional ETFs, ETNs trade on exchanges—so they are bought and sold like traditional ETFs and can be sold short—and the returns are linked to the returns of a benchmark index. But what these products actually issue to investors is unsecured, unsubordinated debt that they can choose to hold until maturity. ETNs do not make interest payments, nor do they offer any principal protection. Unlike with mutual funds (and some ETFs), a benefit of ETNs is that they don't make capital gains distributions to shareholders. However, one thing to be aware of is that the tax treatment for ETNs can differ from product to product. Most ETNs, with the exception of those that track a single currency, are treated, for tax purposes, as prepaid contracts. According to Barclays, this means that investors should realize a taxable capital gain or loss when the ETN is sold, redeemed, or reaches maturity. The gain or loss is equal to the difference between the amount that they receive and their cost basis (this tax treatment is subject to change). The tax treatment for ETNs that track single currencies is different, in that investors must pay taxes on interest accrued during the life of the note, even if that interest is reinvested or not distributed until the ETN is sold or reaches maturity. Gains and losses from these ETNs are not treated as capital gains.

• CREATION/REDEMPTION •

Many of the benefits of ETFs are driven by the way ETF shares come to market. This is known as the creation/redemption process, and it is one of the most important features of ETFs that set them apart from other investment products. The creation and redemption process begins with the help of an authorized participant, or AP. The AP is generally a specialist or large broker enlisted by the ETF sponsor. Here's how it works: To create new shares of ETFs, the AP assembles a large portfolio of securities. For example, to create shares of an ETF that tracks the S&P 500 Index the AP would go out and buy stocks that are represented in it. The AP must buy enough shares of the stock so that they can be divvied up into many baskets called "creation units"; usually they must have enough of the underlying securities to make up at least fifty thousand creation units. These units are then exchanged for ETF shares that can be sold to investors or traded on the open market. To redeem shares of ETFs, the process moves in reverse. The AP buys a large quantity of ETF shares and then exchanges them for the underlying securities, which they can then hold on to or sell. It is important to note that when ETF shares are created or redeemed they are simply being swapped for securities. There is no sale taking place, which means there are no gains or losses. This is important to note as this swap underlies one of the greatest features of ETFs—tax efficiency, which will be discussed shortly.

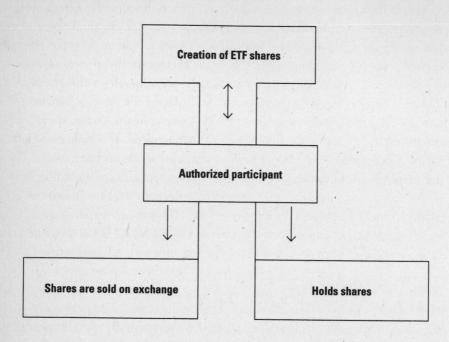

• ELIMINATE SINGLE-STOCK RISK •

Having discussed the way ETFs are structured, created, and redeemed, let's explore the many benefits that these elements provide. The best place to start is with one of the obvious advantages—diversification—as it is one of the greatest benefits ETFs have to offer. By owning shares of an ETF, the investor gets instant exposure to many securities, and this reduces the risk involved in owning individual ones. For instance, suppose that an investor wants exposure to the broad U.S. stock market. To have some diversification, he or she could try to handpick a portfolio of stocks from several different companies representing different segments of the market. But what if one of those companies reports terrible earnings, or declares bankruptcy, causing the stock price to plunge? If each stock accounts for about 10 percent of the portfolio, a meaningful drop in its share price could do major damage. Instead of being exposed to that risk, the investor could buy a broad-market ETF. If any security in the ETF experiences problems, it might still impact the portfolio, but the damage would be far less because most broad-equity ETFs own a significant number of stocks.

For exposure to certain sectors or countries, ETFs can also offer a good way to eliminate the risks involved in trying to buy individual securities. For example, to get exposure to the technology sector an investor might choose one, two, or maybe three technology stocks. But if one of those stocks takes a major hit, that could have a big impact on the portfolio. That's why a better option could be a technology ETF, in which he or she can get instant exposure to many different stocks in the sector, spreading out the risk. An example of one in this category is Technology SPDR ETF (Ticker symbol: XLK). This one includes stocks in companies that are involved with many aspects of information technology, including software, networking, the Internet, and semiconductors. To give an indication of how much diversification this type of ETF offers, at the close of 2008 there were roughly eighty stocks represented in XLK. This is a market cap–weighted ETF, which means that companies with a larger market cap account for a greater portion of the portfolio. By owning this ETF the investor will get substantial exposure to the largest stocks in the category. For instance, AT&T (Ticker symbol: T) accounted for 11.20 percent of the portfolio, Microsoft (Ticker symbol: MSFT) accounted for 10.39 percent of the portfolio, and IBM (Ticker symbol: IBM) made up 7.43 percent. As a result, the investor still has exposure to big-name stocks, but the risk is spread around, especially among the more speculative, smaller stocks. The table below shows that the top ten stocks accounted for more than 60 percent of the portfolio.

TABLE 2.2: TOP TEN HOLDINGS OF THE S&P SELECT TECHNOLOGY SPDR ETF

COMPANY	WEIGHT IN PORTFOLIO (%)
AT&T	11.20
Microsoft Corp.	10.39
International Business Machines Corp.	7.43
Cisco Systems	6.80
Verizon Communications	6.31

COMPANY	WEIGHT IN PORTFOLIO (%)
Hewlett-Packard	5.80
Apple	5.73
Intel	4.77
Oracle	4.41
Google	4.32
Total weight in portfolio	**67.16**

SOURCE: SELECT SECTOR SPDRS

Tax Efficiency

One of the greatest advantages of ETFs is their inherent tax efficiency—a feature made possible because of its unique creation/redemption process. As already explained, the mutual fund redemption process often results in high capital gains distributions to shareholders. However, because of the way ETF shares are created and redeemed, these distributions tend to be rare, even in highly volatile markets. Here's why: When shares of ETFs are sold on the investor level, they are sold on the open market—the same as with stocks. The individual investors selling the ETFs will be taxed on their own sale, but none of the other shareholders will be affected, regardless of how many shares are sold. At the portfolio level, when the AP redeems ETFs, there is no sale of securities. The AP isn't selling back ETF shares but instead swapping them for the underlying securities. Because this is a swap and not a sale, no capital gains are generated. Sometimes, though, an ETF does have to sell securities, for instance if the index that it tracks rebalances and some securities leave the index. But even when this occurs, ETFs have a mechanism in place to minimize capital gains. That is, when ETF shares are redeemed by APs on a day-to-day basis, they swap out the securities that have the lowest-cost basis. That leaves the securities with the highest-cost basis in the portfolio. If there is a rebalancing and the ETF needs to sell some securities, having a portfolio of high-cost-basis stocks will generate fewer capital gains and therefore keep capital gains distributions to a minimum. Several ETF providers have never declared any capital gains distributions.

Another tax advantage ETFs have over mutual funds is their low turnover. Because ETFs are usually passive investments that track indexes, they generally only sell securities if there is a change in the composition of the index. For example, if a stock is removed from the S&P 500 Index, an ETF tracking that index would also sell the stock and, as a result, it could experience a capital gains distribution. However, this tends to be rare. Active mutual funds, by comparison, tend to have much higher turnovers than ETFs or index funds. When there is more selling in the portfolio, that means there is a greater potential to realize capital gains. It also leads to more transaction costs for shareholders.

Trade Close to NAV

In addition to tax efficiency, the ETF creation and redemption process also provides another benefit. It keeps the price of the ETF trading at or very close to its net asset value. It may not seem like a big deal that ETFs trade close to their NAV. It might even be assumed that that is simply how it should be anyway. But that's not necessarily the case. If there is weak demand for an ETF, it can start trading at a price that is less than its NAV. Or, if there is strong demand for an ETF, it could trade at a premium to its NAV. While either of these scenarios is possible, they don't happen very often, and if they do the difference between the trading price and the NAV is generally pretty minimal. Again, that's because of the creation and redemption process. The value of an ETF's underlying securities is calculated every fifteen seconds, which allows the AP to always know the NAV of the ETF. This means that if an ETF begins trading at a discount to the NAV per share, the authorized participant can buy shares of that ETF, redeem them for the underlying securities, and then sell the securities on the market for a profit. If the ETF is trading at a premium, APs can gather up the underlying securities, exchange them for shares of ETFs, and then sell the ETF shares for a profit. This arbitrage mechanism helps keep the price of the ETF shares in line with the NAV.

The following is a simple example to illustrate this process: Consider an ETF composed of one hundred securities. The total market value of those securities is $5,000. If there are one hundred shares of the ETF outstanding, the NAV is $50 per share. Now imagine that there is great demand for the ETF, so it trades at a premium of $2 a share over its NAV, or $52 a share. The authorized participant could go to the market and buy the one hundred underlying securities in the portfolio. This would cost $5,000, as that is equal to one hundred shares at $50 a share. The AP would then exchange those baskets for ETFs and sell the ETF for $52 a share. Selling one hundred ETF shares at $52 a share leaves a profit of $200. The AP's action in selling a big lot of ETFs and reducing the supply/demand imbalance will help to bring the price back in line with its NAV. This arbitrage happens whenever a discrepancy is found between the ETF's share price and its actual underlying value.

This arbitrage mechanism is a significant benefit that ETFs have over closed-end funds, which are close cousins of ETFs. Closed-end funds are also made up of baskets of securities that trade on an exchange. The vast majority of closed-end funds are actively managed, although some do track indexes. But closed-end funds issue only a fixed number of shares. APs don't continuously create or redeem shares, as is the case with ETFs. As a result, if there is strong demand for a closed-end fund, it can start trading at a very large premium to its NAV. But there is no mechanism to bring that price back in line. As a result, closed-end funds often trade at fairly large premiums or discounts.

Costs

Part of the allure of ETFs has been the low expense ratio that they charge investors. The average annual expense ratio for an ETF is estimated to be around 0.4 percent. That compares with an estimated average expense ratio of more than 0.7 percent for indexed mutual funds and almost 1.5 percent for actively managed funds. For broad-based ETFs, the expenses can be significantly cheaper. For instance, the Vanguard Total Stock Market ETF charges only 0.07 percent, compared with the corresponding index fund, the Vanguard Total Stock Market Index Fund, which charges 0.15 percent.

That's not always the case, though. Some ETFs that have been launched in the past few years are pricier. But there's a reason. Unlike the more traditional ETFs, such as the Vanguard Total Market Index ETF, which track broad, well-known indexes, some provide exposure to smaller segments of the market or areas that are difficult to access. That will be discussed in more detail in the next chapter. The cost of an ETF should be considered on a relative basis—i.e., by comparing it to the costs of similar investment products. In many cases the ETF will be a cheaper alternative; or, in some cases, the simplicity offered by the ETF, even at a higher cost, may make it worthwhile. For example, when it comes to investing internationally, ETFs provide exposure to many countries and regions. In some cases, no mutual funds provide the same exposure. One option then is to purchase a portfolio of individual securities that create the same exposure. But, as discussed earlier, it can be very costly, not to mention challenging, to buy enough securities to be well diversified. Another example is the commodities market. Several ETFs offer access to selected commodities, and in many cases there are no corresponding mutual funds. The actual physical commodity could be purchased. While this makes sense for gold, it is not very easy to do with oil or agricultural products. Another alternative would be to open a futures account to trade the commodity. In most cases, though, that is more complex and costly than just buying the ETF, and it is an added step that many retail investors aren't interested in taking. Also, Individual Retirement Accounts and other retirement plan accounts can participate in ETFs but not directly in commodities futures.

Part of the reason ETFs' expense ratios tend to be lower than other products, especially actively managed mutual funds, is their status as passive investments. By tracking indexes, ETFs don't need to pay a portfolio manager to research and select certain stocks. Also, investors in ETFs are spared many of the other costs factored into mutual funds. For instance, because ETFs are traded between investors on the open market, the sponsor does not have to maintain communication with shareholders by sending out annual reports and other literature, as mutual funds do. Also, most ETFs charge low or no marketing fees, also known as 12b-1 service fees. In the event that they do, most ETFs charge a very low fee that is insignificant when compared with mutual funds. Mutual funds can also charge fees for redeeming shares early and can build up high trading costs due to their high turnover rates. Finally, ETFs are not required to hold large amounts of cash to meet redemptions—as mutual funds are—because they don't make cash redemptions. The need to hold cash is another type of cost faced by mutual funds but not ETFs.

Table 2.3 shows the cost advantage that an ETF has over an index fund over a hypothetical ten-year period. In this example, $10,000 has been invested in both funds, each of which tracks the S&P 500 Index. Because they track the same index, we have assumed that they have the same annualized gross returns of 8 percent. The ETF has an expense ratio of 0.09 percent, which is a typical expense ratio for this type of ETF. Meanwhile the index-based mutual fund, a low-cost index fund, charges 0.18 percent. After ten years, the total cost for the ETF, which includes a $10 commission fee to purchase the ETF, would be $193.73. The mounting costs for the index fund would have reached $385.47. Since the funds have the same gross return, it's apparent how these costs impacted the performance of the funds. By the end of the period the ETF hypothetically had accumulated to $21,395.52. The index fund's returns were lower, at $21,203.78.

TABLE 2.3: COMPARISON OF ETF AND INDEX FUND RETURNS

	GROSS ANNUALIZED RETURN (%)	EXPENSE RATIO	TOTAL COSTS OVER TEN YEARS	FINAL VALUE AFTER TEN YEARS
ETF	8	0.09	$193.73	$21,395.52
Index Fund	8	0.18	$385.47	$21,203.78

Let's look at another example of the impact expense ratios can have over a longer period of time. Figure 2.2 illustrates a $10,000 hypothetical investment in two funds over a thirty-year period. Both have gross annual returns of 10 percent. As in the example above, the expense ratio of the ETF is 0.09 percent and the expense ratio for the low-cost index fund is 0.18 percent. As more time passes, the gap in the returns of the two funds widens. After the thirty-year period, the less expensive ETF will grow to about $165,313.20 compared with the index fund, which will be worth $133,042.44. That's a difference of more than $32,000.

Even in this example, which compared an ETF with a low-cost index fund, the impact over time of the higher expense is substantial. So the difference could be much more dramatic when comparing an ETF with a higher cost index fund or an actively managed mutual fund, which on average have expenses that are more than fifteen times that of an ETF in the same category.

Commissions and Spreads

ETFs do incur some costs that mutual funds don't. Because ETFs are bought and sold through brokers, like stocks, investors must pay a commission each time they trade. This can be an issue for someone who is dollar-cost averaging—investing in small, regular increments—as this could cause the brokerage fees to really add up. However, commissions

Figure 2.2: Impact of Expense Ratios on Returns over Thirty Years

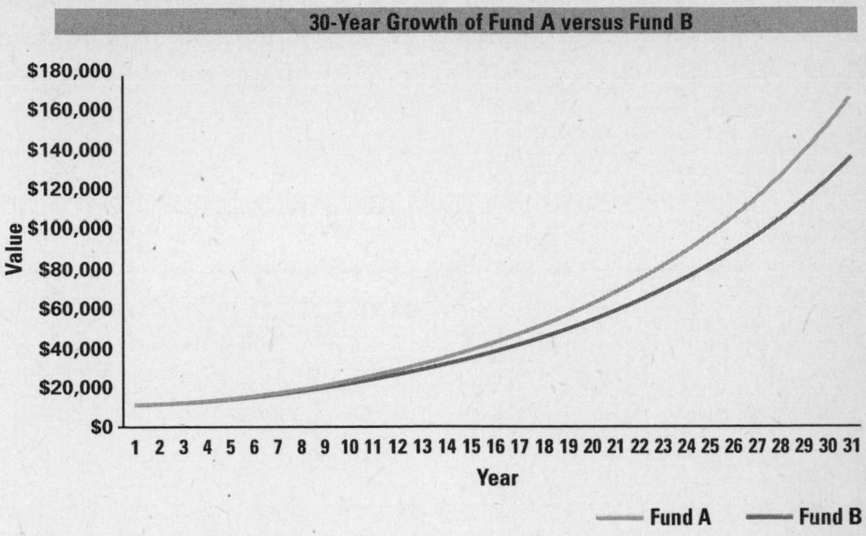

30-Year Growth of Fund A versus Fund B

— Fund A   — Fund B

are a one-time charge, as opposed to mutual funds' management fees and expenses, which are incurred daily. As a result, when investing a lump sum in ETFs the commission is often small, and the longer the ETF is held, the less impact the commission will have, compared with the ongoing fees that mutual funds charge. Even investors who don't invest a huge sum but hold on to their investments for a long time will often benefit, as the lower expense ratio will generally outweigh the cost of the commission.

Another cost that ETFs incur is the bid-ask spread, which is the difference between the price that a buyer is willing to pay for a security (the bid) and the price the seller is asking for it (the ask). With domestic ETFs that are very liquid, spreads tend to be very small. Some ETFs that are less liquid, though, can have higher spreads. Spreads are also sometimes higher for international ETFs. That is largely due to the fact that U.S. markets (where the ETFs trade) may be open when foreign markets (where the underlying securities trade) are closed. Therefore, investors can't always ascertain the relationship between immediate trading trends in the U.S. market and ETFs and underlying securities values. While spreads are more talked about with ETFs, they are costs for mutual funds, as well. That's because the mutual fund portfolio manager must pay a spread each time securities are bought or sold by the portfolio. As with ETFs, the spread may be very small, depending on the security and the number of shares being purchased. However, if the fund manager is buying less liquid stocks (such as microcaps or international stocks) often the transaction volume will cause the cost of the spreads to add up.

No Minimum Investment

Similar to stocks, purchasing an ETF does not require a minimum upfront investment. Investors can buy and sell however many shares they want at any given time, subject to any trading restrictions imposed by the broker. This is unlike mutual funds, which require investors to pony up a minimum investment to buy the fund. These minimum investments can be very low—a few hundred dollars—but they are typically higher, ranging from one thousand to five thousand dollars.

Transparency

Another advantage of ETFs is their transparency. Because ETFs disclose their holdings daily, there is no mystery as to what they contain. Transparency is important because it lets investors and financial professionals know exactly what is inside the ETF at all times, which can help investors choose the ETF that best suits their personal needs. This high level of transparency is also important in helping to reduce or eliminate the unintentional overlap of securities inside a portfolio. For example, even if two ETFs represent different segments of the market, both may own fairly large positions in the same security. By being able to see what is inside the ETF, investors can avoid having too large concentrations in one or more securities.

Liquidity

ETFs benefit from the same liquidity as individual securities. Because shares trade throughout the day, investors can buy and sell at any time. An ETF's liquidity is a combination of two factors: the trading volume of the ETF itself and the volume of the securities that are underlying the ETF. Generally, securities that are thinly traded (less liquid) are riskier, more difficult to trade, and have wider spreads. Domestic, large cap, and broad-based ETFs tend to be among the most liquid, with very small bid-ask spreads. Certain types of ETFs are less liquid and therefore have larger spreads. These often include ETFs that track small and microcaps, specific industries, emerging markets, and fixed income.

Trading Flexibility

Trading ETFs is quick and easy, as they can be bought or sold at any time during the trading day on major stock exchanges. For investors who buy shares with the intention of holding them for years, this level of trading flexibility may not be particularly important. But for others, particularly more active traders, this flexibility is a major selling point of ETFs. Being able to trade ETFs at any time during the trading day eliminates the risk that the price of a security will change dramatically between the time of the trade and the end of the trading day. For example, if an investor owns shares of a telecom ETF and there was a major sell-off in that sector, those shares could be sold quickly, before the price declined further. However, if an investor owned a telecom mutual fund and wanted to sell those shares, regardless of what time in the day the sell order was placed, the price would be based on the day's closing price. In addition, because of intraday pricing, investors also can place limit orders and stop-loss orders on ETFs. That allows them to set the price at which they will buy or sell the ETFs, respectively. Investors can also sell ETF shares short. That means shares can be borrowed and then sold on the bet that they can be bought back later at a lower price. They can also be sold short on a downtick, which means that they can be sold short even if the sale price is higher than the price of the trade immediately preceding their sale.

No Style Drift

Another advantage that ETFs have is their lack of what is known as style drift. Because ETFs track indexes, they must invest according to their intended objective. For instance, the objective of a midcap ETF is to track an index of midcap stocks. What constitutes midcap stocks is defined by the index, and the ETF must adhere to it. If a stock becomes too big and is no longer considered a midcap stock, it will be replaced in the index when it rebalances. As a result, it will no longer be included in the ETF that tracks that index. With actively managed funds, portfolio managers have more flexible guidelines. As a result, this often means that certain securities stay in the fund even when they should no longer be there. Let's use again the example of a midcap stock. Even if that stock experiences significant growth, and has clearly grown out of its midcap status, the portfolio manager may like the stock and continue to keep it inside the fund. Style drift has the potential to impact both the risk level and returns of an investor's portfolio.

• PASSIVE PERFORMANCE •

There is much debate over how the performance of ETFs compares to mutual funds over the long term. The reality is that over longer periods of time, ETFs often outperform comparable mutual funds. This is largely due to the structural differences between ETFs and mutual funds. For instance, as discussed earlier, mutual funds often charge higher fees than ETFs, which can hurt their performance on a net basis. Recall, the average expense ratio for ETFs is around 0.4 percent, compared with about 1.5 percent for actively managed mutual funds. Even the few actively managed ETFs that have come to market—a relatively new development for the ETF industry that will be discussed in more detail later—are able to charge fees that are comparable to passive ETFs. That's because even though they are actively managed, the ETF structure helps keep expenses low. In addition, ETFs, both passive and active, tend to be significantly more tax efficient, reporting little or no capital gains distributions; mutual funds often face substantial tax consequences because of capital gains distributions. These factors often lead to mutual funds' underperforming indexes and ETFs. To a large extent, the underperformance of many actively managed funds makes sense. That's because, as in the fictional town Lake Wobegon, where "all the women are strong, all the men are good-looking, and all the children are above average," statistically, not every manager can be above average. There must be winners and losers. Because ETFs track indexes, they deliver the same or very close to the same returns as the indexes. They cannot significantly outperform the index that they track, but this also means they cannot significantly underperform the index either. Mutual funds, however, strive to outperform their benchmark. However, in any given year, only about one third of equity mutual funds are able to match the performance of their benchmark indexes.

Let's look at a few examples to illustrate. According to Standard & Poor's Mid-year 2008 Indices versus Active Funds Scorecard, over the five-year period ended June 2008, the S&P 500, an index of large cap stocks, outperformed actively managed large cap funds 68.6 percent of the time. Meanwhile, the midcap-focused S&P 400 Index beat actively managed midcap funds 75.9 percent of the time, and the S&P SmallCap 600 Index upstaged active small cap funds 77.8 percent of the time, according to the scorecard. The table below shows how all domestic equity funds performed versus corresponding S&P indexes over one-, three-, and five-year periods as well as the performances of various categories of domestic equity funds. (The complete reports can be found at www.spiva.standardandpoors.com.)

TABLE 2.4: PERCENTAGE OF ACTIVE DOMESTIC STOCK MUTUAL FUNDS OUTPERFORMED BY INDEX

FUND CATEGORY	COMPARISON INDEX	ONE YEAR (%)	THREE YEARS (%)	FIVE YEARS (%)
All Domestic Funds	S&P Composite 1500 Index	48.81	55.53	56.65
All Large Cap Funds	S&P 500	40.80	57.45	68.65
All Midcap Funds	S&P Midcap 400	63.48	63.51	75.87
All Small Cap Funds	S&P SmallCap 600	59.51	59.62	77.80
All Multicap Funds	S&P Composite 1500 Index	43.74	53.73	58.17
LARGE CAP FUNDS				
Large Cap Growth Funds	S&P 500 Growth	43.62	61.76	63.76
Large Cap Core Funds	S&P 500	38.40	59.06	74.25
Large Cap Value Funds	S&P 500 Value	24.00	40.82	62.37
MIDCAP FUNDS				
Midcap Growth Funds	S&P Midcap 400 Growth	73.30	65.68	71.43
Midcap Core Funds	S&P Midcap 400	75.00	76.24	78.18
Midcap Value Funds	S&P Midcap 400 Value	73.75	61.54	78.41
SMALL CAP FUNDS				
Small Cap Growth Funds	S&P SmallCap 600 Growth	65.76	67.74	86.96
Small Cap Core Funds	S&P SmallCap 600	66.82	61.84	73.81
Small Cap Value Funds	S&P SmallCap 600 Value	43.18	41.25	63.11

FUND CATEGORY	COMPARISON INDEX	ONE YEAR (%)	THREE YEARS (%)	FIVE YEARS (%)
MULTICAP FUNDS				
Multicap Growth Funds	S&P Composite 1500 Growth	57.76	45.07	47.18
Multicap Core Funds	S&P Composite 1500 Index	43.01	50.72	55.71
Multicap Value Funds	S&P Composite 1500 Value	40.44	58.60	73.98
REAL ESTATE FUNDS				
Real Estate Funds	S&P BMI U.S. REIT	62.35	54.55	56.94

SOURCE: STANDARD & POOR'S

Data are for periods ended June 30, 2008. Outperformance based on equal weighted fund counts.

A similar trend is evident when comparing how actively managed international funds and fixed income funds have performed against corresponding indexes. In the table below, the same trend exists. While the results are not as dramatic over a one-year period, indexes outperformed on three- and five-year bases between 54 percent and 86 percent of the time.

TABLE 2.5: PERCENTAGE OF ACTIVE INTERNATIONAL STOCK MUTUAL FUNDS OUTPERFORMED BY INDEX

FUND CATEGORY	COMPARISON INDEX	ONE YEAR (%)	THREE YEARS (%)	FIVE YEARS (%)
Global Funds	S&P Global 1200	50.00	61.54	70.10
International Funds	S&P 700	69.71	85.06	86.51
International Small Cap Funds	S&P Developed Ex-U.S. Small Cap	47.92	54.35	55.26
Emerging Markets Funds	S&P/IFCI Composite	45.95	73.02	73.91

SOURCE: STANDARD & POOR'S

Data are for periods ended June 30, 2008. Outperformance based on equal weighted fund counts.

Finally, take a look at how actively managed fixed income funds measure up against corresponding fixed income indexes. In the case of long-term government bonds, over a five-year period the Lehman Brothers Long Government Bond Index outperformed actively managed funds in that category more than 98 percent of the time!

TABLE 2.6: PERCENTAGE OF ACTIVE FIXED INCOME MUTUAL FUNDS OUTPERFORMED BY INDEX

FUND CATEGORY	COMPARISON INDEX	ONE YEAR (%)	THREE YEARS (%)	FIVE YEARS (%)
GOVERNMENT FUNDS				
Government Long Funds	Lehman Brothers Long Government	83.67	71.93	98.39
Government Intermediate Funds	Lehman Brothers Intermediate Government	88.46	94.83	86.76
Government Short Funds	Lehman Brothers 1–3 Year Government	85.71	93.33	91.49
INVESTMENT GRADE				
Investment Grade Long Funds	Lehman Brothers Long Government/Credit	86.73	37.50	89.26
Investment Grade Intermediate Funds	Lehman Brothers Intermediate Government/Credit	91.96	93.36	81.90
Investment Grade Short Funds	Lehman Brothers 1–3 Year Government/Credit	95.95	98.63	96.67
HIGH YIELD				
High Yield	Lehman Brothers High Yield	50.36	69.57	75.56
MORTGAGE-BACKED				
Mortgage-backed	Lehman Brothers Mortgage-backed Securities	83.33	94.55	96.55
GLOBAL				
Global Income Funds	Lehman Brothers Global Aggregate	68.85	74.00	64.71
Emerging Markets Debt Funds	Lehman Brothers Emerging Markets	75.00	38.89	35.00
MUNICIPAL DEBT				
General Municipal Debt Funds	S&P National Municipal Bond	75.00	93.81	90.00
California Municipal Debt Funds	S&P California Municipal Bond	87.18	95.45	91.30
New York Municipal Debt Funds	S&P New York Municipal Bond	87.50	97.30	89.74

SOURCE: STANDARD & POOR'S

Data are for periods ended June 30, 2008. Outperformance based on equal weighted fund counts.

• CHAPTER SUMMARY •

▶ ETFs are similar in some ways to both index funds and stocks. Like index funds, ETFs are passive tools that track the performance of an index. However, ETFs trade like stocks, which means that they can be bought and sold through brokers and traded throughout the day on a stock exchange.

▶ ETFs are most commonly structured in one of two ways: as unit investment trusts, UITs, or open-end funds. In recent years more of the ETFs that have been launched utilize various other structures in order to offer products that provide exposure to other areas of the market, such as commodities or currencies.

▶ The ETF creation/redemption process is behind many ETF benefits, including keeping share prices in line with net asset values and tax efficiency. To create shares of an ETF, an authorized participant, or AP, trades the underlying securities for ETF shares. To redeem ETF shares, an AP exchanges those shares for their underlying securities. Because this is an exchange and not a sale, the creation/redemption process does not generate capital gains distributions.

▶ Because ETFs represent baskets of securities they provide instant diversification and eliminate the risk of owning single stocks. ETFs' benefits also include low costs, transparency, trading flexibility, liquidity, and a lack of style drift.

▶ Index-based products often outperform actively managed products. This is partially because the higher fees charged by actively managed products can hurt net performance.

3

Variety Is the Spice of Life

In addition to the many benefits discussed in the previous chapter, another advantage that continues to add to the appeal of ETFs is the increasingly vast selection of products. The first ETF to launch in the United States was a low-cost product that was designed to provide exposure to the broad U.S. stock market. Since that launch, hundreds of ETFs have been introduced in the United States. These include numerous products designed to track segments of the U.S. stock market, as well as ETFs that provide access to international stock markets, the fixed income arena, and alternative asset classes. This chapter will focus on the first category—ETFs that track U.S. stocks.

Like the original ETF, some of these products are based on broad, well-known, well-established stock indexes, while others provide more precise exposure to specific areas of the U.S. stock market. For instance, there are ETFs that group stocks together according to their market capitalization; others bundle together stocks that reside within the same economic sector or the same country or region, or that have similar style characteristics. This chapter will take a closer look at the varied types of ETFs that represent the U.S. stock market and the differences in the type of exposure that they offer.

• ETFS BY MARKET CAP •

Some of the most popular ETFs on the market are those that track indexes that group stocks together according to their size, or market capitalization, which is calculated by multiplying a stock's price by the number of shares the company has outstanding. Within the category of market cap ETFs the main classifications are: megacaps, large caps, midcaps, small caps, and microcaps. While there are no definitive guidelines as to what constitutes each of these categories, generally speaking, megacaps are stocks of companies that have market caps of more than $100 billion, large caps typically include stocks with a market capitalization between $10 billion and $100 billion (though often megacaps are grouped together with large caps), midcaps generally include stocks valued between $2 billion and $10 billion, small caps are generally valued between $300 million and $2 billion, and microcap ETFs are typically valued at less than $300 million. A good example of a large cap ETF (with megacaps included as well) is the Spyder (Ticker symbol: SPY). It can be seen in the table below that in this ETF, which had more than $77 billion in assets as of December 2008—more than any other ETF—the top ten holdings include such goliaths as ExxonMobil (Ticker symbol: XOM), which has a market cap of more than $409 billion; General Electric (Ticker symbol: GE), whose market cap stands at over $170 billion; and AT&T (Ticker symbol: T), which has a market cap of about $166 billion. The index underlying this ETF determines the weight of each of the underlying stocks according to individual market cap. This means that the larger the market cap of a stock is, the larger its weight in the portfolio. As a result, this ETF is highly skewed in favor of the largest stocks. As the table below shows, the top ten stocks account for about 23 percent of the portfolio as of December 2008. In this case, the performance of these stocks will have a pretty large impact on the performance of the ETF.

**TABLE 3.1: STANDARD & POOR'S DEPOSITARY RECEIPTS
(TICKER SYMBOL: SPY) TOP TEN HOLDINGS**

COMPANY	WEIGHT OF ETF (%)
ExxonMobil	5.44
General Electric	2.34

COMPANY	WEIGHT OF ETF (%)
Procter & Gamble	2.30
AT&T	2.15
Chevron	2.14
Johnson & Johnson	2.13
Microsoft	2.00
Wal-Mart Stores	1.61
Pfizer	1.46
JPMorgan Chase	1.44
Total Weight	**23.01**

SOURCE: STATE STREET GLOBAL ADVISORS

An example of a midcap ETF is the iShares S&P 400 MidCap (Ticker symbol: IJH), which had about $3.5 billion in assets as of December 2008. This ETF has a mean market cap of about $3.16 billion. It's evident from the list below that the companies with the greatest market cap account for the greatest percentage of the portfolio. For instance, in this ETF, the current top holding, Everest Re Group (Ticker symbol: RE), has a market cap of about $4.7 billion, McAfee (Ticker symbol: MFE) has a market cap of around $4.5 billion, and Equitable Resources (Ticker symbol: EQT) has a market cap of $4.1 billion. The stock with the smallest weight in this ETF, Hovnanian Enterprises (Ticker symbol: HOV), which is not listed below, has a market cap of just $165 million and makes up just 0.02 percent of the portfolio.

TABLE 3.2: ISHARES S&P 400 MIDCAP (TICKER SYMBOL: IJH) TOP TEN HOLDINGS

COMPANY	WEIGHT OF ETF (%)
Everest Re Group	0.74
McAfee	0.70
Equitable Resources	0.66
Scana	0.66
WR Berkley	0.64

COMPANY	WEIGHT OF ETF (%)
MDU Resources Group	0.62
Martin Marietta Materials	0.62
O'Reilly Automotive	0.61
New York Community Bancorp	0.61
Dollar Tree	0.60
Total Weight	**6.46**

SOURCE: BARCLAYS GLOBAL INVESTORS

An example of a small cap ETF is the iShares Russell 2000 (Ticker symbol: IWM). This ETF has about $10.5 billion in total assets and a mean market cap of $1.06 billion. The largest holding, Ralcorp Holdings (Ticker symbol: RAH), has a market cap of about $3.08 billion; the market cap of Myriad Genetics (Ticker symbol: MYGN) is about $2.88 billion; and Alexion Pharmaceuticals (Ticker symbol: ALXN) is valued at around $2.56 billion.

TABLE 3.3: ISHARES RUSSELL 2000 (TICKER SYMBOL: IWM) TOP TEN HOLDINGS

COMPANY	WEIGHT OF ETF (%)
Ralcorp Holdings	0.44
Myriad Genetics	0.40
Alexion Pharmaceuticals	0.37
Foundry Networks	0.34
Waste Connections	0.34
Piedmont Natural Gas	0.33
Comstock Resources	0.30
Wabtec	0.29
Westar Energy	0.29
Realty Income	0.28
Total Weight	**3.38**

SOURCE: BARCLAYS GLOBAL INVESTORS

• STYLE-BASED ETFS •

Growth and value are the leading style categories into which stocks are divided. As mentioned in the first chapter, value stocks are generally considered to be less expensive in relation to earnings or book value, and they are also thought to have higher average dividend payouts. Growth stocks typically have consistent, above average earnings growth and higher price-to-earnings and price-to-book ratios. Dow Jones, S&P/Barra, and Russell are three well-known style-based indexes upon which various ETFs are based. These indexes can vary significantly in their definitions of growth and value stocks, in their methodology for including and omitting stocks from the index, and in how often the indexes reconstitute. Because of this, in some cases an investor might find the same securities present in both a value and a growth index. To avoid this overlap there are also ETFs based on "pure" style indexes, which strive to avoid this. The S&P/Citigroup Pure Style Indices are examples of pure style indexes. These indexes focus on companies that exhibit either strong growth or value characteristics. In doing this they let investors more closely target a specific style box by eliminating overlapping stocks. Within these pure style indexes, stocks are weighted according to their style scores rather than by market cap, in an attempt to eliminate size bias. Let's use the Rydex S&P Pure Value ETF (Ticker symbol: RPV) as an example. The top ten holdings of this ETF are shown below. In this ETF, the majority of the stocks that make up the top ten holdings represent the consumer discretionary area of the market, which is a group that is currently considered by many to be a good value play.

TABLE 3.4: RYDEX S&P PURE VALUE ETF (TICKER SYMBOL: RPV) TOP TEN HOLDINGS

COMPANY	WEIGHT OF ETF (%)
KB Home	3.21
DR Horton	2.71
Energy Group	2.62
Lennar	2.53
Spectra Energy	2.50

COMPANY	WEIGHT OF ETF (%)
AmerisourceBergen	1.99
DTE Energy	1.93
Nisource	1.91
Autonation	1.72
Progress Energy	1.71
Total Weight	**22.83**

SOURCE: RYDEX SGI

• SECTOR ETFS •

These ETFs are based on indexes that divide the market into different slices according to the sector that they represent. While different indexes have different ways of dividing up the broad sectors of the market, the following categories are commonly used: basic materials, consumer goods, consumer services, energy, financials, health care, industrials, natural resources, technology, telecommunications, transportation, and utilities. Most sectors of the market have several ETFs tracking them. In some cases there are dozens of ETFs available to track the same sector. The following example is the Select Sector Energy SPDR (Ticker symbol: XLE), an ETF that tracks energy companies that primarily develop and produce crude oil and natural gas, and provide drilling and other energy-related services. This ETF is market-cap weighted, so the large stocks in the sector account for the greatest weight in the portfolio. The top ten companies account for more than 70 percent of the portfolio.

TABLE 3.5: SELECT SECTOR ENERGY SPDR (TICKER SYMBOL: XLE)
TOP TEN HOLDINGS

COMPANY	WEIGHT OF ETF (%)
ExxonMobil	25.93
Chevron Corp	16.20
ConocoPhillips	7.92
Occidental Petroleum	4.98

COMPANY	WEIGHT OF ETF (%)
Devon Energy	3.54
Schlumberger	3.41
Apache Corp	2.98
XTO Energy	2.64
EOG Resources	2.25
Transocean	2.21
Total Weight	72.06

SOURCE: SELECT SECTOR SPDRS

• INDUSTRY/SUBSECTOR ETFS •

Industry ETFs are a little different from sector ETFs in that they track indexes that follow even narrower slices, or subsectors, of the market. Some examples might include a software ETF that's within the broader category of technology or an insurance-focused ETF within the category of financials. There was quite a stir in the market in early 2007 when a company called XShares came out with a family of ETFs that track small pieces of the health care industry such as cardio devices, patient care services, and the development of medical devices. Some industry observers have questioned whether many of these very narrow products are necessary, though the companies that have created them believe they can occupy a niche in some investors' portfolios. (At the time this book was published, many of these products had closed.) One example of an industry ETF is the HealthShares Cancer ETF (Ticker symbol: HHK) that tracks an index composed of companies in the health care, life science, and biotechnology sectors that are engaged in the research, clinical development, and commercialization of therapeutic agents treating a wide variety of cancers. The following are the top ten holdings in this ETF, which make up more than 57 percent of the portfolio.

• • •

TABLE 3.6: HEALTHSHARES CANCER ETF (TICKER SYMBOL: HHK) TOP TEN HOLDINGS

COMPANY	WEIGHT OF ETF (%)
Geron	5.50
Nektar Therapeutics	5.37
Enzon Pharmaceuticals	3.78
PDL BioPharma	3.56
Cephalon	3.49
Kyowa Hakko Kirin	3.45
Ligand Pharmaceuticals	3.42
GTX Inc.	3.37
BTG	3.35
Chugai Pharmaceuticals	3.33
Total Weight	**38.62**

SOURCE: XSHARES

• FUNDAMENTAL ETFS •

A fundamental index selects and weighs components based on a combination of fundamental factors such as dividends, earnings, and sales. Fundamental indexing, introduced in 2005, was based on research conducted by Rob Arnott, chairman of the firm Research Associates, as a joint venture between the FTSE Group and Research Associates. The initial showcase for this index was a new broad-based U.S. equity index, the FTSE RAFI US 1000, which selects one thousand stocks based on a rules-based model that includes sales, cash flow, book value, and dividends. In 2006, PowerShares launched a family of fundamentally weighted ETFs based on FTSE RAFI indexes that select and weigh securities according to sales, cash flow, book price, and dividends. Let's look at the top ten holdings for the PowerShares FTSE RAFI US 1000 ETF (Ticker symbol: PRF), which holds the one thousand largest U.S. stocks weighted by size, according to each firm's book value, cash flow, dividends, and sales.

TABLE 3.7: POWERSHARES FTSE RAFI U.S. 1000 ETF
(TICKER SYMBOL: PRF) TOP TEN HOLDINGS

COMPANY	WEIGHT OF ETF (%)
ExxonMobil	4.11
Wal-Mart Stores	2.22
Chevron	2.19
General Electric	2.16
JPMorgan Chase	2.02
Verizon Communications	2.00
AT&T	1.88
Microsoft	1.85
Pfizer	1.84
Wells Fargo	1.57
Total Weight	**21.84**

SOURCE: INVESCOPOWERSHARES

• DIVIDEND ETFS •

Dividend ETFs track indexes that select securities based on their dividend payouts. This methodology became a hot topic of conversation in 2006 after ETF provider WisdomTree launched a family of dividend-weighted ETFs. This firm believes that selecting securities according to their dividend payouts will, in general, generate higher cumulative returns with lower volatility than comparable indexes that weigh securities according to market cap. There are other dividend ETFs that work by including stocks that have consistently increased their dividends without ever missing or cutting a payout. A popular dividend ETF is the iShares Dow Jones Select Dividend Index ETF Fund (Ticker symbol: DVY). This ETF is made up of the one hundred highest-dividend yielding stocks in the Dow Jones U.S. Total Stock Market Index. The stocks are selected based on their dividend yield and screened based on their dividend-per-share growth rate, dividend-payout percentage rate, and average daily trading volume. The top ten stocks in this ETF are in the following table. The majority of stocks in the index are from the financial, utility, and consumer goods sectors, which tend to pay more dividends than other sectors of the market.

TABLE 3.8: ISHARES DOW JONES SELECT DIVIDEND INDEX ETF (TICKER SYMBOL: DVY) TOP TEN HOLDINGS

COMPANY	WEIGHT OF ETF (%)
DTE Energy	2.67
Pinnacle West Capital	2.63
PNC Financial Services Group	2.61
FirstEnergy	2.53
Chevron	2.46
Nicor	2.28
Genuine Parts	2.20
Mercury General	2.00
Zions Bancorporation	1.88
PPG Industries	1.87
Total Weight	**23.13**

SOURCE: BARCLAYS GLOBAL INVESTORS

• EARNINGS ETFS •

Similar to dividend ETFs, these ETFs track indexes that represent stocks that are selected based on their earnings. These ETFs can be attractive to investors who want to focus on companies that are doing the best job producing consistently increasing earnings. These ETFs took the spotlight when WisdomTree introduced a family of ETFs that tracked earnings-based indexes. One ETF that fits into this category is WisdomTree's broad market, earnings-weighted ETF, the WisdomTree Total Earnings Fund (ETF) (Ticker symbol: EXT). According to WisdomTree, this ETF should track the performance of companies within the broad U.S. stock market that have had positive cumulative earnings for the four fiscal quarters prior to each index rebalancing date.

TABLE 3.9: WISDOMTREE TOTAL EARNINGS FUND (ETF)
(TICKER SYMBOL: EXT) TOP TEN HOLDINGS

COMPANY	WEIGHT OF ETF (%)
ExxonMobil	6.40
Wal-Mart Stores	2.70
Chevron	2.62
JPMorgan Chase	2.11
General Electric	1.75
Berkshire Hathaway	1.66
Johnson & Johnson	1.59
Procter & Gamble	1.52
Microsoft	1.47
Wells Fargo	1.42
Total Weight	**23.24**

SOURCE: WISDOMTREE

• INTELLIGENT ETFS •

Intelligent ETFs are based on indexes that use a consistent screening method to select index components that are considered the most likely to appreciate. They aim to generate better returns than their corresponding, passive benchmark. PowerShares was the first player in this area with its family of ETFs based on intelligent indexes, or Intellidexes. These indexes seek to hold the securities that have the greatest investment merit. In 2007, First Trust followed up with the launch of several sector and style-based ETFs based on indexes known as the AlphaDEXes. Intelligent ETFs are still passive products, as they track indexes and lack human intervention in selecting index components. However, because the indexes vary more than traditional indexes by changing index components mechanically whenever the ETFs rebalance, generally quarterly, they are considered more active products. With these indexes, at each rebalancing event, turnover can be relatively high compared to purely passive ETFs. Let's look at the Power-Shares Dynamic Market (ETF) (Ticker symbol: PWC) as an example. This ETF tracks an index composed of one hundred U.S. stocks selected each quarter by the American Stock Exchange, according to the proprietary Intellidex methodology. The methodology looks for stocks with superior risk-return profiles. The companies are ranked according to various criteria including fundamentals, valuation, risk, and overall investment potential, and the ETF is rebalanced quarterly. When a rebalancing occurs, the universe is evaluated based on twenty-five "merit factors." The goal of this ETF is to create an index and paired ETF that provide U.S. core equity market exposure with the potential to outperform other similar indexes, such as the S&P 500, through individual stock selection. The top ten holdings are in the table below.

TABLE 3.10: POWERSHARES DYNAMIC MARKET (ETF) (TICKER SYMBOL: PWC) TOP TEN HOLDINGS

COMPANY	WEIGHT OF ETF (%)
Occidental Petroleum	4.39
Altria Group	3.95
Anadarko Petroleum	3.89
Kroger	3.83
Fluor	2.73
Lockheed Martin	2.61
Air Products & Chemicals	2.58
Dover	2.57
FirstEnergy	2.55
Amgen	2.50
Total Weight	**31.60**

SOURCE: INVESCOPOWERSHARES

• LEVERAGED ETFS •

Leveraged ETFs hit the market in 2006 to allow investors to make big bets on the market. By using instruments such as swap agreements, futures contracts, and options on securities indexes, leveraged ETFs seek to magnify the results of the underlying securities by a prescribed multiple (usually two times). Assuming an ETF uses leverage to double the performance of an index, if the index rises 1 percent in a given trading day, the ETF could be expected to rise 2 percent. ProShares's Ultra S&P 500 (Ticker symbol: SSO) is an example of a leveraged ETF that tracks the S&P 500. Its performance goal is to generate returns that are double that of the index. That means that if the index falls, this ETF can be expected to fall twice as much on a daily basis. The following are the top ten holdings for the ProShares Ultra S&P 500.

TABLE 3.11: PROSHARES ULTRA S&P 500 (TICKER SYMBOL: SSO) TOP HOLDINGS

COMPANY	WEIGHT OF ETF (%)
ExxonMobil	5.43
General Electric	2.33
Procter & Gamble	2.30
AT&T	2.16
Chevron	2.11
Johnson & Johnson	2.08
Microsoft	1.98
Wal-Mart Stores	1.59
Pfizer	1.48
JPMorgan Chase	1.48
Total Weight	**22.94**

SOURCE: PROSHARES

• INVERSE ETFS •

Inverse ETFs, which were also introduced in 2006, allow investors to make bets against a certain segment of the market by seeking returns that are the opposite of an index that tracks that market. For example, if an index were to fall 1 percent in a given day, the inverse ETF, also referred to as a short ETF, that tracks the index would rise 1 percent. There are also leveraged inverse ETFs, which combine both the leveraging and inverse concepts. These ETFs aim for returns that are opposite the index and are also magnified. For example, if an index falls 1 percent, a leveraged inverse ETF that tracks it could be expected to rise 2 percent. ProShares was the first company to offer such strategy-based ETFs, and they have done very well since then in terms of assets raised and trading volumes. An example of an inverse ETF is the ProShares Short (Ticker symbol: PSQ), which aims to provide results that are the inverse of the NASDAQ-100 Index. The following table lists the holdings for the Short.

TABLE 3.12: PROSHARES SHORT (TICKER SYMBOL: PSQ) HOLDINGS

SECURITY	NOTIONAL VALUE	SHARES/CONTRACTS
NASDAQ-100 Swaps	−80,851,117.33	−67,044.62
NASDAQ-100 20/03/09	−12,888,090.00	−534
Net Other Assets/Cash		93,724,290.99

SOURCE: PROSHARES

While these examples of leveraged and inverse ETFs track broad indexes, there are also a variety of narrower ETFs on the market that provide leveraged and inverse exposure to sector-, style-, and market cap–based indexes.

• ACTIVE ETFS •

Active ETFs essentially merge features of actively managed funds with the highly beneficial ETF structure. As with actively managed mutual funds, active ETFs incorporate a human element into selecting securities, whereby a portfolio manager is behind the scenes creating a portfolio of equity or fixed income designed for specific goals, such as performance or risk management. Like other ETFs, though, these products trade like stocks, trading on exchanges throughout the day and benefiting from the lower costs and tax advantages that are inherent with the ETF structure.

After much waiting and a lot of hype, the first active ETF made its way to the market in 2008. In March of that year, Bear Stearns launched the Bear Stearns Current Yield Fund (Ticker symbol: YYY), a fixed income–based fund that gives a portfolio manager the discretion to pick the underlying securities. The idea was to invest mostly in short-term debt, including U.S. government securities, corporate debt, and mortgage-backed securities. The ETF, however, was liquidated in October 2008 after managing to attract only $50 million in assets. Soon after that initial active ETF was launched, PowerShares came out with four active ETFs: three equity-based ETFs and one fixed income. The equity-based PowerShares Active AlphaQ Fund (Ticker symbol: PQY) and the PowerShares Active Alpha Multi-Cap Fund (Ticker symbol: PQZ) are similar in that they both include U.S. stocks with a market cap greater than $400 million that are updated weekly based on a proprietary screening done by the fund's sub-adviser, AER Advisors. The PowerShares Active Mega-Cap Fund (Ticker symbol: PMA) includes stocks from the Russell Top 200 Index as well as other megacap stocks. They are chosen by Invesco Institutional's proprietary stock selection model. Meanwhile, the active fixed income ETF, the PowerShares Active Low Duration Fund (Ticker symbol: PLK), has at least 80 percent of its assets invested in U.S. government, corporate, and agency debt securities. Generally, the fund's effective duration will be in the range of zero to three years. The idea of active ETFs is to maintain the benefits that the ETF structure provides, including low expenses, tax efficiency, transparency, near instant liquidity, flexibility, and the ability to purchase on margin and to place market, stop, or limit orders. But there are also benefits that they are looking to provide above those that can be achieved through traditional ETFs, such as higher returns than a comparable passive benchmark index, greater risk management, reduced volatility, and more consistent returns.

Let's look at the PowerShares Active Mega-Cap Fund. The holdings of this ETF include stocks of the Russell Top 200 Index as well as other megacap stocks that are evaluated by Invesco Institutional's proprietary stock selection model and meet certain liquidity requirements. The following are the top ten holdings as of December 2008.

TABLE 3.13: POWERSHARES ACTIVE MEGA-CAP FUND (TICKER SYMBOL: PMA) TOP HOLDINGS

COMPANY	WEIGHT OF ETF (%)
ExxonMobil	11.09
Pfizer	8.25
Eli Lilly	6.10
Biogen Idec	5.65
Symantec	5.28

COMPANY	WEIGHT OF ETF (%)
Occidental Petroleum	5.06
eBay	4.72
Verizon Communications	4.68
ConocoPhillips	4.63
IBM	4.42
Total Weight	**59.88**

SOURCE: INVESCOPOWERSHARES

Many in the industry expect active ETFs to continue to be rolled out in a variety of different shapes and sizes. While active ETFs are still very new, and many variations on the model are expected to be rolled out in the future, these new products could have a big impact on industry growth by attracting more investors that are advocates of active investing but like the ease and simplicity of the ETF structure.

There have been some hurdles in creating active ETFs, which is why it took a while for the first product to debut. One of the biggest obstacles has been transparency. Traditional ETFs are transparent, so it is always known exactly what securities they hold. The holdings don't change unless the index is rebalanced, and the rebalancing changes are also transparent. However, with active products, portfolio managers don't want the world to know exactly what they are doing. After all, why bother investing in an active fund or ETF if the investor could just see exactly what the fund manager is doing and mirror the same strategy? The other side of the argument is that if transparency is lost, investors would forfeit one of the biggest benefits of ETFs. For instance, if authorized participants could not see what is held in the ETF, they could lose the ability to arbitrage and keep share pricing efficient. The result could look more like a closed-end fund, with large premiums and discounts, than an ETF.

The PowerShares active ETFs sought to overcome these issues by disclosing the portfolio's holdings daily on the fund's Web site after the close of trading on the NYSE Arca (the NYSE's all-electronic securities platform) and prior to the opening of trading on the NYSE Arca the following day. In addition, the portfolio will make changes only once per week, on the last business day of each week, and the changes will be reflected on the funds' Web site prior to the opening of trading on the next business day. This process maintains some transparency, though not as much as traditional ETFs, which constantly provide investors access to the holdings as well as disclose their net asset value every fifteen seconds.

There are various other issues with active ETFs, such as costs. One of the benefits of ETFs is that their expense ratios are lower than actively managed mutual funds. While investors do pay brokerage fees to trade ETFs, those are usually offset over time due to the lower expense ratio. However, adding active management to ETFs could come with higher management fees and expenses. If that's the case, not only must investors pay a brokerage fee, but they will have a higher expense ratio. The Power-Shares active equity ETFs have an expense ratio of 0.75 percent, which is higher than many traditional broad equity ETFs though still significantly lower than the average expense ratio of actively managed mutual funds, which tracks around 1.5 percent. The expense ratio for the active bond ETF is 0.29 percent. In addition, if the performance of these products proves to be substantially better than passive ETFs, the higher expense ratio will not matter.

If active ETFs prove to be successful, many more companies could be lured into the ETF space, including more mutual fund companies, which have steered clear of it so far. In the past, ETFs were less profitable for them, and it was thought that they threatened to cannibalize part of their profitable mutual fund businesses. Active ETFs, though, could change these dynamics. These companies would be able to continue using their active managers and also charge the higher expense ratios they are accustomed to. An actively managed ETF structure also could mean a major increase in the ETF industry's assets. The majority of mutual fund assets are in active funds—in fact, roughly 85 percent of the total. With such a large market interested in some form of active management, it clearly appears that the active ETF structure could attract meaningful assets.

• LIFE CYCLE AND LIFESTYLE ETFS •

In October 2007, the first family of life cycle ETFs was introduced by XShares Advisors and a TD Ameritrade subsidiary, Amerivest Investment Management. The funds, known as TDX Independence Funds, invest in a combination of equities and fixed income securities and change their allocation over time to become more conservative by selling stocks and moving into fixed income. The ETFs track the Zacks Lifecycle Indexes, and have expense ratios of 0.65 percent, which is significantly lower than the average target date fund, which typically charges upward of 1.2 percent. In May 2008, PowerShares launched a group of ETFs—the PowerShares Autonomic Balanced NFA Global Asset Portfolio—that are essentially risk-based ETFs designed to provide the best possible returns for varying levels of risk. These ETFs track indexes of ETFs designed by Boston-based advisory firm New Frontier Advisors. The asset allocation of the ETFs ranges from 60 percent equity and 40 percent fixed income for the more conservative ETF, to 75 percent equity and 25 percent fixed income for the more moderately allocated ETF, and 90 percent equity and just 10 percent fixed income for the most aggressive of the group. These ETFs do not adjust their asset allocations like target date funds, though they offer a diversified basket of stocks and bonds to investors targeting varying levels of risk. Each of these funds charges an expense ratio of just 0.25 percent.

In November 2008, iShares also came out with a family of risk-based and target date ETFs. These products invest primarily in other iShares ETFs, though there may be small allocations to individual securities. These include conservative, moderate, aggressive, and growth allocation funds. In addition, they offer target date funds that range in ten-year increments from 2010 to 2040, and an additional fund, the iShares S&P Target Date Retirement Income Index Fund, which is a very conservative fund for investors who are close to retirement. The expense ratios for these funds range from 0.29 percent to 0.34 percent. The way these risk-based and target date funds function will be discussed later in the book.

Let's look at the TDX Independence 2030 ETF (Ticker symbol: TDN). The table below lists the holdings of this ETF and its allocation between equities and fixed income.

TABLE 3.14: TDX INDEPENDENCE 2030 ETF (TICKER SYMBOL: TDN) TOP HOLDINGS

COMPANY	WEIGHT OF ETF (%)
ExxonMobil	3.95
U.S. Treasury Note 4.5%	2.14
Wal-Mart Stores	1.82
Chevron	1.64

COMPANY	WEIGHT OF ETF (%)
Microsoft	1.64
AT&T	1.53
Procter & Gamble	1.50
General Electric	1.41
U.S. Treasury N/B 4.75% 5/15/2014	1.37
Johnson & Johnson	1.34
Total Weight	**18.34**

SOURCE: TDX INDEPENDENCE FUNDS

• WEIGHTING INDEXES •

In addition to grouping stocks together based on different features such as size, style, or sector, another element that can distinguish one index-tracking ETF from another is how the index that it tracks assigns weights to its underlying securities. For instance, most ETFs are based on indexes that allocate the greatest percentage to stocks with the largest market cap, though some disperse the weight evenly among all of their stocks and some base each stock's weight on its share price. Below are descriptions of various different weighting schemes.

Market Cap Weighting

Market cap weighting has already been referenced several times in this chapter, since the majority of ETFs on the market track indexes that are market cap weighted. In an index that is market cap weighted, the components with the largest market cap make up the largest weight in the index. One advantage of such a market cap weighted index is simplicity. As stock prices change each trading day, the weightings of index components automatically adjust. However, this method also has a disadvantage. That is, the resulting index often has an overweight position in stocks that are overvalued and an underweight position in stocks that are undervalued. Some argue that because of this, these indexes are inefficient and could result in underperformance. The S&P 500 is a market cap weighted index. Also, recall from the earlier example, the top ten stocks in this index account for about 20 percent of the portfolio. Because this index is so top heavy, the performance of these few large stocks will have a pretty significant impact on the overall performance of the ETF.

Market cap is generally determined by multiplying the share price of a stock by the number of shares outstanding. But there is also another, slightly different way to do this, known as free float methodology. This approach determines the market cap by multiplying the stock price by the number of shares on the market that are readily available. Unlike traditional market cap weighted indexes, this excludes certain shares that are not accessible, such as those held by governments.

Equal Weighting

ETFs that use an equal weighting scheme are based on indexes that diverge from the traditional market cap weighting methodology by assigning all securities in the index the same or similar weight. The object behind equal weight indexes is to overcome some shortcomings of market cap weighted benchmarks, such as overweighting overvalued stocks and underweighting stocks that are undervalued. The thinking is that this can improve index performance, because the stocks that would have otherwise been undervalued have a greater weight in the portfolio, and therefore have more potential to appreciate. Meanwhile, the stocks that are overvalued already make up a smaller portion of the index. An equal weight index tends to perform better than a market cap weight index in environments that favor mid- and small cap stocks. Also, the equal weighting has the advantage of avoiding excessive valuations during momentum-driven markets.

Some investors believe the choice between a market cap weight index and equal weight index is trivial. However, the difference in performance can be surprisingly large. Let's use an example to illustrate: the broadest of all U.S. stock market indexes, the Wilshire 5000 index, which includes 5,400 component stocks that collectively account for more than 99 percent of all U.S. publicly traded equities. The table below compares the performance of the equal weight version of this index with the market cap weighted version—both of which hold the same components. Over a one-year period the index, when weighing all the securities equally, had significantly worse performance than the market cap weighted index. However, the annualized ten-year performance of the equally weighted index was substantially greater than that of the market cap weighted index.

TABLE 3.15: PERFORMANCES OF WILSHIRE 5000 INDEXES FOR PERIODS ENDING MARCH 31, 2008

INDEX	1 YEAR	3 YEARS ANNUALIZED	5 YEARS ANNUALIZED	10 YEARS ANNUALIZED
Wilshire 5000 Equal Weight	-18.77%	3.44%	20.75%	12.94%
Wilshire 5000 (Market Cap Weighted)	-5.76%	6.37%	12.45%	3.95%

SOURCE: WILSHIRE ASSOCIATES

One issue with equal weighted ETFs is that they need to be rebalanced periodically to maintain their weighting, and this has the potential to increase expenses. One example of an equal weighted ETF is the Rydex S&P 500 Equal Weight (Ticker symbol: RSP), which has about $1.4 billion in assets. This ETF also tracks the S&P 500 but assigns an equal weight at periodic rebalancing events to all index components. As the table below shows, even the top holdings make up only about between 0.30 percent and 0.40 percent of the ETF's assets.

TABLE 3.16: RYDEX S&P 500 EQUAL WEIGHT ETF (TICKER SYMBOL: RSP) TOP TEN HOLDINGS

COMPANY	WEIGHT OF ETF (%)
SSGA Funds SSGA Government Money Market	0.40
Archer Daniels	0.37
Apollo Group	0.37
Constellation Energy	0.34
Bristol Meyers Squibb	0.32
Intercontinental Exchange	0.32
ExxonMobil	0.31
Autozone	0.30
Verizon Communications	0.30
Tellabs	0.30
Total Weight	**3.33**

SOURCE: RYDEX SGI

Price Weighting

The best-known price weighted index is the Dow Jones Industrial Average. ETFs based on price weighted indexes are designed to give stocks with the highest share prices the greatest weighting in the index and the stocks with the lowest share prices the lowest weighting. The overall value of the index is determined by adding the stocks' prices and dividing them by the number of stocks. The stocks with the highest share prices will have the greatest impact on the performance of the index. A well-known ETF in this category is the Diamonds Trust Series, also known as the Dow Diamonds, which is based on the Dow Jones Industrial Average (Ticker symbol: DIA). The Dow Jones Industrial Average comprises thirty of the largest stocks that are considered leaders in their industries. It then weighs those stocks according to their prices. The table below lists the top ten holdings in the Dow Diamonds ETF, which has about $8.6 billion in assets. As of September 2009, IBM had the greatest weight in this ETF, 9.33 percent, followed by ExxonMobil, which accounted for 6.25 percent, and Chevron, which made up 5.92 percent.

TABLE 3.17: DOW DIAMONDS (TICKER SYMBOL: DIA) TOP TEN HOLDINGS (WEIGHTED BY PRICE)

COMPANY	WEIGHT OF ETF (%)	STOCK PRICE (AS OF DECEMBER 12, 2008)
IBM	7.49	$82.20
ExxonMobil	7.44	$80.45
Chevron	7.38	$79
McDonald's	5.66	$60.59
Procter & Gamble	5.44	$58.94
Johnson & Johnson	5.41	$57.25
3M	5.12	$56.04
Wal-Mart Stores	5.09	$54.63
United Technologies	4.37	$48.82
Coca-Cola	4.11	$44.57
Total Weight	57.51	

SOURCE: STATE STREET GLOBAL ADVISORS

• CHAPTER SUMMARY •

▶ The majority of ETFs that trade in the United States represent some segment of the U.S. stock market. Some are broad-based ETFs that track well-known indexes, while others slice the stock market into narrow segments.

▶ ETFs representing the U.S. stock market can be divided into different categories. Stocks can be grouped together according to the market cap of the underlying stocks, the style that they represent, or their sector, industry, or fundamental factors. ETFs also can be classified by the strategy that is used with them, such as intelligent indexing, or by the techniques used, such as leverage, shorting, or active portfolio management.

▶ Traditional index-based ETFs also can be differentiated based on the way that the stocks in the index are weighed. Most commonly this is done according to market cap, so the stocks with the greatest market cap make up the greatest weight in the portfolio. However, some ETFs are based on indexes that use other methodologies, such as weighing the stocks equally or according to their stock price.

4

ETFs Aim Abroad

Exposure to the U.S. stock market is a crucial piece of any investment portfolio, but it is only one piece of the puzzle. Having exposure to the international stock market is also essential in developing a well-diversified portfolio. While the U.S. stock market has continued to increase in size and sophistication, markets across the rest of the world have grown even faster. Investors have taken note and have been responding by increasing their focus on markets around the world, both in developed areas as well as in emerging markets. The introduction of foreign ETFs has made it even easier for U.S. investors to gain access to these markets by allowing them to invest broadly in a range of foreign investments or gain specific exposure to certain areas of foreign markets. In recent years investors have become increasingly aware of the benefits that these ETFs have to offer. In fact, through 2007, global and international equity ETFs accounted for almost 30 percent of the U.S. ETF industry's total ETF assets. This chapter will look at the many benefits of investing in international equities. It also will focus on the rapid growth in international ETFs, the various international ETF options that are available to investors, and some of the important differences that exist between U.S. and international equity ETFs.

• THE BENEFITS OF INTERNATIONAL INVESTING •

Financial advisers often recommend that investors allocate at least 10 percent of their portfolios to international equities, and some experts suggest international allocations that are even higher. Harvard University, for example, reportedly has increased its portfolio's international allocation to 40 percent. While that allocation may not be appropriate for everyone, there are various reasons investors should take a closer look at international investments. The following are some of the benefits these investments can have on a portfolio:

Boost Portfolio Performance

Including foreign investments has the potential to boost the performance of a portfolio. Consider the period from 1970 through 2007. Developed foreign markets (measured by the MSCI EAFE Index) outperformed the U.S. market (measured by the S&P 500 Index) in twenty-two of thirty-eight years. While the *annualized* rate of return of both indexes was fairly balanced over the full thirty-eight-year period—11.2 percent for MSCI EAFE and 11 percent for the S&P 500—investors could have benefited from having an allocation to both domestic and international equities—specifically if they had more tailored exposure to certain foreign markets that produced better returns than the U.S. market during various periods of time.

In addition, emerging market equities in recent years have produced some of the most attractive returns of any asset class in the world. For example, for the three-year period 2005 through 2007, the four BRIC markets—Brazil, Russia, India, and China—together achieved an annualized performance of 25.19 percent in U.S. dollars, according to MSCI Barra. Recall, the BRIC countries are considered to have very rapidly developing economies; however, over the same period, even a broader emerging markets index published by MSCI returned 22.77 percent. While emerging markets can be volatile, having some emerging market exposure gives an investment program a greater ability to tap into high rates of local market growth.

A Value Play

Another beneficial element of including foreign stocks in a portfolio is that they are often good value investments. While this is not always the case, as price-to-earnings ratios can change significantly over time, at times overseas stocks can be undervalued relative to U.S. stocks. When price-to-earnings ratios are lower in international markets than in the United States, investors have an opportunity to capitalize on attractive foreign equity prices.

Dividend Income

Investing in international equities also can be a good way to add dividend income to a portfolio. In the U.S. stock market, high dividends often can be hard to find, and in many cases, particularly recently, U.S. dividend payouts have been considerably lower than they've been abroad. The average dividend yield around the time this book was written was 2.2 percent, compared with 3.6 percent for the FTSE 100, which is an index that tracks the 100 largest U.K. companies, in terms of market cap, listed on the London Stock Exchange. That is why broadening the universe of potential stock choices to include global markets can help dividend-minded investors increase yields without sacrificing quality.

Diversification

Adding international investments to a portfolio also will serve to increase diversification, as discussed in Chapter 1. Even when investors have diversified their portfolios across investment styles, market caps, and sectors of the U.S. market, they may lack foreign exposure. Adding an international element to a U.S.-heavy portfolio can help to reduce overall portfolio volatility. During periods of domestic economic uncertainty or weakness, the strength of foreign markets often can offset lower returns or losses in U.S. positions. The following table shows the correlations between the U.S. market, as measured by the S&P 500 Index, and various foreign market benchmarks for the fourteen-year period through 2006.

**TABLE 4.1: MARKET CORRELATION WITH THE U.S. STOCK MARKET,
1992–2006**

COUNTRY/REGION	CORRELATION
(S&P 500 Index) United States	1.00
Europe (MSCI Europe Index)	0.75
All developed markets (excluding United States) (MSCI EAFE Index)	0.69
Asia Pacific (excluding Japan) (MSCI AC Asia Pacific Ex-Japan Index)	0.61
Emerging markets (MSCI Emerging Markets Index)	0.64
Japan (MSCI Japan Index)	0.36

SOURCE: STYLEADVISOR

The larger developed economies of Europe have the highest correlations to the U.S. markets, while emerging markets and Asian markets have modestly low correlations. Notice that Japanese equities have a particularly low correlation with the U.S. market, which has historically been the case. As a result, Japanese investments have the potential to offer investors particularly strong diversification benefits inside their portfolios.

• THE DEVELOPMENT OF INTERNATIONAL ETFS •

The first internationally focused ETFs came to market in 1996 when Barclays Global Investors launched a suite of country-specific ETFs. These ETFs initially were called World Equity Benchmark Shares (WEBS), but were later renamed iShares. These ETFs represented 17 developed markets. They were the only international ETFs traded on U.S. exchanges until 2000, when an era of rapid expansion began. Through 2008 there were roughly 150 international ETFs. ETFs offer investors many options when it comes to investing abroad, and as products continue to be rolled out, the menu keeps getting better and better. There are global ETFs, which provide broad diversification by tracking indexes of the largest companies around the world. There are ETFs that only track stocks from developed countries, or from emerging markets, or from specific countries, and there are ETFs that provide exposure to certain sectors of the global market.

While there are various ways investors can gain access to international markets, ETFs allow investors to gain broad international exposure easily by buying even a single ETF, or to gain precise exposure to certain niches of the world by investing in a variety of more targeted international products. And because these ETFs track indexes, they eliminate the need for investors to either rely on a portfolio manager to select specific stocks or, alternately, do the time-consuming research themselves.

Global ETFs typically offer broad exposure to some of the largest companies around the world. One example is the SPDR Dow Jones Global Titans ETF (Ticker symbol: DGT), which provides exposure to fifty such stocks. As the table below shows, this ETF provides exposure to various countries, though, because it is a global ETF, U.S. stocks still account for a significant portion of the holdings.

TABLE 4.2: COUNTRIES REPRESENTED IN SPDR DJ GLOBAL TITANS ETF (TICKER SYMBOL: DGT)

COUNTRY	WEIGHT IN PORTFOLIO (%)
United States	60.21
United Kingdom	14.99
Switzerland	7.63
France	3.62
Germany	2.73
Spain	1.87
Italy	1.24
The Netherlands	1.17
South Korea	1.15

SOURCE: STATE STREET GLOBAL ADVISORS

The following table shows the top holdings in this ETF. These holdings include some of the largest companies in the world, many of which are U.S. companies, such as ExxonMobil (Ticker symbol: XOM) and General Electric (Ticker symbol: GE); this accounts for the disproportionate weight in U.S. stocks.

TABLE 4.3: TOP HOLDINGS OF SPDR DJ GLOBAL TITANS ETF

COMPANY	WEIGHT IN PORTFOLIO (%)
ExxonMobil	6.74
General Electric	5.47
Microsoft	3.50
AT&T	3.42
Procter & Gamble	3.19
Nestlé SA	2.92
HSBC Holdings	2.89
BP	2.82
Johnson & Johnson	2.72

SOURCE: STATE STREET GLOBAL ADVISORS

There are also ETFs that are focused on providing exposure to a variety of developed countries, which are countries with large, highly developed economies. A good example is the iShares MSCI EAFE ETF (Ticker symbol: ETA), which, with more than $47 billion in assets, is the largest ETF in the category. This ETF tracks the MSCI EAFE Index. Owning this ETF gives exposure to twenty-one different countries; each country and its weight in the portfolio is listed below.

TABLE 4.4: COUNTRIES REPRESENTED IN ISHARES MSCI EAFE ETF (TICKER SYMBOL: ETA)

COUNTRY	WEIGHT IN PORTFOLIO (%)
United Kingdom	21.34
Japan	19.93
France	10.68
Germany	9.11
Switzerland	7.20
Australia	6.36
Spain	4.47
Italy	3.87

COUNTRY	WEIGHT IN PORTFOLIO (%)
The Netherlands	3.02
Sweden	2.44
Hong Kong	2.16
Finland	1.85
Belgium	1.38
Singapore	1.15
Norway	1.04
Denmark	1.04
Ireland	0.71
Austria	0.59
Greece	0.50
Portugal	0.41
United States	0.02

SOURCE: BARCLAYS GLOBAL INVESTORS

Because this is a market cap weighted ETF, its top holdings include many of the same companies as the holdings of the global ETF, with the exception of U.S. stocks. The weights of the stocks are more evenly dispersed, however, because there are roughly twelve hundred stocks represented in this ETF. The following is a list of the top holdings of the iShares MSCI EAFE ETF.

TABLE 4.5: TOP HOLDINGS OF ISHARES MSCI EAFE ETF

COMPANY	WEIGHT IN PORTFOLIO (%)
BP	1.73
HSBC Holdings	1.54
Nestlé SA	1.37
Total SA	1.36
Vodafone Group	1.25
Royal Dutch Shell	1.10

COMPANY	WEIGHT IN PORTFOLIO (%)
Toyota Motor	1.03
Banco Santander SA	1.02
BHP Billiton	1.00

SOURCE: BARCLAYS GLOBAL INVESTORS

Another category of international ETF that has become popular is that of emerging markets. These focus on investing in companies whose economies are not yet as large as those of the developed countries; however, they have the potential for growth. The iShares MSCI Emerging Markets ETF (Ticker symbol: EEM) is a popular emerging markets ETF with roughly $26.5 billion in assets. This ETF invests in twenty-three different countries. The table below shows how the portfolio's allocation is divided among these countries.

TABLE 4.6: COUNTRIES REPRESENTED IN ISHARES MSCI EMERGING MARKETS ETF (TICKER SYMBOL: EEM)

COUNTRY	WEIGHT IN PORTFOLIO (%)
Brazil	14.18
China	12.89
South Korea	12.36
Taiwan	10.55
Russian Federation	9.34
South Africa	7.40
Mexico	6.20
India	5.96
Israel	3.57
Thailand	2.27
Czech Republic	2.26
Chile	2.13
Indonesia	2.11
Hungary	1.46

COUNTRY	WEIGHT IN PORTFOLIO (%)
The Philippines	1.43
Hong Kong	1.29
Egypt	0.86
Turkey	0.80
Argentina	0.79
Peru	0.58
Malaysia	0.57
United States	0.40
Colombia	0.11

SOURCE: BARCLAYS GLOBAL INVESTORS

The following is a list of the top holdings in this ETF. The weights of these stocks are also fairly evenly dispersed as there are more than 930 stocks represented in this ETF.

TABLE 4.7: TOP HOLDINGS IN ISHARES MSCI EMERGING MARKETS ETF

COMPANY	WEIGHT IN PORTFOLIO (%)
OAO Gazprom ADS	3.80
Samsung Electronics	3.45
Taiwan Semiconductor	2.63
China Mobile	2.55
Petroleo Brasileiro ADR/A	2.41
Chunghwa Telecom ADR	2.38
Posco ADR	2.37
Petroleo Brasileiro ADR	2.24
Cia Vale Do Rio Doce—SP ADR	2.02
Cia Vale Do Rio Doce—ADR	1.72

SOURCE: BARCLAYS GLOBAL INVESTORS

So far, each of the international ETF categories discussed has been similar in that they represent a fairly broad group of stocks: the largest stocks from around the world; stocks from developed countries; or stocks from emerging markets. But there are also international ETFs that can provide more specific exposure by allowing investment in stocks from an individual country or a particular area of the international market. Let's look first at country-specific ETFs, using the iShares Japan ETF (Ticker symbol: EWJ) as an example. This ETF, which has about $8.5 billion in assets, offers exposure to Japanese stocks by tracking the MSCI Japan Index. This ETF includes stocks from a variety of different sectors of the Japanese market. The table below shows how the ETF is allocated among different sectors.

TABLE 4.8: SECTOR BREAKDOWN OF ISHARES JAPAN ETF (TICKER SYMBOL: EWJ)

SECTOR	WEIGHT IN PORTFOLIO (%)
Financials	19.44
Industrials	19.36
Consumer Discretionary	18.89
Information Technology	14.00
Materials	8.99
Health Care	5.31
Consumer Staples	5.19
Utilities	4.09
Telecommunication Services	2.81
Energy	1.11

SOURCE: BARCLAYS GLOBAL INVESTORS

The ETF holds almost four hundred Japanese stocks. It is market cap weighted, giving the most weight in the portfolio to the largest stocks. Table 4.9 shows the top holdings of this ETF.

• • •

TABLE 4.9: TOP HOLDINGS OF ISHARES JAPAN ETF

COMPANY	WEIGHT IN PORTFOLIO (%)
Toyota Motor	5.04
Mitsubishi UFJ Financial Group	3.46
Nintendo	2.07
Sumitomo Mitsui Financial Group	2.06
Canon	1.95
Mizuho Financial Group	1.84
Honda Motor	1.84
Matsushita Electric	1.78
Sony	1.68
Takeda Pharmaceutical	1.59

SOURCE: BARCLAYS GLOBAL INVESTORS

• GROWTH IN INTERNATIONAL ETFS •

As demand for international exposure has increased, so has the demand for ETFs representing these various segments. According to the Investment Company Institute, assets of international ETFs that are traded on U.S. exchanges rose to almost $180 billion in 2007, up from just $252 million in 1996. The rapid expansion of this category is evident in the table below. Notice the particularly strong growth that began after 2000.

TABLE 4.10: GROWTH OF INTERNATIONAL ETFS ACCORDING TO PRODUCTS AND ASSETS

YEAR	NUMBER OF U.S. TRADED INTERNATIONAL ETFS	NET ASSETS OF U.S. TRADED INTERNATIONAL ETFS ($ MILLIONS)
1996	17	252
1997	17	506
1998	17	1,026
1999	17	1,992

YEAR	NUMBER OF U.S. TRADED INTERNATIONAL ETFS	NET ASSETS OF U.S. TRADED INTERNATIONAL ETFS ($ MILLIONS)
2000	25	2,041
2001	34	3,016
2002	39	5,324
2003	41	13,984
2004	43	33,644
2005	49	65,210
2006	85	111,194
2007	159	179,702

SOURCE: INVESTMENT COMPANY INSTITUTE

As is the case with the rest of the ETF market, assets in international ETFs are highly concentrated among just a few products. The table below shows that the assets of the top five international ETFs account for more than $88 billion in this category. That's roughly half of all international ETF assets.

TABLE 4.11: TOP FIVE INTERNATIONAL ETFS (ASSETS)

ETF NAME	TOTAL ASSETS ($ MILLIONS)
iShares MSCI EAFE (Ticker symbol: EFA)	47,362.90
iShares MSCI Emerging Markets (Ticker symbol: EEM)	26,329.30
Vanguard Emerging Markets (Ticker symbol: VWO)	7,059.10
iShares S&P Latin 40 (Ticker symbol: ILF)	4,016.50
iShares MSCI ex-Japan (Ticker symbol: EPP)	3,832.80

SOURCE: INDEXUNIVERSE.COM

Why have assets of international ETFs taken off like a rocket in the past few years? There are two basic answers. The first has to do with U.S. investors' ever-expanding awareness of international markets. More U.S. citizens are traveling outside the country, and both awareness and understanding of international economic trends is on the rise. The net purchases by

Americans of long-term foreign securities such as stocks and bonds, which are tracked by the U.S. Treasury, were virtually zero from 1999 through 2002. Then, from 2003 through 2007, net foreign purchases increased steadily and sharply. In December 2006, they reached a high of $51.2 billion. This trend indicates a strong and sustained demand by Americans to diversify their portfolios to include foreign investments. Another factor that has spurred interest in international ETFs has to do with currencies. During this same period, 2003 through 2007, the value of the U.S. dollar experienced a major decline against several other major world currencies. This diminished value of the dollar helped to enhance the performance of most foreign markets when their returns are converted back into dollars.

• ACCESS TO EMERGING MARKETS •

Emerging market ETFs have become a particular favorite among investors in recent years. Companies in many emerging markets often are difficult to research, making essential information less readily available than that of stocks from developed countries, and investors may lack the time or ability to participate in these markets by picking individual stocks. As a result, many have turned to actively managed mutual funds as a solution. However, these funds often have high management fees because of the extra costs involved in researching foreign companies. In addition, these funds don't always track closely with index returns of a given emerging market. That's why ETFs often provide the best solution. They offer lower-cost exposure to emerging markets benchmarks and eliminate the need to research and select individual stocks.

• GLOBAL SECTOR OR THEME INVESTING •

Another benefit of international ETFs is that they allow investors to participate in various themes or trends, which in many cases emerge abroad before they are accepted in the United States. A good example of this is the clean energy movement. Across the world more than 160 nations have already ratified the international agreement known as the Kyoto Protocol, which dictates standards for reducing greenhouse gas emissions through more efficient use of clean or alternative energy sources. Among developed nations, the only major nonsigners of the agreement are the United States and Australia. The need to comply with the Kyoto Protocol has stimulated innovative technologies and helped to launch public companies involved in clean energy. Currently, many of these companies are traded outside the United States, and they can be accessed through global ETFs dedicated to this theme.

Another example of global theme investing is that of water resources. In the United States, a large amount of water is still developed or distributed by public agencies. However, in Europe, Asia, and other parts of the world that is often not the case; water resources are developed by private enterprises. As China's economy continues to thrive, a major issue it is likely to face is the provision of enough water to quench its population's thirst and supply its agricultural lands and industries. Water is also critical to the vast populations and emerging economies of the third world. One way to engage in this potential growth area is to invest in an ETF that provides exposure to the international water market. An example of an ETF that provides this exposure is the PowerShares Global Water ETF (Ticker symbol: PIO). The aim of this ETF is to represent companies around the world that focus on the provision of potable water, the treatment of water, and the technology and services that are directly related to global water consumption. The table below shows the various countries that are represented in this ETF.

TABLE 4.12: COUNTRIES REPRESENTED IN POWERSHARES GLOBAL WATER ETF (TICKER SYMBOL: PIO)

COUNTRY	WEIGHT IN PORTFOLIO (%)
United States	27.36
Japan	10.60
Italy	9.72
Austria	8.02
Canada	6.80
Finland	5.32
United Kingdom	5.07
The Netherlands	4.50
Germany	3.87
Singapore	3.83

SOURCE: INVESCOPOWERSHARES

• DIFFERENCES BETWEEN DOMESTIC EQUITY AND INTERNATIONAL EQUITY ETFS •

International ETFs are a great way to get exposure to non-U.S. stocks. And they function mostly in the same way as ETFs that track the U.S. market. However, there are some differences with international ETFs of which investors should be mindful. Some examples include the way that the prices of international ETFs are quoted and the impact that different currencies can have on these ETFs. In the following sections these differences between domestic equity and international equity ETFs will be delved into a little deeper.

Currency Conversion

Because ETFs track indexes, their performances should be approximately similar after accounting for fees and expenses. However, one difference with international ETFs that can arise is the way in which the indexes that they track are quoted. International indexes can be quoted in one of two ways. One way is according to their local currency. In this case, the index that the ETF tracks reflects the change in the values of the securities in their local markets, without currency adjustments. The other is according to U.S. dollars, in which the index is adjusted to account for changes in relative currency values between local currencies and the U.S. dollar. U.S. investors who buy ETFs listed on U.S. exchanges should generally expect that their investments will track the latter version of the index.

To take a specific example, several ETFs listed on U.S. exchanges seek to track the performance of the MSCI EAFE Index. The table below compares the performance of this index in local currency and U.S. dollars, as of December 31, 2007.

TABLE 4.13: PERFORMANCE FOR MSCI EAFE INDEX IN U.S. DOLLARS AND LOCAL CURRENCY

	U.S. DOLLARS (%)	LOCAL CURRENCY (%)
1 Year	11.63	3.97
3 Years	17.32	16.35
5 Years	22.08	16.56
10 Years	9.04	6.49

SOURCE: MORGAN STANLEY CAPITAL INTERNATIONAL

For each period shown in the table, the performance was lower in local currency terms than in U.S. dollar terms. This shows that the dollar was weak compared with local currencies during the periods shown. When the returns produced in foreign markets were converted to U.S. dollars, investors received an extra component of performance. This is an illustration of how international ETFs can help investors hedge against periods of weakness in the U.S. dollar.

However, U.S. investors also should realize that currency conversion has risks. If the dollar appreciates against foreign currencies for a period of time, currency conversion would subtract from total return performance. Currency conversion risk should always be carefully considered before making international investments.

American Depositary Receipts (ADR)

A number of ETFs hold baskets of American Depositary Receipts (ADR) that trade in U.S. markets, and they also may track indexes composed of ADRs. ADRs are negotiable U.S. securities that represent a set number of shares of a foreign stock. Approximately five hundred ADRs are listed on U.S. stock exchanges. U.S. accounting, disclosure, and regulatory requirements apply to ADRs listed on a U.S. national exchange, and all trades clear and settle in U.S. dollars. Among the major advantages of investing in ADRs compared to purchasing the corresponding shares on foreign exchanges are their convenience, cost-efficiency, and adherence to U.S. exchange regulations and conventions. They can also help minimize the difficulties involved in buying and selling stocks on thinly traded emerging market exchanges. An ADR's share price is dependent on supply-and-demand forces in the U.S. market. However, prices rarely deviate very far from the equivalent price of the linked foreign shares, due to arbitrage trading opportunities.

The return on an ADR equals its own return (in the local market where the linked stock trades) plus any appreciation of the home market currency versus the U.S. dollar or minus any foreign currency depreciation. In addition to currency risk, ADRs also face the same political risk that underlies shares traded abroad. If a government collapses and its stock market suffers, the loss also will be reflected in the ADRs traded in the United States.

An example of an ETF that tracks ADRs is the PowerShares BLDRS

Asia 50 ADR Index Fund (Ticker symbol: ADRA), which is an ETF that participates in many of the largest and strongest companies in Asia via ADRs. It tracks the Bank of New York Asia 50 ADR Index. Among the components of this index are Toyota Motor (Ticker symbol: TM), BHP Billiton (Ticker symbol: BHP), Honda Motor (Ticker symbol: HMC), and Sony (Ticker symbol: SNE). Exposure to these companies is gained through ADRs that trade on U.S. exchanges. Therefore, the index is quoted in U.S. dollars. If the dollar is weak against Asian currencies, all of these companies stand to perform somewhat better, so the currency influence remains.

One issue with ETFs that invest in ADRs is that they pose some currency risk. That's because these ETFs have the same issue with currency conversion as other international ETFs. However, in ADR-based ETFs there is no confusion about whether the index return is quoted in U.S. dollars or local currency. ADR-based ETFs always reflect the actual return to a U.S. investor in U.S. dollars.

Price Spreads

The majority of international ETFs listed on U.S. exchanges are highly liquid, trading throughout the market day at competitive bid-ask spreads. However, that's not always the case. Sometimes the underlying securities inside these ETFs are not as liquid in their domestic markets. This can be true for a number of reasons. For instance, some Asian markets celebrate holidays during which U.S. markets remain open for trading. In addition, because of differing time zones, trading on Japanese exchanges closes about eight hours before trading on U.S. exchanges opens. In these cases, how do the prices of ETFs reflect underlying domestic securities' prices on a timely basis?

A study conducted by Dr. Robert F. Engle of New York University and Dr. Debo Sarkar of the Analysis Group/Economics found that for international ETFs a normal range of bid-ask spreads was 10 to 35 basis points—a bit higher than in comparable domestic ETFs. But their study also found that these larger spreads can arise temporarily in international ETFs, but usually disappear in a few hours or (at the most) several days.

There are ways, though, that investors can avoid paying these larger spreads. One idea is to use limit orders to buy or sell international ETFs at stated prices. This can be effective in some cases if the order placed can trigger when relatively high bid-ask spreads narrow. In addition, frequent ETF traders who are concerned about transaction costs, including bid-ask spreads, may want to consider ETFs that track ADRs. These may be more cost-efficient than those that don't, as ADRs trade in U.S. markets and as a result are priced simultaneously with the ETFs that track them.

Liquidity

Another potential issue with international ETFs is liquidity, stemming from the creation/redemption process. Recall from an earlier discussion, ETFs are created and redeemed when an authorized participant (AP) exchanges baskets of underlying securities for shares, or vice versa. This means that arbitrage traders can generate profits when the prices of ETFs deviate very far from their net asset values (NAV). In some international markets (especially the smaller emerging markets), political, military, or currency crises have sometimes made markets illiquid for intervals of time. If such an event were to happen in the future, APs might be reluctant to provide liquidity until underlying securities prices settle. Keep in mind, though, that ETFs increase diversification relative to owning individual securities. So, an event that affects a few securities in the portfolio may not have a great impact on the price or liquidity of the whole fund.

Taxes on Dividends

Like mutual funds, ETFs pass on the income that they receive from companies in their portfolio to investors as dividends. Under current U.S. tax law, certain dividends qualify for more favorable treatment as "qualified" dividends. These currently are taxed at a maximum rate of 15 percent for federal income tax purposes. Dividends that are not considered qualified can be subject to higher tax rates. For a dividend from a foreign company to be considered a qualified dividend, it must meet one of three tests: (1) be incorporated in a U.S. possession; (2) be located in a country that participates in an approved U.S. tax treaty; or (3) be traded in the U.S. market, like ADRs. In addition, to be eligible to claim qualified dividend status, the specific investment must have been held for at least 61 days during a preceding 121-day period.

In some cases dividends from foreign companies may not meet these criteria, and investors may be surprised to see their tax bite is greater than they expected. ETFs report annually on Form 1099-DIV the portion of each distribution that is a qualified dividend. But in order to be completely aware of all tax implications early on, it's a good idea for investors to consult their personal tax advisers.

Deduction for Foreign Tax Withholding

Another point to be aware of with international ETFs is that some countries require tax withholding on income paid to foreign investors. This is only an issue when an ETF trades in foreign markets—and this does not include ADRs in U.S. markets. ETF sponsors provide annual details on any foreign income withholding amounts. Investors who are affected by such withholding should consult their personal tax advisers for details on a U.S. federal tax deduction that can help to offset foreign tax withholding.

• CHAPTER SUMMARY •

▶ Having exposure to the international stock market is essential in developing a well-diversified portfolio. ETFs provide a great way to gain exposure to foreign markets.

▶ Investing in international ETFs can have many benefits, including the potential to boost performance, act as value investments inside a portfolio, provide dividend income, and increase diversification.

▶ International ETFs also can be useful tools for getting exposure to emerging markets and for engaging in global sector or theme investing.

▶ Through 2007, global and international equity ETFs accounted for almost 30 percent of the U.S. ETF industry's total ETF assets. Global markets had to produce rewarding investment returns.

▶ Differences exist between domestic equity and international ETFs. These include the way the ETFs are quoted because of different currencies, the inclusion of ADRs, wider price spread, and differences in liquidity and tax laws.

5

Expanding Beyond Equities

So far this book has focused on domestic and international equity ETFs, but as mentioned earlier, equity investments should only make up a portion of a well-diversified portfolio. To enhance diversification and manage risk, it is also important to include allocations to fixed income, and for some, investments in alternative asset classes such as commodities and currencies. In the early years of the ETF evolution, investors had very limited or no options when it came to getting exposure to these categories. Recently, however, things have changed. There are now many ETFs on the market that allow investors to tap into numerous segments of the fixed income market as well as a wide variety of alternative asset classes. These ETFs are able to provide this exposure in an easy and cost-effective way, which is particularly beneficial to investors who have had, in the past, difficulty when trying to gain access to these areas. This chapter will discuss the benefits of enhancing diversification by adding fixed income and alternative assets to a portfolio. In addition, the various fixed income and alternative asset ETFs that are available to investors will be discussed.

• THE IMPORTANCE OF THE FIXED INCOME MARKET •

The fixed income market in the United States is a huge market—unbeknownst to some, it is even larger than the U.S. equity market. Through 2007, it accounted for more than $30 trillion in assets, more than half of total U.S. market cap. It is also a highly segmented market. Assets are divided fairly evenly between various fixed income investments: corporate and high yield bonds; mortgage-backed securities; money markets; municipal bonds; asset-backed securities; federal agency securities; and treasuries.

As discussed in Chapter 1, because fixed income as a group often performs differently in comparison to equities, their addition to a portfolio tends to act as a good diversifier and helps in managing overall volatility. Fixed income can also provide more stability because the returns produced are generally more consistent than those of equities, because bonds offer a guaranteed income stream, and because in the event that a company goes bankrupt, bond holders will be recompensated before equity shareholders. It is important to recognize, though, that there can be a lot of variation among different fixed income investments, frequently causing them to perform quite differently from one another. That's why including a combination of fixed income investments also can serve to lower volatility and, in some cases, boost returns. The following table shows the differing performances of fixed income indexes between 2002 and 2006. Notice how the performance of these investments varied over time. This is particularly evident between 2002 and 2003, when high yield performed negatively—only to rebound the next year with a nearly 29 percent gain.

TABLE 5.1: PERFORMANCE OF VARIOUS FIXED INCOME INVESTMENTS (2002–2006)

FIXED INCOME INVESTMENT	2002 (%)	2003 (%)	2004 (%)	2005 (%)	2006 (%)
Treasury	11.79	2.24	3.54	2.79	3.08
Corporate	10.12	8.24	5.39	1.68	4.30
Municipal	9.60	5.31	4.48	3.51	4.84
High Yield	−1.41	28.97	11.13	2.74	11.85
Mortgage-backed Securities	8.75	3.07	4.70	2.61	5.22

SOURCE: LEHMAN BROTHERS

Fixed Income ETFs

The creation of fixed income ETFs was a major boon to investors—specifically individual investors. Because bonds are primarily traded over-the-counter, they often lack liquidity, trading flexibility, and price transparency—which have generally only been available on the institutional level. The creation of bond ETFs resolved these issues, making the bond market significantly more accessible to mainstream investors, and provided institutional investors with an additional bond trading mechanism. In addition, trading bonds inside the ETF wrapper brought along with it the other benefits inherent in trading ETFs mentioned earlier in this book, including tax efficiency, substantially lower costs than comparable actively managed bond funds, instant diversification, and trading flexibility.

Despite the obvious benefits of bond ETFs, it took a while to get these products going, as the ETF providers had to figure out a way to overcome the issues with liquidity and pricing. But eventually they did. The solution was to track a sampling of the largest and most liquid bonds within a particular index. Unlike stock ETFs, where most if not all of the stocks in the index are represented in the ETF, when it comes to bond ETFs, generally there is just a percentage of the bonds in the index that is actually represented in the ETF. Bond ETFs had very slow beginnings, though in recent years the menu has grown significantly to include everything from ETFs that track broad bond indexes to those that are focused on more specific types of bonds such as government, corporate, municipal, Treasury, international bonds, and more.

• THE BEGINNING OF BOND ETFS •

The first batch of bond ETFs was launched by Barclays in July 2002. These bond ETFs offered four options: the iShares iBoxx $ Investment Grade Corporate Bond ETF (Ticker symbol: LQD); the iShares Lehman 7–10 Year Treasury Bond ETF (Ticker symbol: IEF); the iShares Lehman 1–3 Year Treasury Bond ETF (Ticker symbol: SHY); and the iShares Lehman 20+ Year Treasury Bond ETF (Ticker symbol: TLT). (There was also another company that launched two fixed income ETFs in 2002, though those ETFs were unable to garner enough assets and closed within months.)

The following year Barclays came out with two more fixed income ETFs. In September 2003, it launched the iShares Lehman Aggregate Bond ETF (Ticker symbol: AGG), and in December the company introduced the iShares Lehman U.S. Treasury Inflation Protected Securities Bond ETF (Ticker symbol: TIP). Those six ETFs remained the only fixed income ETFs on the market until 2007, even while hundreds of equity ETFs continued to be rolled out.

But even though these products were slow to take off, in 2007 the dam broke, and new fixed income products started to pour in—and that is expected to continue in the foreseeable future.

As of October 2008, there were sixty bond ETFs, according to the Investment Company Institute, and assets in these products had increased to more than $48 billion. The table below shows how the industry has grown in terms of products and assets. Notice that it wasn't until 2007 that the number of products jumped significantly; however, assets have continued to increase steadily since the first products came to market.

TABLE 5.2: GROWTH OF FIXED INCOME ETFS BY PRODUCTS AND ASSETS

YEAR	NUMBER OF ETFS	ASSETS ($ MILLIONS)
2002	8	3,915
2003	6	4,667
2004	6	8,516
2005	6	15,004
2006	6	20,514
2007	49	34,648
October 2008	60	48,175

SOURCE: INVESTMENT COMPANY INSTITUTE

Assets in fixed income ETFs still make up a small piece of the ETF pie. The majority of assets that are in these products are currently found in ETFs that track government bonds. However, as fixed income ETFs continue to be rolled out and gain traction among investors, assets are expected to increase in the group as a whole, as well as become more evenly distributed among various fixed income products. The following table shows the breakdown of the assets in each category of fixed income ETFs.

TABLE 5.3: BREAKDOWN OF ASSETS AMONG FIXED INCOME ETFS

TYPE OF FIXED INCOME ETF	ASSETS ($ BILLIONS)	TOTAL ETF ASSETS (%)
Government and Credit	11.8	2
Government (Excluding Munis)	23.9	4
Municipals	1.3	< 1
Credit	5.5	1
Total	42.4	7

SOURCE: INVESTMENT COMPANY INSTITUTE

There are now several ETF sponsors that offer fixed income products, providing a good selection of options for investors, though Barclays* continues to have the most ETFs in this category and offers a diversified menu, ranging from investment grade and high yield corporate ETFs to mortgage-backed security, credit, and municipal bond ETFs. The iShares Lehman Aggregate Bond ETF (Ticker symbol: AGG) is the largest fixed income ETF, with more than $9 billion in assets. This ETF, which has an expense ratio of 0.24 percent, offers diverse fixed income exposure, investing in a combination of U.S. investment-grade government bonds, investment-grade corporate bonds, mortgage pass-through securities, and asset-backed securities. The bonds underlying this ETF range in terms of credit ratings and maturity, though the vast majority are assigned an agency, U.S. government, AAA, or Aaa rating and have maturities of less than 10 years. Another popular fixed income ETF is the iShares Lehman TIPS ETF (Ticker symbol: TIP). This one, which has more than $8 billion in assets and an expense ratio of 0.20 percent, invests almost entirely in U.S. government or agency-rated securities with an average maturity of 8.39 years.

PowerShares has several products, including a one- to thirty-year laddered Treasury ETF (Ticker symbol: PLW) that measures the potential returns of the U.S. Treasury yield curve based on about thirty equally weighted U.S. Treasury issues with fixed coupons that are scheduled to mature in a proportional, annual, laddered structure. They also have among their selection an ETF that invests in emerging markets sovereign debt, municipal bond ETFs, and an actively managed bond ETF that invests in U.S. government, corpo-

---

* At the time this book was written, Barclays agreed to sell its investment unit, which includes the iShares ETF unit, for $13.5 billion to BlackRock Inc., making BlackRock the world's largest money manager.

rate, and agency debt securities. In addition, State Street has various fixed income ETFs, ranging from long-term treasuries and short-term municipal bond ETFs to an international government inflation-protected bond ETF. Vanguard, meanwhile, offers a handful of these ETFs, including short-, intermediate-, and long-term bond ETFs, as well as a total bond ETF.

• INTERNATIONAL FIXED INCOME ETFS •

With the influx of bond ETFs came the arrival of international Treasury bond ETFs, offering investors yet another vehicle to enhance their diversification. As discussed earlier in the book, each investment's diversification benefit is dependent on its correlation to other investments within a portfolio. Even in the wake of the economic crisis, the low correlations between international bonds and the broad U.S. market have stayed largely intact. In addition, international bond ETFs have proven to be a good hedge against shifts in U.S. interest rates.

The most popular ETF in this category is State Street's SPDR Barclays Capital International Treasury Bond ETF (Ticker symbol: BWX), which rolled out in October 2007. This ETF, which has over $1 billion in assets and an expense ratio of just 0.50 percent, tracks the Barclays Capital Global Treasury Ex-US Capped Index, which follows fixed-rate local currency, investment grade sovereign debt of countries outside the United States, with the largest holdings in Japan, Italy, and Germany, and an average maturity of just over eight years. A similar product offered by State Street is the SPDR Barclays Capital Short Term International Treasury Bond ETF (Ticker symbol: BWZ), which is the shorter-term version, tracking fixed rate, investment grade debt issued by foreign governments of developed countries with one- to three-year remaining maturities. Assets in this ETF, as of June 2008, were only around $10 million.

Barclays also offers two international bond ETFs that were introduced in 2009. One is the iShares S&P/Citigroup International Treasury Bond Fund (Ticker symbol: IGOV), which tracks the S&P/Citigroup International Treasury Bond Index Ex-US, a broad index of treasury bonds from developed countries outside the United States issued in local currencies. Maturities vary, though the majority are from one to ten years. This ETF has an expense ratio of 0.35 percent, and has assets of under $20 million. Japan, Italy, and France are the dominant countries represented in this ETF. Like State Street, Barclays also offers a comparable shorter-maturity ETF, the iShares S&P/Citigroup 1–3 Year International Treasury Bond

Fund (Ticker symbol: ISHG), which tracks the S&P/Citigroup International Treasury Bond Index Ex-US 1–3 Year. The expense ratio on this ETF is also 0.35 percent, and assets are under $10 million.

· ALTERNATIVE ASSET CLASS ETFS ·

While stocks and bonds should be represented in every investor's portfolio, over the past several years investors have been catching on to the diversification benefits of including alternative asset classes such as currencies and commodities in their portfolios. In the past, investors often have avoided these areas, as it was too difficult or costly to get access to them, or they have gained access indirectly by, for instance, purchasing shares of oil companies in order to get exposure to the oil market. However, because these asset classes are now accessible through ETFs, investors can get direct exposure in an easy and cost-efficient way. The rest of this chapter will focus on two alternative asset classes, commodities and currencies, the benefits of including them in a portfolio, and some of the ETF options that are available to investors looking to tap into these areas.

· COMMODITIES ·

Commodities are products that can be traded on the financial markets. Some of the more popular commodities that are traded include oil, gasoline, natural gas, precious metals, industrial metals, grain/food supplies, livestock, timber, and lumber.

There are various ways to invest in companies that exploit commodities. One way is to purchase individual stocks of commodity companies such as the stock of an energy company like ExxonMobil, or by investing in a fund or ETF that invests in various commodity stocks. However, these investments are not considered pure commodity plays. While the price movement of the commodity likely will affect the stock, it is also affected by other issues, such as the market's overall direction, company management decisions, and quarterly earnings.

To add pure commodity exposure to a portfolio, investors traditionally have had to invest in them directly, which can be done in a variety of ways.

1. **Physical Possession.** One way is to physically possess the commodity. Some individual investors have owned gold or

silver bullion or coins. The problem is that for most investors, physically accumulating supplies of commodities is generally not very practical.

2. **Spot Market Purchases.** Another solution is to make spot market purchases. The spot market is the immediate market where commodities are bought and sold at their current price. For instance, when a car is filled up at the gas station, technically the purchaser is making a spot market purchase of gasoline. This market is more geared toward professional traders who generally buy and sell very large quantities of commodities in the spot market, and don't necessarily take physical possession of them.

3. **Futures Contracts.** A more common method for trading commodities is by using forward contracts and futures market purchases. A forward contract is an agreement to trade a specified quantity of a commodity at a given date and price in the future. For example, a farmer might agree to deliver ten thousand bushels of corn to a food manufacturer in September for four dollars a bushel. This transaction allows the farmer to plan ahead, because he or she knows what the price will be once the product is delivered. It also helps the food manufacturer budget its costs and avoid sharp price increases due to adverse weather. Some forward contracts are negotiated privately, and a variety of forward contracts trade on over-the-counter (OTC) markets.

Futures markets create liquidity by trading contracts with uniform terms for the volume of the commodity to be delivered, the date of delivery (expiration), and the price. The leading U.S. futures markets include the Chicago Board of Trade, the Chicago Mercantile Exchange, and the Chicago Board of Options Exchange. All futures exchanges in the United States are regulated by the Commodities Futures Trading Commission (CFTC). These exchanges serve a valuable role by providing market liquidity, uniform contract terms, and regulatory oversight.

Getting Commodities Exposure Through ETFs

When it comes to commodity ETFs, there are generally two categories: ones that hold physical commodities, such as gold and silver, inside a vault, and ones that hold futures contracts on commodities such as corn, wheat, and pork bellies.

The first commodity ETF to come to market was the StreetTRACKS Gold Trust ETF (Ticker symbol: GLD), which has since been renamed SPDR Gold Shares. It was launched by State Street in November 2004. This ETF, which is characterized as a physical commodity ETF, is structured as a grantor trust and holds just one asset, gold bullion, in a vault. It works by issuing shares that are each equal to one tenth of an ounce of the gold bullion. An investor who bought one hundred shares of this ETF would own the equivalent of ten ounces of gold, and this investment could be expected to perform about the same over time as if the equivalent physical gold had been purchased.

The other type of commodity ETF invests in futures contracts for various commodities. These effects exist largely because certain commodities aren't easy to physically obtain or store. Just try to imagine a vault full of pork bellies or barrels of oil. The storage space would be expensive to maintain, not to mention unsanitary or hazardous. So instead, these products track the futures contracts on these commodities. Generally, they do this via a basket of varied commodities that may contain anything from agricultural products to metals to livestock.

A growing number of ETFs track indexes composed of either physical commodities or commodities futures contracts. Through these ETFs, investors can participate in buying and selling these commodities as easily as they buy and sell shares of stock. They also can do this while avoiding the complexities or extra costs of owning physical assets—for instance, it is simpler and more secure to liquidate a gold ETF than to take ten ounces of physical gold to a dealer—or of participating in the futures market. Currently, the leading providers of commodities ETFs are Barclays, PowerShares, and State Street.

The types of commodity ETFs on the market include those that track energy, precious metals, base metals, and agricultural products. Let's take a look at some examples of ETFs that fall into these categories.

Oil and Energy

ETFs have made ownership of oil and energy commodities accessible to every investor. Through ETFs, it is as easy to add ten barrels of oil to a portfolio as it is to buy one hundred shares of stock. The ETFs closely track the price of oil in leading financial markets, just as equity ETFs track the price of stock market benchmarks. Some of the most popular energy-based commodity ETFs focus on crude oil pumped from the earth and products refined from crude oil—principally gasoline and heating oil. Natural gas, a common by-product of oil exploration, is also a valuable commodity used worldwide in heating and the production of electricity. Other energy commodities include propane, coal, kerosene, diesel fuel, electricity, and a new class of "emissions credits," which are being used to control energy consumption and global warming.

Energy ETFs can be useful in short-term or long-term investment strategies. In the short term, investing in energy can help investors profit from short-term or seasonal gains in energy prices, such as the typical increase in gasoline prices as the summer driving season approaches. Energy ETFs also can help to hedge against higher consumer costs for heating oil, natural gas, or gasoline.

On a long-term basis, allocating part of a portfolio to energy ETFs can help investors participate in "peak oil"—the time when the highest rate of oil is being pumped—over time. Energy ETFs also can help long-term investors ride through difficult economic or geopolitical events, such as a war in the Middle East or a recession in the United States. This is because these energy investments, particularly oil, historically have had a very low correlation with U.S. stocks. Because high energy prices can contribute to a softening economy, having some exposure to this asset class may help to stabilize portfolios when stocks are weak.

One example of an ETF that provides direct exposure to energy—and specifically oil—is the United States Oil Fund (Ticker symbol: USO). This ETF, which was launched by Victoria Bay Asset Management (now United States Commodity Funds), tracks the price movements of West Texas Intermediate light, sweet crude oil delivered to Cushing, Oklahoma, which is the main benchmark in the United States for crude oil. It invests in futures contracts for this and other petroleum-based fuels that are traded on regulated futures exchanges. It also can invest in cash-settled options on oil futures contracts, forward contracts for oil, and over-the-counter transactions that are based on the price of oil.

Precious and Base Metals

Gold and silver are the main precious metals that have become accessible to investors through ETFs. Metals are considered precious either because they have a higher per weight value than other metals and are used in making jewelry or coins, or because historically they have been considered the purest form of money. Even today, in countries where there is weak faith in paper currencies, gold and silver are prized as money substitutes. In India and China, two ancient civilizations that are rapidly modernizing, many people of modest means hold a large part of their personal wealth in gold and silver.

Until the arrival of ETFs, most individual gold and silver investors owned the physical metals. But to own and trade metals requires storage, transport, and insurance to protect against damage or theft. Dealers often charge markups of 2 percent to 4 percent on each purchase or sale. ETFs have made precious metals ownership far more efficient and accessible, and this has added demand to the precious metals investment market.

Historically, silver and gold prices have moved somewhat parallel, with silver's price recently being somewhat more volatile (on a percentage basis) than gold's. For U.S. investors, four primary factors influence the direction of gold and silver prices:

▶ **Supply and Demand.** The major source of demand for gold is for jewelry and coins. For silver, some demand comes from jewelry and coins, though much of the demand is a result of its usefulness in a variety of industrial applications, such as in making electrical contacts, switches and fuses, and medical instruments. In recent years the introduction of the gold and silver ETFs has also been responsible for an increased demand for these metals.

▶ **Investor Confidence.** Another factor that can influence the direction of the price of these metals is overall confidence in financial markets. Gold and silver historically are considered to be safe investments in times when financial markets are in turmoil, thus generally experiencing price increases during times of falling stock prices. They also tend to react favorably in times of high inflation.

▶ **Currency Moves.** The price of gold and silver also can be impacted by movements in currencies, as they tend to perform well during times when the dollar is weak, because it takes more weak dollars to purchase a constant quantity of precious metals.

► **Industrialization.** The base metals, also referred to as industrial metals, include aluminum, copper, zinc, nickel, lead, iron, steel, and uranium. These all have lower per weight value than the precious metals but are essential components of many industrial processes and products. The rapid industrialization of formerly undeveloped countries, especially China, has fueled increased demand for base metals. For example, over the past decade, China's share of world copper and nickel consumption has increased from about 2 percent to more than 20 percent, according to the investing Web site SaveHaven.com.

Base metals prices are driven largely by supply-demand influences. In many cases periods of strong demand are followed by increased supplies, as producers open new mines to meet demand. Base metals tend to perform well in periods of high economic growth, and they work modestly well as inflation hedges; however, they are prone to price volatility and can decline sharply during recessions or periods of weak commodities prices.

There are also a variety of base metals ETFs that hold futures contracts. For instance, the PowerShares DB Base Metals ETF (Ticker symbol: DBB) is based on the Deutsche Bank Liquid Commodity Index—Optimum Yield Industrial Metals Excess Return Index. This index is made up of futures contracts on some of the most liquid and widely used base metals, such as aluminum, zinc, and copper. The index is intended to reflect the performance of the industrial metals sector.

Agricultural

Major agricultural products include corn, soybeans, wheat, cattle, hogs, cocoa, coffee, sugar, cotton, and orange juice. Agricultural products were the original commodities that traded on futures exchanges. For many decades, futures contracts have helped farmers and food producers hedge against natural disasters, such as floods or droughts, while better planning prices. ETFs currently make baskets of several agricultural commodities accessible to investors, and in the future it is possible that individual agricultural products may be available in ETFs.

While agricultural products can be grown all over the world, and prices can vary among geographic regions, trends affecting these commodities have become more globalized. For example, in recent years a growing share of the U.S. and Brazilian corn crops has been allocated for the production of ethanol, and this has reduced the supplies of corn available for food and feed, driving up corn prices all over the world. In Mexico, people have demonstrated in the streets because the price of corn tortillas more than tripled. Shortages of corn for animal feed, in turn, produced higher prices for cattle and hogs. A large part of the cost paid by consumers for agricultural products goes for transportation and water. Thus, exposure to agricultural products can be an indirect way of hedging against shortages of oil (required for transportation) and water resources.

There are a variety of ETFs that invest in either specific agricultural products or a diversified bunch of them. An example of a broadly diversified agricultural ETF is the PowerShares DB Agricultural ETF (Ticker symbol: DBA). This one tracks the Deutsche Bank Liquid Commodity Index—Optimum Yield Agriculture Excess Return, which is composed of futures contracts on some of the most liquid and widely traded agricultural commodities, such as corn, wheat, soybeans, and sugar.

Taxes on Commodity ETFs

While commodities ETFs function in much the same way as ETFs that track stocks or bonds, there are some differences worth noting, one of which is how commodity ETFs are taxed. ETFs that physically hold commodities like gold and silver are considered "collectibles," and are taxed as such. That means that on any capital gains realized by holding the ETF—for instance, if some gold bullion is sold to pay expenses—the investor is subject to a maximum tax of 28 percent if the bullion was held for at least a year.

Meanwhile, for ETFs that hold futures contracts, gains are taxed as 60 percent long-term gains and 40 percent short-term gains—the tax rates on long-term gains are lower than on short-term gains. The tax code that applies says that at the end of each day open futures positions must be "marked to market" for tax purposes. This basically means that futures are considered to have been sold on the last business day of the year and reestablished on the first business day of the following year. For those in the highest tax bracket, that results in a maximum tax rate of 23 percent.

Benefits of Investing in Commodities

As with any investment, one of the most important questions to ask before investing in commodities is how will it benefit the portfolio? There are four main reasons to consider investing in commodities.

- ► **Participation in Global Growth.** Most commodities represent similar value all over the world. Therefore, they trade independently of any country's domestic economic or market conditions. For example, to participate in the U.S. stock market, an investor generally should feel confident that the U.S. economy will keep growing and that U.S. stock market performance will stay strong. But commodity investing does not require such faith in any economy, market, or political system. Commodity prices are determined largely by global supply/demand forces. In today's globalizing economy, increased demand for a given commodity in one part of the world can lead to higher prices everywhere. As developing nations such as China and India industrialize, they are placing huge demand pressures on finite supplies of some commodities.

- ► **Inflation Hedge.** Inflation is a measurement of the amount of currency required to purchase goods and services. Because commodities represent the value of goods, they have a special value in protecting investment portfolios against inflation. Generally, when inflation is tracking above average, commodities prices tend to rise. Commodities such as gold and silver are generally considered to be particularly good hedges against rising inflation. However, in recent decades other commodities also have proven their inflation-hedging abilities. For example, according to U.S. Department of Energy data, the average price of a barrel of oil increased from $2.51 in 1950 to more than $130 in 2008, and this represented an annual rate of increase of 7 percent. Over the same period, the U.S. Consumer Price Index, which is the leading measure of inflation, increased an average of 3.9 percent per year.

- ► **Diversification.** As previously discussed, including commodities in a portfolio also can serve to increase diversification. As an asset class, commodities have produced low correlations with most types of financial instruments, including U.S. stocks and bonds, foreign stocks, and Treasury Bills. The table below shows the correlations between these asset classes and commodities as represented by the Goldman Sachs Commodities Index for the period 1970–2003.

TABLE 5.4: CORRELATION BETWEEN COMMODITIES AND VARIOUS ASSET CLASSES

ASSET CLASS	INDEX	CORRELATION WITH COMMODITIES
U.S. Stocks	S&P 500 Index	–0.27
U.S. Bonds	Long-term government bonds	–0.20
Foreign Stocks	MSCI EAFE Index	–0.13
Cash	U.S. Treasury Bills	0.00

SOURCE: INVESTORSSOLUTIONS.COM

These correlations indicate that including commodities in a portfolio has the potential to increase its risk-adjusted returns, because they can help reduce portfolio volatility. Having some exposure to commodities also can help to reduce the impact of declines in the stock market.

► **Currency Hedge.** Commodities also can be valuable in protecting a portfolio against currency depreciation. This is because commodities enable investors to protect against the rapid depreciation or devaluation of currencies. This is particularly true for investors outside the United States. For example, in 1994 and 1995, Mexico experienced a currency crisis that caused the value of the peso to decline sharply against the U.S. dollar. By investing in gold during this period, some Mexicans avoided a steep decline in purchasing power. This hasn't been as much of an issue for U.S. investors, as the dollar generally has been considered among the world's strongest currencies for decades. However, it should be noted that in recent years the dollar has shown periods of extended weakness against many other major world currencies.

• CURRENCY ETFS •

Currency investing used to be reserved for financial professionals and big-time investors. With the introduction of currency ETFs, however, this has changed. Now, not only can retail investors make bets on the direction of different currencies using ETFs, but financial professionals and big-time investors have a new and simple way to participate in this market.

Currency ETFs help investors participate in strong currencies while also hedging against weak ones. Some financial advisers view currencies as a separate asset class and suggest that investors allocate perhaps 5 percent to 10 percent of their portfolios to it for diversification.

Currency ETFs invest directly in foreign currencies. They provide a way for investors to gain exposure to international markets without having to own individual companies that issue stocks and bonds. The first currency ETF, the CurrencyShares Euro Trust (Ticker symbol: FXE), was rolled out in December 2005. The product was the first of several CurrencyShares introduced by Rydex Investments—now Rydex SGI, after Rydex merged with Security Global Investors following the 2008 purchase of Rydex by Security Benefit Corp. The CurrencyShares Euro Trust is designed to track the price of the euro. In this ETF, each share is equal to one hundred euros. At the time this book was written, there were nine CurrencyShares in all, with others designed to track the Australian dollar, the British pound sterling, the Canadian dollar, the Japanese yen, the Mexican peso, the Russian ruble, the Swedish krona, and the Swiss franc. In addition, there are ETFs from other providers that offer exposure to a basket of various currencies and others that take a positive or negative stance on the U.S. dollar against other currencies. In affiliation with Deutsche Bank, PowerShares launched a multicurrency basket ETF, called the PowerShares DB G10 Currency Harvest Fund (Ticker symbol: DBV), in September 2006. This ETF works by using a popular technique called the carry trade. From a pool of the leading currencies of the world, this ETF buys those with the highest yields and sells short those with the lowest yields. In February 2007, PowerShares introduced a pair of funds that allow investors to take either bullish or bearish positions in the U.S. dollar versus a basket of leading foreign currencies.

Benefits of Investing in Currencies

In the past the vast majority of Americans conducted virtually all of their financial and investment transactions in U.S. dollars. Now, more Americans are traveling or living in other countries and investing in markets around the world. If the U.S. dollar is weak against foreign currencies, it costs Americans more to travel or live abroad. Conversely, if the U.S. dollar is strong against foreign currencies, the investment returns earned in foreign markets will not be as rewarding.

Investors can benefit from directly participating in currency ETFs in several ways. For instance, by purchasing an ETF that represents a single currency, such as the euro CurrencyShares, they can profit from the strength or weakness of one specific currency versus another. Currencies trade like commodities—in spot markets and in forward and futures markets. Owners of a given currency are considered to have a long position in the currency. Meanwhile, those who owe that currency are considered to be short. For example, an American tourist taking a vacation to France upon arrival in the Paris airport may change American dollars into euros. During the vacation, the tourist is essentially "long" the euro. For the trip home, if the tourist converts the euros back into dollars he or she would be "short" the dollar.

As is the case with stocks, those with a long position in a currency will benefit when the currency appreciates. Those short the currency will benefit if the currency declines against a benchmark currency. It is possible to profit by being either long or short any currency trade; it generally will depend on the relationship between pairs of currencies—in other words, on what is happening with the local currency versus the currency in which the investor has either a long or short position.

Investors also can profit from the strength or weakness in a specific currency compared with a basket of other currencies. By using ETFs instead of trading one currency versus another, investors can establish a long or short position in one currency versus a basket or average of other leading currencies. An example of ETFs that enable this are the previously mentioned bullish and bearish ETFs: the PowerShares DB U.S. Dollar Negative Fund (Ticker symbol: UDN) and the Powershares DB U.S. Dollar Positive Fund (Ticker symbol: UUP). The Dollar Negative Fund allows an investor to go short the dollar against a basket that consists of currencies shown in the following table, while the Dollar Positive Fund allows the investor to go long.

TABLE 5.5: REPRESENTATIVE BASKET OF CURRENCIES IN DOLLAR POSITIVE AND NEGATIVE ETFS

CURRENCY	WEIGHT IN BASKET (%)
Euro	57.6
Japanese Yen	13.6
British Pound	11.9
Canadian Dollar	9.1
Swedish Krona	4.2
Swiss Franc	3.6

SOURCE: POWERSHARES CAPITAL MANAGEMENT, AS OF FEBRUARY 20, 2007

One of the greatest benefits of these products is their ability to enhance portfolio diversification. Owning or shorting a basket of securities helps to average the ups and downs of dollar fluctuations versus individual currencies. In addition, in some emerging markets, currencies often are used as a way of diversifying assets to prevent financial losses due to the domestic currency's rapid depreciation or devaluation. (Both of these terms mean a decline in currency value. "Depreciation" connotes losses in trading value and "devaluation" connotes losses due to government or central bank policies.) At times, a currency can become vulnerable to all of the factors described above, leading to catastrophic declines in currency value. Even within the domestic economy, the currency may become almost worthless. To understand how such a scenario can develop over several years, the example of Argentina in 1999–2002 is illustrative. In the mid-1990s, Argentina had been a showcase for capitalism in South America, with a GDP growth rate of 8 percent, rising personal incomes, and large amounts of foreign investment. But then, a spiral of chaos began, starting with unprecedented amounts of foreign borrowing by the national government. As its deficit increased, Argentina's economy slid into a recession in 1999. In 2001, the inflation rate soared from 4 percent to 40 percent and short-term interest rates increased from 7 percent to 32 percent. A year later, the crisis peaked as the government implemented capital and currency restrictions, foreigners stopped providing loans, and riots broke out in the streets. The value of Argentina's peso (versus the U.S. dollar) declined by 83 percent in one year, as half of the country's population fell into poverty.

While this situation is not likely to happen in most developed economies, it serves as a warning that any currency can be vulnerable to a combination of negative events that accumulate over time. In a dynamic global economy, having some currency diversification makes as much sense as having a well-diversified investment portfolio.

Changes in Currency

So what causes one currency to change in relation to another? There are several possible factors, one being interest rates.

► **High Interest Rate Opportunities.** As investment markets have become more global, investors often look for opportunities to invest in high interest rate paying currencies. For example, countries such as Australia and New Zealand in recent years have gained a reputation for paying high interest rates on bank deposits and bonds. The official interest rates of New Zealand and Australia were set at 8 percent and 6.25 percent, respectively. Japan, on the other hand, has paid the lowest interest rates of any major nation—through mid-2006, the Bank of Japan's official interest rate was set at 0 percent, and it was increased gradually over the next year to 0.5 percent. This has led to persistent weakness in the yen versus other currencies. Because of the gap in rates, sophisticated investors have been able to go short the yen and invest the proceeds in a high-yield currency such as New Zealand or Australian dollars.

► **Low Interest Rate Opportunities.** While high interest rates attract investors to currencies, low rates can cause investors to seek higher returns in currencies outside of their local one. This has been the case in Japan, where some investors have executed what is known as the yen carry trade. This means that they have transferred their yen-denominated savings into foreign investments denominated in foreign currencies. By doing this they are able to benefit by essentially shorting their own currency. Keep in mind, however, that while interest rates can have a major impact on currency values, in cases where a currency's value is highly inflated or deflated because of interest rates, other factors can cause it to revert back to its "intrinsic value." Using Japan again as an example, from

August 1998 through December 1999, Japan's currency gained 41 percent versus the U.S. dollar, as the Japanese economy emerged from a lengthy recession. This was largely a result of intervention by the U.S. government to support the yen.

▶ **Inflation.** Inflation can also influence the direction of a currency—more specifically, when inflation is high it often can cause weakness in a currency. Once a currency weakens, making it more difficult to pay for imports, the supply of goods and services available to consumers can dry up, fueling even more domestic inflation. Some governments use a tactic to inflate the domestic money supply: exchanging local currency that they get from exports for the foreign currency, and then holding the foreign currency as government reserves. Some observers believe that China's yuan has been maintained at a value well below its intrinsic value through this process, which is referred to as sterilization.

▶ **Imports and Exports.** The amount that a country imports and exports also can influence the value of a currency. Generally, countries that export more goods and services than they import maintain strong currencies. A current account is used to measure changes in the country's net foreign assets produced by its balance of trade. When the current account is consistently positive it will cause a country's government and companies to hold large quantities of foreign assets. As foreign assets are exchanged for the local currency, supply-and-demand forces increase the value of the local currency. On the flip side, when a country's current account is consistently negative, it basically exports a large amount of the country's currency abroad. Since 2000, the United States has produced by far the largest negative current account balance of any nation in history. From 2005 to 2007 the U.S. trade deficit soared to an average of more than $700 billion per year—in total, more than $2 trillion over three years. This is perhaps the most important factor behind the continued weakness of the U.S. dollar.

▶ **Economic Cycles.** Economies that are growing at a healthy rate often have stronger and more stable currencies, while weaker economies tend to produce weaker currencies. However, governments sometimes take actions to deliberately weaken their own currency to stimulate exports or discourage imports. This is done as a way of maintaining growth in domestic economic output.

Now let's take a look at some of the major currencies around the world.

The U.S. Dollar

For decades, the U.S. dollar has been considered one of the strongest currencies in the world, and it has been the dominant currency used in international financial transactions. Globally, investors have wanted to own assets denominated in U.S. dollars, or the U.S. currency outright, for three main reasons: the stability of the U.S. political system and growth of the U.S. economy; the integrity and liquidity of U.S. financial markets; and faith that the U.S. government and its central bank, the Federal Reserve, will maintain policies that protect the value of dollars and debt instruments denominated in dollars, especially U.S. Treasuries.

As measured by a trade-weighted index against other major currencies of the world, the dollar has experienced four significant phases over the past quarter century, as shown in the table below.

TABLE 5.6: THE U.S. DOLLAR'S HISTORIC PHASES

UP/DOWN DOLLAR PHASE	DIRECTION OF THE DOLLAR	GAIN OR LOSS OF THE DOLLAR VERSUS TRADE-WEIGHTED EXCHANGE INDEX (%)
1980–83 (4 years)	Up	+36.3
1984–94 (11 years)	Down	–34.8
1995–2001 (7 years)	Up	+28.5
2002–7 (6 years)	Down	–33.7

SOURCE: ST. LOUIS FEDERAL RESERVE ECONOMIC RESEARCH

In March 2008, the dollar fell to its lowest level versus the Trade-Weighted Exchange Index since the Federal Reserve began keeping this data in 1973. The previous up-down dollar cycle (1980–94) lasted fifteen years in total and was somewhat symmetrical, with the up phase of the cycle (+36.3 percent) about matching the down phase (–34.8 percent). The current cycle has lasted thirteen-plus years and produced up and down phases that were roughly symmetrical through 2007.

The Euro

As the official currency of the European Economic Union (EU), the euro is currently used by thirteen nations—Austria, Belgium, Finland, France, Germany, Greece, Ireland, Italy, Luxembourg, the Netherlands, Portugal, Spain, and Slovenia. Another twenty-one members of the EU have not yet officially adopted the euro but may do so in the future. The major EU members that have not yet adopted the euro include Sweden, the U.K., and Denmark. Each country that has adopted the euro may print banknotes with its own distinctive mint marks; however, all euros are interchangeable across national borders. For the purposes of redeeming older currencies used before the euro, frozen exchange rates apply. For example, old French francs are exchangeable at a rate of 6.56 francs per euro.

In recent years the euro has come to be regarded as the equal of the U.S. dollar in international financial transactions and foreign reserves. In part, the euro's prominence has been driven by its steady appreciation versus the dollar since 2001. The euro also benefits from the growth and diversity of the EU as it has continued to expand by adding member countries.

The Yen

The yen is the official currency of Japan, the second largest national economy in the world (behind the United States). However, since the start of 2005, the yen has been fairly weak against most other major currencies. Why? The short answer is Japan's very low interest rates, by far the lowest of any major country. Japanese savers and investors convert yen to foreign currencies to earn higher rates, and sophisticated investors borrow yen and then invest in foreign markets (i.e., participate in the yen carry trade).

The Pound Sterling

The U.K. is the most important member of the European Union that has not yet accepted the euro. Instead, the U.K. continues to use the pound sterling as its official currency. (For the U.K. to adopt the euro in the future would require approval of Parliament and the British people via referendum.) The pound sterling generally moves somewhat parallel with the euro on currency markets; however, it has enough variation in price to be considered a worthy addition to diversified baskets of global currencies.

The Canadian Dollar

The Canadian dollar (sometimes called the loonie because of the loon's image on a one-dollar coin) is important because Canada is the United States' largest trading partner and a major source of oil and commodities imports. During the 1990s and into 2000, the Canadian dollar was very weak, compared with the U.S. dollar. By the end of 2001, $1 U.S. could buy $1.59 Canadian. However, that gap has largely closed. As of September 2009, $1 U.S. was worth $1.07 Canadian.

The Swiss Franc

Although Switzerland is a tiny country, its financial system is considered one of the strongest and most stable in the world. The Swiss franc has commonly been referred to as the hardest of the world's hard currencies. (A hard currency has validity in international commerce.) Swiss currency was among the last in the world to be on the gold standard, and it currently benefits from very low inflation and stable government policies.

Investing in Currency ETFs

There are varied ways that currency ETFs can be structured. For instance, Rydex's CurrencyShares hold actual currencies that are deposited in an interest-bearing account. These ETFs do not engage in trading derivatives such as currency swaps, options, or futures. One benefit of holding actual currencies, similar to physically holding gold like the gold ETF, is that there is total transparency. Investors know exactly what is underlying their shares. The PowerShares DB Currency Harvest ETF works differently from the CurrencyShares in that it trades futures contracts on the currencies that make up the Deutsche Bank G10 Currency Future Harvest Index Excess Return. The index itself takes both long and short futures positions—long and leveraged currency futures positions for currencies associated with relatively high-yielding interest rates and short currency futures positions for certain currencies associated with relatively low-yielding interest rates. Currency ETFs that participate in futures contracts typically invest most of their assets into high-quality interest-bearing debt instruments, and the interest income can be a significant part of the ETF's total return. A relatively small part of ETF assets are used to satisfy futures margin requirements. The ability to profit from interest earned on cash is a feature found in virtually all ETFs that invest in futures contracts. Using futures contracts also can help lower the potential risk of default. Some types of investments in currencies, such as asset-linked notes, carry the risk that the issuer of the note will fail to make a payment. In futures contracts traded on regulated exchanges, clearinghouses act as the counterparty for each position, greatly reducing default risk.

There are various benefits to using ETFs to invest in currencies. One such benefit is cost, which can be substantially lower when using currency ETFs compared with directly buying and selling currencies. According to Rydex Investments, individual investors looking to trade currencies directly have had to pay commissions as high as 3 percent to effectuate their transactions. This compares with CurrencyShares, which have an annual expense ratio of 0.40 percent in addition to the standard brokerage fees. PowerShares DB G10 Currency Harvest Fund, which tracks a basket of various currencies, also has a more modest fee, of about 0.75 percent. Currency ETFs, because they trade on an exchange, also provide investors with easy access to a variety of currencies, as well as provide investors with the opportunity to implement various trading strategies. For instance, margin accounts can be used, which allow investors to borrow money to buy shares of the ETF. These ETFs also offer near instant liquidity and portfolio transparency, and they trade at or very close to their net asset value. And compared with directly buying and selling different currencies, they offer investors simplicity by allowing them to easily make trades in their regular brokerage accounts. These ETFs also give investors the opportunity to purchase relatively small amounts of currencies efficiently.

• CHAPTER SUMMARY •

▶ Including allocations to commodities and currencies can be a good way to add an increased level of diversification to a portfolio.

▶ With the rollout of ETFs that track commodities and currencies, investors now have a new way to invest in these asset classes that is easier and in most cases more cost-effective than methods that they have been forced to rely on previously.

▶ These correlations indicate that including commodities in a portfolio has the potential to increase its risk-adjusted returns because they can help reduce portfolio volatility. Having some exposure to commodities also can help reduce the impacts of declines in the stock market.

▶ Some commodities ETFs work by tracking indexes composed of either physical commodities or commodities futures contracts, though there are a few ETFs that track precious metals that allow investors to actually own the underlying commodity.

▶ Investing in foreign currencies is also a beneficial way to increase diversification inside a portfolio. It can help to smooth out dollar fluctuations versus individual currencies. In addition, currencies can be used in some emerging markets to help prevent financial losses due to the domestic currency's rapid depreciation or devaluation.

▶ Currency ETFs allow investors to make bets on the direction of varied currencies. They can help investors participate in strong currencies while also hedging against weak ones. Some financial advisers view currencies as a separate asset class and suggest that investors allocate perhaps 5 percent to 10 percent of their portfolios to it for diversification.

▶ Cost-effectiveness is one of the greatest benefits in using ETFs to invest in currencies. Individual investors looking to trade currencies directly have had to pay as much as a 3 percent commission to effectuate their transactions, compared with certain currency-based ETFs that have annual expense ratios as low as 0.40 percent.

6

Evaluating ETFs

The previous chapters discussed the many ETF options that are available, ranging from those that track various slices of the stock market in the United States and abroad to ETFs that provide exposure to the fixed income market, commodities, and currencies. Among these categories, through the end of 2008, there were more than 740 different ETFs to choose from. So how does an investor know which ETFs will best fit inside his or her portfolio? In any given category there could be dozens of different ETFs. Some ETFs that fall under the same category are actually pretty similar. Others, however, have major differences in terms of the types of securities that they track, costs, tax efficiencies, and more. That's why investors need to take a close look under the hood to understand exactly what they're getting with each ETF. This chapter will discuss the importance of examining and evaluating various ETF components, from the more basic and easily identifiable differences that any investor should note before purchasing to the more sophisticated processes used by financial professionals and ETF rating services.

• THE ETF CHALLENGE •

Choosing the best ETF from the ever-growing universe of products is tough and keeps getting tougher. It's not the same as choosing an actively managed mutual fund, in which case investors are mostly concerned with the past performance of the fund as an indicator of how the portfolio manager has done over time, and how it has performed in relation to the overall market or to other funds in its category. With ETFs, past performance may be one factor to consider. But because ETFs are based on indexes, they are not designed to significantly underperform or outperform their benchmark.

Choosing an ETF is more akin to choosing an individual security. There are many technical and fundamental components that can be evaluated to determine the merits of a particular security, and the same is true for ETFs. One challenge in choosing an ETF is the fact that there are often many choices in the same category. For instance, there are more than two dozen ETFs that track the technology sector. While many of these products seem very alike, there are some underlying differences that could have a substantial impact on the role they play in a portfolio, whether they are being used for asset allocation or another strategy. The following section will look at many of the metrics that investors can use to compare ETFs.

• EXPENSE RATIO •

The expense ratio is as straightforward a metric as there is. It is the annual cost that a shareholder has to pay to own an ETF, expressed as a percentage. Because these expenses can take away from performance, the more expensive an ETF is, the less likely it is that it will be successful in adding value above the benchmark that it tracks. The expense ratio of an ETF also plays a secondary role: It gauges how well the ETF manager handles the operational issues of the underlying securities and how well the ETF producer is reducing costs over time. Expense ratios are one of the first metrics to look at when comparing ETFs. This information can be found easily, either on the ETF sponsor's Web site, in a product prospectus, or on any number of financial data Web site services. A comparison of technology ETFs can be used to illustrate how seemingly similar products can differ even in something as basic as cost. The following table is a list of diversified technology ETFs. Notice that the expense ratios range from 0.23 percent all the way up to 0.71 percent.

• • •

TABLE 6.1: DIVERSIFIED TECHNOLOGY

ETF	EXPENSE RATIO (IN %)
PowerShares Dynamic Technology	0.71
First Trust Technology AlphaDEX	0.7
First Trust NASDAQ 100 Technology	0.6
Rydex S&P Equal Weight Technology	0.5
SPDR MS Technology	0.5
iShares Goldman Sachs Technology	0.48
iShares Dow Jones Technology	0.48
Technology SPDR	0.23

• UNDERLYING SECURITIES •

It is also essential for investors to examine the securities that are underlying the ETFs to see exactly what they are getting by buying the ETFs. This includes knowing what types of stocks are represented in the index, as there may be differences in the types of stocks that are included. For example, while most technology ETFs include kingpin companies like Microsoft and Apple, some may choose to include companies in the telecommunications industries, while others do not. It is important for investors to read the prospectus to get a sense of the exact kind of exposure they would be getting by purchasing the ETF. The following table shows the top ten holdings of three of the largest technology ETFs—the Technology SPDR, the iShares Dow Jones Technology ETF, and the Rydex S&P Equal Weight Technology ETF. Even by taking a small sample of just the ten largest holdings, it is evident that there are discrepancies among the underlying holdings of the ETFs.

TABLE 6.2: TOP TEN HOLDINGS

TECHNOLOGY SPDR	ISHARES DOW JONES U.S. TECHNOLOGY	RYDEX S&P EQUAL WEIGHT TECHNOLOGY
Microsoft	Microsoft	Tellabs
AT&T	IBM	Oracle
IBM	Cisco Systems	Automatic Data Processing

TECHNOLOGY SPDR	ISHARES DOW JONES U.S. TECHNOLOGY	RYDEX S&P EQUAL WEIGHT TECHNOLOGY
Cisco Systems	Apple	Citrix Systems
Hewlett-Packard	Intel	Akamai Technologies
Apple	Google	EMC
Intel	Oracle	Verisign
Verizon Communications	Hewlett-Packard	Lexmark International
Google	Qualcomm	Fidelity National Information
Oracle	Dell	Paychex

SOURCE: SELECT SECTORS SPDRS

• CONCENTRATION •

Another good way to get a sense of what is underlying the ETF is to look at its top ten holdings and the weight of each in the portfolio. This not only gives the investor an idea of the type of companies the ETF is focused on, but also how concentrated the ETF is. Concentration measures how diversified an ETF is by looking at each security inside it and then taking into account how much weight it holds in the ETF. To measure concentration, the average weight of each security in the index can be measured, as well as how much the weights of other securities in the index vary, based on the total number of securities in the ETF. It's better to have lower weights for each security, or more securities within the ETF. The lower the concentration risk, the better it is for the investor. That's because low concentration risk implies that the ETF is not overly sensitive to the performance of any single security. The table below illustrates the concentration of the top ten holdings of the three technology ETFs mentioned above. Note how the weights of these companies vary—particularly in the equal weight ETF, which is designed so its holdings will be more evenly distributed.

TABLE 6.3: COMPARISON OF HOLDINGS AMONG TECHNOLOGY ETFS

TECHNOLOGY SPDR (XLK)	APPROXIMATE WEIGHT IN PORTFOLIO (%)
Microsoft	10.80
AT&T	8.50
IBM	8.20

SOURCE: BARCLAYS

TECHNOLOGY SPDR (XLK)	APPROXIMATE WEIGHT IN PORTFOLIO (%)
Cisco Systems	6.90
Hewlett-Packard	5.85
Apple	5.20
Intel	4.85
Verizon Communications	4.75
Google	4.40
Oracle	4.10
Total	**63.55**
ISHARES DOW JONES U.S. TECHNOLOGY (IYW)	
Microsoft	13.20
IBM	8.85
Cisco Systems	8.05
Apple	6.70
Intel	6.30
Google	5.70
Oracle	5.00
Hewlett-Packard	4.90
Qualcomm	4.60
Dell	1.70
Total	**65.00**
RYDEX S&P EQUAL WEIGHT TECHNOLOGY (RYT)	
Tellabs	2.01
Oracle	1.87
Automatic Data Processing	1.78
Citrix Systems	1.77
Akamai Technologies	1.74
EMC	1.70
Verisign	1.68
Lexmark International	1.66

TECHNOLOGY SPDR (XLK)	APPROXIMATE WEIGHT IN PORTFOLIO (%)
Fidelity National Information	1.66
Paychex	1.65
Total	**17.52**

SOURCE: STATE STREET GLOBAL ADVISORS, BARCLAYS GLOBAL INVESTORS, RYDEX INVESTMENTS

Both XLK and IYW are highly concentrated, with about two thirds of the assets held in the top ten stocks. However, even between these two ETFs there are differences in the actual holdings and how they are weighted. RYT is markedly different, in terms of its significantly lower concentration, the actual holdings that make up the top ten, and how they are weighted.

In addition to knowing the top ten holdings, it is also important to know how many stocks are included in the index, which is an indication of how diversified the portfolio is. In the case of technology ETFs mentioned, the number of holdings ranges from as few as 39 underlying stocks to as many as 212. The number of holdings for each ETF is included in the table below.

TABLE 6.4: HOLDINGS OF VARIOUS TECHNOLOGY ETFS

ETF	NUMBER OF HOLDINGS
PowerShares Dynamic Technology	61
First Trust Technology AlphaDEX	74
First Trust NASDAQ 100 Technology	39
Rydex S&P Equal Weight Technology	83
SPDR MS Technology	36
iShares Goldman Sachs Technology	212
iShares Dow Jones Technology	182
Technology SPDR	85

SOURCE: INDEXUNIVERSE.COM

In an ETF such as the First Trust NASDAQ 100 Technology ETF, which has just thirty-nine underlying securities, the performance of even a few stocks will have a much greater impact on the performance of the ETF compared with ETFs that are less concentrated. The performance of each stock will have a proportional impact on the ETF.

• PERFORMANCE •

Because ETFs are index-based, their performance does not determine the ETF's merit as it does for actively managed mutual funds, for which the performance is largely a reflection of the portfolio manager's skill. However, it can be an important factor, particularly when comparing similar ETFs, as it indicates how the underlying indexes are performing against one another. The following table lists the annualized performance of technology ETFs over one-, three- and five-year periods. (Some ETFs listed do not have a long enough track record.) Within a one-year period, losses ranged from 28.28 percent to 34.95 percent.

TABLE 6.5: PERFORMANCE OF VARIOUS TECHNOLOGY ETFS

ETF	1 YEAR (%)	3 YEAR (%)	5 YEAR (%)
PowerShares Dynamic Technology	−34.95	N/A	N/A
First Trust Technology AlphaDEX	−35.08	N/A	N/A
First Trust NASDAQ 100 Technology	−29.1	−4.24	N/A
Rydex S&P Equal Weight Technology	−32.29	N/A	N/A
SPDR MS Technology	−28.56	−4.03	−1.38
iShares Goldman Sachs Technology	−28.88	−3.16	−1.64
iShares Dow Jones Technology	−28.38	−3.48	−1.44
Technology SPDR	−29.2	−3.74	−1.45

SOURCE: INDEXUNIVERSE.COM

• TAX EFFICIENCY •

Capital gains distributions are a good indicator of tax efficiency. Recall that with ETFs, capital gains can largely be avoided because of their unique creation and redemption process. When capital gains are distributed, they can eat into performance. While capital gains are sometimes unavoidable, when they are incurred they should be minimized as much as possible. How large or small the capital gains distributions are is often an indication of how well or how poorly the ETF provider is doing in minimizing the tax inefficiencies that accompany the distribution of capital gains. Capital gains distributions are disclosed by ETF sponsors yearly. Historical information can be found on the sponsor's Web site.

• SPREADS •

The spread of an ETF is measured by comparing the difference that the bidding investor is willing to pay for an ETF to the price that the owner of the shares is asking—in other words it serves to gauge the transaction costs that are hidden within each ETF. When buying an ETF at its asking price and selling at its bid price, the loss incurred is the difference between the two prices. The lower the bid-ask ratio of an ETF, the better it is for investors, as it indicates lower transaction costs and higher liquidity. As seen in the table below, the spreads for the various technology ETFs range from one cent to five cents, or, as a percentage, 0 to 0.2 percent.

TABLE 6.6: SPREADS FOR VARIOUS TECHNOLOGY ETFS

ETF	SPREAD	SPREAD %
PowerShares Dynamic Technology	0.03	0.2
First Trust Technology AlphaDEX	0.03	0.2
First Trust NASDAQ 100 Technology	0.03	0.2
Rydex S&P Equal Weight Technology	0.05	0.2
SPDR MS Technology	0.05	0.1
iShares Goldman Sachs Technology	0.03	0.1
iShares Dow Jones Technology	0.02	0
Technology SPDR	0.01	0.1

SOURCE: INDEXUNIVERSE.COM

• TRACKING ERROR •

All ETFs have a stated benchmark. The goal of most ETFs is to match their performance to their benchmarks as closely as possible. But sometimes they don't. When that happens it can be an indication that the ETF manager is not doing a great job. That is where the tracking error comes into play as it measures how well the ETF manager is matching the benchmark. One simple way tracking error can be evaluated is by looking at the absolute returns of an ETF versus its benchmark. The lower the tracking error, the better the ETF manager is doing replicating the stated benchmark. According to Morgan Stanley, in 2008 the average tracking error was 0.52 percent.

• YIELDS •

Average earnings and dividend yields can also be used in evaluating equity ETFs. Earnings yields are a measure of the growth that you can expect from stocks. They can be calculated for each stock by taking the earnings per share divided by the share price. A high average earnings yield for an ETF is better than a low earnings yield. Average dividend yields can also be used when evaluating equity ETFs. An average dividend yield is a measurement of the amount of dividends a company pays to its investors. As is the case with earnings yield, a higher average dividend yield for an ETF is better than a lower dividend yield. Dividend yields can be calculated for each stock by taking the annual dividend paid by a stock and dividing it by the current stock price.

• STANDARD DEVIATION •

Standard deviation of returns is another metric that is helpful in assessing ETFs. As discussed in Chapter 1, standard deviation looks at the dispersion of returns from the average. The list below illustrates the range of standard deviations among technology ETFs over a three- and five-year period. (Many of these ETFs do not have long enough track records.)

TABLE 6.7: STANDARD DEVIATION OF VARIOUS TECHNOLOGY ETFS

ETF	3 YEARS	5 YEARS
PowerShares Dynamic Technology	N/A	N/A
First Trust Technology AlphaDEX	N/A	N/A
First Trust NASDAQ 100 Technology	27.08	N/A

ETF	3 YEARS	5 YEARS
Rydex S&P Equal Weight Technology	N/A	N/A
SPDR MS Technology	26.6	23.45
iShares Goldman Sachs Technology	24.03	21.41
iShares Dow Jones Technology	23.63	20.92
Technology SPDR	21.85	20.78

SOURCE: INDEXUNIVERSE.COM

• LIQUIDITY •

An ETF's liquidity is also an important factor to consider when evaluating ETFs, as it can have an impact on how easily the ETF can be traded as well as on bid/ask spreads. ETFs that are less liquid generally have higher spreads and are more difficult to trade than ETFs that are more liquid. A good indicator of an ETF's liquidity is its trading volume. Higher trading volume indicates greater demand for the ETF. When evaluating ETFs, both the volume of the ETF itself and the volume of the underlying stocks are good indicators of liquidity. Volume of ETFs can vary dramatically. The table below illustrates the average volume of technology ETFs in terms of both dollar and share volume.

TABLE 6.8: DOLLAR AND SHARE VOLUME OF VARIOUS TECHNOLOGY ETFS

ETF	DOLLAR VOLUME	SHARE VOLUME
PowerShares Dynamic Technology	4.5 million	264,000
First Trust Technology AlphaDEX	1.98 million	158,000
First Trust NASDAQ 100 Technology	9.58 million	636,000
Rydex S&P Equal Weight Technology	9.76 million	291,000
SPDR MS Technology	27.58 million	654,000
iShares Goldman Sachs Technology	170.36 million	4.29 million
iShares Dow Jones Technology	482 million	11.67 million
Technology SPDR	2.44 billion	141 million

• ONLINE ETF TOOLS •

There are several online services available to investors, which offer useful information and evaluation tools to help better understand the differences among ETFs. Some evaluate various criteria and then offer ratings for specific ETFs while others simply offer data that investors can use to come to their own conclusions. One popular ratings service is offered by the research firm Morningstar, which is well known for its mutual fund rating service. Morningstar rates ETFs primarily on their risk-adjusted returns. Using star ratings, the Morningstar service looks at ETFs with three years of returns and assigns a star rating of 1 through 5 to them, depending on their performance. Another ratings service is offered by Marco Polo XTF and can be found on the Web site XTF.com/ratings. This is also a great resource for individual investors and financial professionals looking to invest in ETFs, as it assesses more than a dozen metrics. It groups the metrics into two broad categories: structural integrity and investment metrics. Structural integrity is used to measure the operational efficiencies of each ETF, while investment metrics looks at factors such as risks, returns, and momentum. Within each category, the service evaluates numerous individual metrics to assess each ETF compared with its specific peer groups and against the broader universe. The idea is to obtain a complete understanding of what makes up each ETF and how it functions. Both Morningstar and XTF offer free basic rating services, though they charge for premium information.

Among the sites that simply offer ETF data, one of the most comprehensive can be found at IndexUniverse.com. This service allows users to select from a range of ETF categories and assess ETFs based on more than 45 data points including returns, net assets, spreads, standard deviation, and more. This site also offers thorough information on the ETF industries such as ongoing developments, new products, and evaluations of different products. There are also a lot of great sites that offer ETF screens and helpful industry updates, tools, and articles. These include:

- ► ETFtrends.com
- ► ETFguide.com
- ► ETFconnect.com
- ► SmartMoney.com

► TheStreet.com
► SeekingAlpha.com
► Morningstar.com

• CHAPTER SUMMARY •

► With hundreds of ETFs on the market and more being launched all the time, being able to distinguish the merits of each ETF has become increasingly important.

► There are various metrics to consider when evaluating an ETF. These include expense ratios, underlying holdings, concentration, tracking error, spreads, yields, standard deviation, returns, and liquidity.

► There are many ETF rating services that use various criteria to evaluate and rate different ETFs. Several other services allow investors to research and compare ETFs by selecting certain data points with which to evaluate ETFs on their own.

► There are numerous Web sites that provide useful articles, updates, and tools to investors interested in understanding, researching, and evaluating ETFs.

7

The ETF Explosion

ETFs have boomed over the past several years, both in terms of the number of products on the market and the total assets in these products. The former is due largely to the entrance of more ETF sponsors in the space looking to satisfy a wide array of investor needs. What began with a single ETF provider in 1993 has blossomed into more than a dozen different companies offering among them more than 740 products. The growth in assets, meanwhile, is due largely to an increased awareness of their benefits by both retail investors and financial professionals. For instance, some retail investors are putting together a simple, low-cost portfolio using a few broad-based ETFs in order to obtain exposure to the total market, while others are using ETFs to fill in gaps in their current portfolios or tap into areas of the market that may be tough to access in other ways. And that's just the start. ETFs also can be used to serve various strategic functions. They can help cut down a potentially hefty year-end tax bill, serve as a place to park excess cash, or hedge risk in a portfolio. This chapter will look at the proliferation of ETFs from a single product to where they stand today. It will look at some of the major ETF players, the types of products they are offering, and the varied ways that both retail investors and financial professionals are using ETFs to manage investment portfolios. It will also examine where the bulk of ETF assets have been going, including the types of products that assets are flowing into, how the growth of ETF assets compares with other financial products on the market, and the growth in ETFs worldwide.

• ETFS: THE EARLY YEARS •

The S&P 500 Depository Receipts, nicknamed the Spyder, was the first ETF to launch, in 1993, and it was designed to track the five hundred largest U.S. stocks, which make up the S&P 500 Index. It remained the only ETF on the market for two years, until the Mid-Cap SPDR (Ticker symbol: MDY) was introduced. This product of the Bank of New York was similar to the original Spyder, except it tracked an index of four hundred midsized stocks. In 1996, the menu of ETFs broadened when Barclays Global Investors launched the first international ETFs. These were based on the Morgan Stanley Capital International indexes and provided exposure to seventeen countries; they were initially called WEBS, which stood for World Equity Benchmark Shares. Later they were renamed iShares to align with the branding of the rest of Barclays's ETFs. In 1998, State Street launched nine more ETFs, each of which represented a different economic sector of the S&P 500—the "sector Spyders." They were the first ETFs that let investors tap into a narrower cut of the U.S. stock market.

In 1999, Merrill Lynch came on the scene with two Holding Company Depository Receipts (Holdrs)—the Internet Holdrs (Ticker symbol: HHH) and BioTech Holdrs (Ticker symbol: BBH). The Holdrs, more of which were later launched, offer beneficial ownership of a specified group of stocks within a particular sector or industry and are sold in hundred-share lots. A handful of other ETFs followed, but as the millennium came to a close there were still only 32 ETFs available on the U.S. market. However, in 2000 everything started to change. In the following table it's clear that by the end of 2000 the number of ETFs had almost tripled. By 2005, the number of ETFs had grown to 220. But it was in 2006 that the ETF industry really caught people's attention. In 2006 alone, 156 new ETFs came to market. The big spike of 2006 continued into 2007. Through the end of 2007 there were 629 ETFs trading in the United States, according to the Investment Company Institute. As of September 2008 there were roughly 800 ETFs—including exchange-traded products such as Holdrs and exchange-traded notes—trading in the United States, and hundreds more are expected to come to market over the next few years.

TABLE 7.1: NUMBER OF ETFS LAUNCHED

YEAR	TOTAL	BROAD U.S. STOCK ETFS	SECTOR U.S. EQUITY ETFS	INTERNATIONAL EQUITY	HYBRID	BOND ETFS
1993	1	1	-	-	-	-
1994	1	1	-	-	-	-
1995	2	2	-	-	-	-
1996	19	2	-	17	-	-
1997	19	2	-	17	-	-
1998	29	3	9	17	-	-
1999	30	4	9	17	-	-
2000	80	29	26	25	-	-
2001	102	34	34	34	-	-
2002	113	34	32	39	-	8
2003	119	39	33	41	-	6
2004	152	60	43	43	-	6
2005	204	81	68	49	-	6
2006	359	133	135	85	-	6
2007	629	197	219	159	5	49

SOURCE: BLOOMBERG, STATE STREET RESEARCH

• THE PLAYERS •

Much of the growth in products has been due to competition among players, who have been increasingly launching new and innovative products that have enabled the industry to evolve into the diverse marketplace that it is today. Some of the companies that entered the ETF market already had made their footprint with index mutual funds. Others saw ETFs as an extension of their experience with UITs or closed-end funds, which have characteristics similar to ETFs. At the time this book was written, there were about two dozen ETF providers in the United States and more companies were expected to enter the space in the future. However, it's important to note that while the landscape is becoming increasingly diverse in terms of the various companies that are providing ETFs, a few companies continue to dominate. Following is a brief description of the top players in the ETF space.

Barclays Global Investors: Barclays has been involved in index investing since 1971, so it was no surprise when the company entered the ETF space in 1996 with the launch of seventeen WEBS, which, recall, were ETFs that provided exposure to individual countries. After that launch Barclays stayed on the ETF sidelines until 2000. However, once they reentered the game, they did it in a big way. In 2000, Barclays launched thirty-eight ETFs, tracking everything from the broad markets in the United States and abroad to specific sectors, countries, and regions. In 2002, Barclays launched the first four ETFs to track fixed income, and later the company introduced two more. It wasn't until 2007, though, that Barclays launched an additional nine fixed income ETFs, greatly expanding its fixed income offerings, which remained the only fixed income ETFs until later in 2007, when several other players joined that market. In 2005, Barclays also introduced a commodity ETF, the iShares COMEX Gold ETF (Ticker symbol: IAU), which was designed to track the price of gold. The following year the company launched two more commodity ETFs, iShares Silver Trust (Ticker symbol: SLV) and iShares GSCI Commodity Index Trust (Ticker symbol: GSG). The iShares Silver Trust was similar to the gold ETFs except that it tracks the price of ten ounces of silver. The iShares GSCI Commodity Index Trust, meanwhile, tracks a diverse basket of commodities, from energy and livestock to precious metals and agriculture. This ETF was also interesting in that the index it tracks does not invest in stocks but in futures contracts. In 2006, Barclays launched a handful of exchange-traded notes, or ETNs. These products, which go by the iPath brand name, are similar to ETFs. However, they are actually unsecured debt instruments. Barclays is now the largest ETF company in the United States in terms of both the number of ETFs it has on the market and its ETF assets under management. According to Citigroup Global Markets, by May 2009 the company commanded about 49 percent of all ETF assets and 213 exchange-traded products on the market. At the time this book was written, Barclays had agreed to sell its iShares ETF business to Black-Rock Inc. (Ticker symbol: BLK).

State Street Global Advisors: State Street claimed the "first-mover" advantage in the ETF space thanks to its 1993 launch of the Spyder, which has gone on to become the largest ETF in terms of assets. Since its debut State Street has continued to develop ETFs at a steady pace. Initially, State Street launched most of its ETFs under two brand names, Spyders and StreetTRACKS. The company later decided to streamline its offerings and converted several ETFs to the Spyder brand. In 2005, the company spiced up the ETF market when it introduced the first-ever commodity-based ETF, StreetTRACKS Gold Trust. This ETF doesn't mimic an index like most of the ETFs that came before it. Instead, it participates directly in ownership of gold bullion, and each ETF share equals one tenth of an ounce. In 2007, the company launched its first set of fixed income ETFs. Through May 2009 State Street commanded about 24 percent of all ETF assets and had eighty-six ETFs on the market.

Vanguard Group: An established player in the index mutual fund space since the 1970s, Vanguard joined the ETF fray in 2001 with the launch of the Total Stock Market Index VIPER (Ticker symbol: VTI), which follows the Morgan Stanley Capital International U.S. Broad Market Index of large, mid-, and small cap stocks. VIPER is an acronym for Vanguard Index Participation Receipts. Several other ETFs were launched under the VIPER name, but it was later dropped. For the first few years Vanguard stuck to launching broader, more traditional ETFs. However, in 2007, the company introduced four fixed income ETFs, making it among the first to rival Barclays fixed income ETFs. Since then they have continued to roll out a variety of products, though the majority are a combination of broad U.S. market, sector, style, and regional ETFs. Vanguard's ETFs are different from other ETF providers, as they are not stand-alone entities but actually share classes of Vanguard's mutual funds. The expectation is that this structure will lead to economies of scale, which will benefit investors. Vanguard's claim to fame continues to be its ability to launch and maintain many of the lowest-cost ETFs. As of 2009, Vanguard had thirty-nine ETFs, and is third in line behind Barclays and State Street, with almost 10 percent market share.

PowerShares Capital Management: PowerShares entered the ETF market in 2003 with the launch of two ETFs: PowerShares ETF Dynamic OTC (Ticker symbol: PWO) and PowerShares ETF Dynamic Market (Ticker symbol: PWC). Unlike most other ETFs that previously had launched based on well-known, established indexes, PowerShares ETFs were based on proprietary indexes that it developed with the American Stock Exchange. The indexes, called Intellidex, were designed to beat traditional indexes by using a quantitative model to pick stocks with the greatest potential to outperform. In 2004, the company launched two more ETFs. During the following two years PowerShares made a big move, launching more than thirty ETFs each year. In addition to its use of the Intellidexes, in 2006 PowerShares also piqued interest with its fundamentally weighted ETFs, which track indexes that weigh securities based on fundamental factors. PowerShares also has added to the lineup of commodity- and currency-based ETFs: In 2006 and 2007, in conjunction with Deutsche Bank, the company launched several ETFs to provide exposure to those areas. In 2006, asset manager Amvescap PLC acquired PowerShares.

In 2007, PowerShares launched its first batch of fixed income ETFs, and it also took over sponsorship of the well-known Qs ETF, which is based on the NASDAQ-100 Index, as well as the four BLDRs, or "Builders" ETFs, which are based on the Bank of New York ADR Index. They are designed to provide international equity exposure by tracking indexes that represent American Depositary Receipts, or ADRs, which are certificates issued by U.S. banks that represent shares in foreign stocks. In 2008, PowerShares made another splash with the introduction of five actively managed ETFs as well as a family of asset allocation funds. As of May 2009, PowerShares was the second largest company in terms of total ETFs with 105 products and about 4.1 percent of total ETF assets.

ProShares Advisors: ProShares debuted its first family of ETFs in 2006. These products were interesting in that they used leverage strategies to enhance returns and shorting strategies to produce reciprocal returns of a given index. These ETFs, which were the first to let investors make bets on where the market, or certain segments of the market, is heading, raised some eyebrows. The first batch of ProShares were based on broad indexes. The company has since come out with a wide variety of leverage and inverse products that track specific sectors and styles. Through May 2009, ProShares had seventy-six ETFs, and had a market share of 4.4 percent.

Merrill Lynch: The Holdrs were the first two ETFs launched by Merrill Lynch. Holdrs, which are structured as grantor trusts, start out with twenty stocks, though they can include fewer if underlying stocks merge or go private. Holdrs provide access to certain sectors or industries of the market and function differently from most other ETFs. For instance, they can be purchased in only one-hundred-share lots, and investors can exchange them for the underlying stocks. Through 2001, Merrill Lynch had launched seventeen Holdrs; none have been launched since. As of

May 2009, Merrill Lynch's ETF assets accounted for less than 1 percent of the total ETF market.

Rydex: Also a known player in the mutual fund space, Rydex launched its first ETF in 2003, the Rydex S&P Equal Weight ETF (Ticker symbol: RSP). This ETF tracks an index that contains the same stocks as those in the S&P 500. But instead of weighting the stocks in the index by their market cap, this ETF gives all stocks an equal weighting. Two years after introducing RSP, Rydex launched a second ETF, the Rydex Russell Top 50, which represents the fifty largest U.S. companies in the Russell 3000 index based on market cap. As of May 2009, Rydex offered a variety of equal and market cap weighted ETFs. In 2005, Rydex launched the first currency-based ETF, CurrencyShares Euro Trust (Ticker symbol: FXE), a grantor trust that tracks the price of the euro. Through the first half of 2009, the company had launched eight additional CurrencyShares. These ETFs are similar in some ways to money market funds, though they track the value of the currencies that they represent. In addition to currency ETFs, Rydex also has several style-based ETFs and various inverse and leverage ETFs, which provide exposure to the broad market and specific sectors. As of May 2009, the company had forty ETFs and accounted for less than 1 percent of ETF assets.

VanEck Associates: VanEck launched its first three ETFs in 2006, and later followed up with several more, including equity ETFs that tap into various countries or regions as well as specific niches of the market such as coal, global alternative energy, steel, and nuclear and solar energy. They also offer a handful of municipal bond ETFs, including a high-yield municipal ETF, a Pre-Refunded Municipal ETF, and municipal ETFs of varying durations. As of May 2009, VanEck had twenty ETFs and held 1.45 percent of total ETF assets.

WisdomTree Asset Management: The first lot of ETFs from this company hit the market in 2006 to track indexes that used a rules-based methodology to weigh stocks, the idea being that the stocks in these indexes had greater potential to outperform. The first of these ETFs were based on indexes that selected stocks according to dividends. The company later launched another series of fundamentally weighted ETFs that selected and weighed stocks based on their earnings. WisdomTree's ETFs were the first fundamentally weighted ETFs. WisdomTree's ETF menu has since grown to include a variety of U.S. and international equity ETFs, a fixed income product, and currency income ETFs that track the currencies of various developed and emerging markets. As of May 2009, WisdomTree had fifty-one ETFs with assets accounting for less than 1 percent of total ETF assets.

Claymore Advisors: Claymore Advisors, which had also made a name for itself in the UIT and closed-end fund space, launched its first ETFs in 2006, and they all had an interesting spin. One ETF tracked an index of stocks that were experiencing heavy trading among company executives and insiders, while another followed stocks that were thought to be flying under the radar screen of Wall Street analysts. Their most recent lineup includes various domestic, international, and global ETFs as well as an aggregate bond and short-term bond ETF. They also offer a country rotation ETF, which adjusts its allocation to different countries depending on various factors, as well as a similar version that rotates around sectors of the U.S. stock market. Country and sector will be talked about in greater detail later in the book. Claymore had thirty-four ETFs as of mid-2009 and less than 1 percent of ETF assets.

First Trust: A player in the UIT, variable annuity, and closed-end fund spaces, First Trust launched a single ETF in 2005, the First Trust Dow Jones Select MicroCap ETF (Ticker symbol: FDM). In 2006 and 2007, the company followed up with several more ETFs. These included the family of enhanced ETFs based on indexes called AlphaDEXes, which also strive to produce returns above those of traditional, passive indexes. The company offers U.S. style, size, and sector ETFs as well as international and global ETFs. They also have a handful of specialty ETFs, tracking dividend leaders, the water industry, clean energy, and recent Initial Public Offerings. As of May 2009, the company had thirty-eight ETFs and less than 1 percent of ETF assets.

XShares Advisors: Xshares entered the ETF game in early 2007. They began by launching a slew of health-industry-related ETFs, targeting very specific segments of that market. However, the company later ended up closing down those ETFs. Not long afterward, the company came out with a new ETF called AirShares EU Carbon Allowances Fund (Ticker symbol: ASO), which is a commodity pool that tracks a basket of exchange-traded futures contracts for European Union Allowances (EUAs). EUAs are an entitlement to emit one metric ton of carbon dioxide equivalent that is transferable under the European Union Greenhouse Gas Emissions Trading Scheme. The company also has a family of ETFs called TDX Independence Funds, which are target date ETFs that adjust their allocation to become more conservative as the target date nears. As of May 2009, the company had six ETFs and less than 1 percent of total ETF assets.

Fidelity: This giant mutual fund group launched its first and only ETF in 2003. The Fidelity NASDAQ Composite Index Track (Ticker symbol: ONEQ) is designed to replicate the roughly eighteen hundred stocks in the NASDAQ Composite. There has been no word on whether the company will launch additional ETFs. ONEQ has less than 1 percent in ETF assets.

Deutsche Bank: Using the PowerShares brand, Deutsche Bank offers a wide range of commodity ETFs and ETNs, including a range of inverse and leverage energy, oil, and metals ETFs. The company also has three currency ETFs—a basket product that holds long futures contracts on the G10 currencies that have the highest interest rates and short contracts on those with the lowest interest rates, another ETF that plays on the strength of the dollar, and another that plays on the weakness. While the company is one of the largest ETF sponsors in Europe, in the United States it commands about 1.4 percent of the ETF market share, as of May 2009.

Direxion: This company came on the ETF scene in 2008 and offers a range of bullish and bearish ETFs. These ETFs use short selling and leverage strategies on broad segments of the market, specific sectors, developed and emerging markets, and Treasuries. As of May 2009, Direxion had twenty ETFs and less than 1 percent market share.

Elements: Elements are a family of ETNs focused on equities and commodities including metals, energy, livestock, and agriculture. As of May 2009, there were fourteen Elements ETNs, which comprised less than 1 percent of ETF assets.

There are a handful of other ETF sponsors that at the time this book was written had very few ETFs and accounted for a very minimal share of the total ETF market.

While the number of ETF sponsors continues to expand, the ETF market remains very concentrated among a few top players in terms of assets as well as the number of products on the market. This is even more evident in the following chart, which shows the top ten ETF sponsors according to their market share. In terms of assets, Barclays is by far the largest contender, with more than half of all ETF assets. The graph below shows that collectively the top five ETF providers account for more than 90 percent of all ETF assets.

Figure 7.1: Top ETF Sponsors by Market Share

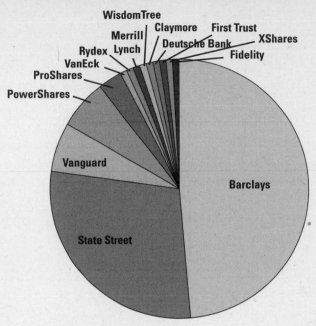

While there is more dispersion in terms of the number of ETFs that each sponsor has on the market, the graph below shows that sponsorship is still highly concentrated. The top five ETF companies in terms of the number of products are behind almost five hundred ETFs.

Figure 7.2: Top ETF Sponsors by Number of ETFs

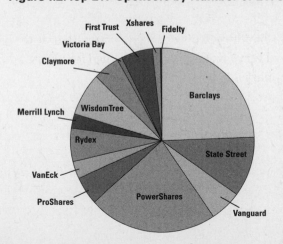

• ASSET FLOWS AND DISTRIBUTION •

As the number of ETFs has continued to increase, so have the assets in these products, though it took a while for this process to catch on. By 1996, three years after the first ETF was launched, ETFs had accumulated just over $2 billion in assets; by 1998 that had increased to $15.6 billion, and by 2000 assets had risen to $65.6 billion. ETF assets have continued to escalate, surging to more than $420 billion by the end of 2006, and as of mid-2009, assets had risen to about $700 billion. Table 7.2 shows the growth in ETF assets between 1995 and 2008, and how they have continued to experience fairly strong growth overall.

TABLE 7.2: NET ASSETS OF ETFS (1995–2007)

YEAR	TOTAL ETF ASSETS ($ MILLIONS)
1995	1,052
1996	2,411
1997	6,707
1998	15,568
1999	33,873
2000	65,585
2001	82,993
2002	102,143
2003	159,983
2004	227,540
2005	300,820
2006	422,550
2007	608,442
2008	531,000

SOURCE: INVESTMENT COMPANY INSTITUTE

The table above tracks *net* ETF assets, including assets that accumulated based on performance. Because performance of the market can have a big impact on asset growth, perhaps a more accurate way to measure asset flows into ETFs is by looking at the net issuance of ETFs, which can give a better sense of the new money flowing in. The table below shows that between 1993 and 2008, with the exception of 1994, new money has flowed into ETFs each year. In 2006, most of the new money went into global and international ETFs, which was not the case just two years prior. Broad-based domestic ETFs were second in line, followed by sector-based products. Fixed income ETFs attracted by far the least amount of assets. But remember, they only came on the scene in 2002, and until 2007 there were only a small handful of those available.

TABLE 7.3: NET ISSUANCE OF ETF SHARES (1993–2008)

YEAR	TOTAL ($ MILLIONS)
1993	442
1994	–28
1995	443
1996	1,108
1997	3,466
1998	6,195
1999	11,929
2000	42,508
2001	31,012
2002	45,302
2003	15,810
2004	56,375
2005	56,729
2006	73,995
2007	150,617
2008	177,220

SOURCE: INVESTMENT COMPANY INSTITUTE

• CONCENTRATED ASSETS •

The majority of ETF assets are still concentrated in only a few segments. For instance, more traditional ETFs, such as those that are market cap–based and international stock ETFs, account for more than half of all ETF assets. The table below shows the breakdown of ETF assets in each of the categories.

TABLE 7.4: ETF ASSETS BY CATEGORY THROUGH 2008 (IN $ MILLIONS)

ETF CATEGORY	TOTAL ASSETS ($ MILLIONS)	ETF ASSETS (%)
U.S. Market Cap/Style	239	45
Sector	58	11
International/Global	114	21.3
Fixed Income/Hybrid	57	10.6
Commodities	36	6.7
Other	29	5.4
Total	532	100

SOURCE: INVESTMENT COMPANY INSTITUTE

As of September 2009, the Vanguard Total Stock Market ETF was the largest ETF, with $104 billion in assets, having finally knocked the Spyder out of first place. The Spyder had about $72 billion, followed by the Vanguard Total Bond ETF with $61 billion and the MSCI EAFE with $33 billion.

TABLE 7.5: TOP 10 ETFS ACCORDING TO ASSETS

ETF	TICKER	CATEGORY	TOTAL ASSETS ($ MILLIONS)
Vanguard Total Stock Market	VTI	Total Stock Market	104.9
SPDR	SPY	Large Cap	72.60
Vanguard Total Bond Market	BND	Total Bond Market	61.30
iShares MSCI EAFE	EFA	International Developed Markets	33.50
SPDR Gold Trust	GLD	Commodities: Gold	32.60
iShares MSCI Emerging Markets	EEM	Emerging Markets	30.3
Vanguard Emerging Markets	VWO	International Emerging Markets	22.1
iShares S&P 500	IVV	Large Cap	19.8
Vanguard MidCap	VO	Mid Caps	17.0
PowerShares QQQQ	QQQQ	Large Cap	16.4
Total			410.50

SOURCE: INDEXUNIVERSE.COM

• BROAD ASSET ALLOCATION •

Much of the growth of ETF assets is due to the fact that investors and financial professionals are increasingly becoming aware of the many benefits they have to offer, either for constructing an entire portfolio or to fill a certain niche or execute a particular strategy. The following pages will explore many of the uses of ETFs. For investors who aren't interested in putting much time into creating portfolios, purchasing just a few core ETFs can create an easy and inexpensive one that will provide exposure to the total market. For instance, the S&P 500 Index has been mentioned several times throughout this book. Including an ETF based on this index, such as the Spyder (Ticker symbol: SPY), can be a good way to gain exposure to the broad U.S. stock market. This ETF has an expense ratio of just 0.10 percent. For exposure to the bond market, an ETF that tracks the broad-based Lehman Brothers U.S. Aggregate Index might be a good choice. Recall from Chapter 1 that this index tracks the investment-grade bond market in the United States. The iShares Lehman Aggregate Bond

ETF (Ticker symbol: AGG) is an example of an ETF based on this index, and it has an expense ratio of 0.24 percent. To round out the portfolio, an investor could also buy an ETF that tracks the MSCI EAFE Index. This is among the indexes most widely used to gauge the performance of international equities. The iShares MSCI EAFE ETF (Ticker symbol: EFA) is a very popular ETF that tracks this index, and it has an expense ratio of 0.34 percent. With just three ETFs an investor can get low-cost exposure to the U.S. and international equity markets as well as the fixed income market.

• CORE AND EXPLORE •

Commonly, ETFs are used by individual investors and financial professionals to allocate assets using a "core-and-explore" portfolio approach, also sometimes referred to as core/satellite. This type of portfolio starts out with one or two broad market ETFs, which are used as the main holdings of the portfolio. For instance, core holdings may be products that track the S&P 500 or the Lehman Aggregate Bond Index. The rest of the assets in the portfolio are then used to explore other areas of the market, including narrow investments that often carry more risk. The portion of the portfolio dedicated to exploring can be done with ETFs that track different sectors or countries, or ETFs that represent alternative asset classes. If an investor is interested in taking on even more risk, he/she could also include some individual stocks or actively managed mutual funds in this portion of the portfolio.

• FILLING IN A GAP •

ETFs make it very easy to get access to varied areas of the stock market and, increasingly, the fixed income market. But, as explored earlier in this book, they also can provide exposure to segments of the market that previously have been difficult for investors to access, including commodities and currencies. There are numerous ETFs that track the commodities market, from individual commodities like precious metals or oil to baskets of commodities that represent everything from corn and wheat to pork bellies and natural gas. Accessing commodities in the past was challenging for individual investors, in part because it was generally done by trading commodities via a separate futures trading account. The commodity-based ETFs eliminate that extra step by allowing investors to buy and sell a range of commodities just as they would an individual stock.

Investors also can use ETFs to get exposure to currencies. The foreign exchange, or forex, market is an over-the-counter market where securities are not traded publicly on an exchange. The currency-related ETFs that are currently on the market, though, trade on major stock exchanges, so investors can trade currencies easily at any time during the trading day. Through these ETFs, investors can get exposure to the euro, the yen, the pound, and several other currencies. Investors also can make bets on the direction of the U.S. dollar.

• MAKING BIG MARKET BETS •

ETFs also can be used to make bets on the market by using strategies such as leverage and shorting. Leverage ordinarily entails borrowing money to purchase securities in the hopes that they will rise and the returns will be magnified. Shorting is a bet that a security is going to fall. In order to short a security, investors have to borrow that security from a third party and then sell it, betting that the price will fall and allowing the investor to buy it back at a cheaper price and earn a profit. A leveraged ETF works by amplifying the returns of the index that it is tracking. For instance, with a leveraged ETF that works by doubling returns, if the underlying index rises 1 percent per day, the leveraged ETF could be expected to rise 2 percent. ETFs that engage in short selling, known as inverse ETFs, do the opposite. If the underlying index rises 1 percent, the inverse ETF would fall 1 percent. There are also leveraged-inverse ETFs that provide inverse results that are then magnified. So, if an index rises 1 percent the leveraged inverse ETF could be expected to fall 2 percent. These ETFs can be risky, but for more educated investors they offer a convenient way to implement these strategies.

• TAX STRATEGIES •

ETFs also can offer a way to minimize the tax bite at the end of the year. Suppose an investor owns a technology stock that has major losses embedded in it. At the end of the year the investor could sell that stock at a loss to lower his/her taxable income for the year, reducing the taxes due to Uncle Sam. This is known as tax-loss harvesting. But what if the investor still wants exposure to that stock or the area of the market that it represents? The investor could sell that stock and then buy it back. However, there is a rule, known as the wash-sale rule, which says that if an investor buys back the same stock within thirty days of selling it, he/she cannot recognize the loss immediately. Instead of sitting on that money in cash for thirty days and risk losing out on any potential upside in the market, the investor could sell the stock and put the proceeds in an ETF that represents the same sector or industry. This allows the investor to maintain similar exposure while still being able to recognize the tax loss. For example, let's say the investor owns shares of a technology stock that has unrealized losses. The stock could be sold to generate a loss that will lower the taxable income and then shares of a technology ETF could be bought. If the technology stock rose after it is sold, the investor would still be able to participate in the gain by owning the technology ETF. And thirty days after the sale, the investor could decide whether to stay in the ETF or sell it and buy back shares of the technology stock. Realize, of course, that there will be a taxable event when the ETF is sold, as there would be with any security. The individual tax impact should be weighed for each transaction.

• PARKING CASH •

Mutual fund portfolio managers often use ETFs as a temporary place to park excess cash. If a manager sells a big position in one or more securities but isn't going to replace it right away, that means they have excess cash lying around, creating a potential drag on performance. If the market rises, a fund with a lot of cash will not benefit entirely, since it is not fully invested in the market. To avoid this, portfolio managers will often purchase an ETF instead. This could be a broad market ETF that represents the sector that they plan on investing in eventually, or even a short-term fixed income ETF. This process, known as cash equitization, isn't done just by portfolio managers. For instance, say an investor receives a big payment from a real estate investment transaction or a retirement plan payout but hasn't yet decided what to do with that money. A good option could be to invest it in an ETF. That way, instead of just sitting on the sidelines, the cash has the possibility of appreciating while the investor decides what to do with it.

• HEDGING STRATEGIES WITH ETFS •

Hedge funds are popular among sophisticated investors because they offer access to strategies that hedge specific risk exposures in the stock market.

Because of the various features ETFs have to offer, they are often effective tools for executing many of the strategies commonly used inside these hedge funds. One reason is that ETFs offer easy trading. Recall, because ETFs trade on exchanges like stocks, shares can be bought or sold throughout the trading day using familiar types of orders. Even a relatively small portfolio can achieve diversification among several ETFs. ETFs also can be sold short on a downtick. This basically means that shares of ETFs can be sold short even when they are trading at a price that is below the previous trade. In addition, investors can benefit greatly from the ETFs' tax efficiency when using them for hedging. That's because ETFs normally do not make taxable distributions of capital gains as mutual funds do, and gains on positions held more than a year currently qualify for favorable long-term capital gains treatment. Finally, the performance of most ETFs tracks close to their benchmarks, allowing investors to hedge part or all of the systematic risk of specific benchmarks. For example, if an investor owns an actively managed stock portfolio and simultaneously sells short an ETF that tracks the S&P 500 Index, the total position stands to profit to the extent that the active portion outperforms the index.

In many cases, these benefits actually make them more effective products than hedge funds themselves. One reason is because of the heavy costs charged by hedge funds. A typical cost structure in a hedge fund includes a management fee of 2 percent, plus an incentive allocation equal to 20 percent or more of the annual appreciation. Hedge funds also tend to be tax inefficient, as few hedge fund managers try to minimize the tax impact on individual investors. Because most hedge funds trade securities often, a large part of their returns consist of short-term gains that are taxed as ordinary income. Hedge funds also tend to be complex and lack transparency, leaving many investors unsure of their specific holdings, and they may not understand the complexities of their manager's strategy. Finally, hedge funds generally are available to only the wealthiest of investors. They require very high minimum investments—often $500,000 or more per investor—and only the very wealthiest individual investors can afford to diversify money among several hedge funds.

• LONG/SHORT STRATEGIES •

One hedging strategy that could be achieved easily using ETFs is a long/short equity strategy, also referred to as a pairs trade. This strategy basically entails pairing two securities—one that an investor wants to buy on the bet that it is going to rise and one that an investor wants to sell short on the expectation that it will fall. The idea is to try to protect a portfolio from downturns in certain weak segments of the market. For example, a pairs trade might work if one stock is expected to fall but its sector is going to rise. In this case, the investor could short the stock that is expected to fall and buy an ETF that represents the sector that is expected to rise.

Long/short paired trades were among the first popular strategies developed by hedge funds, in part because they take advantage of research and insights on both sides of the market—up and down. For example, suppose an investor does not have an opinion on whether the stock market as a whole will rise or fall and wishes to hedge against the risks in either direction. A basic long/short strategy is to buy an attractive stock in a given industry while shorting an unattractive stock in the same industry. If the two positions are balanced in size (e.g., a paired trade) the combination is insulated from overall movements in the stock market and the particular industry. The return of a paired long/short trade will be positive to the extent that the attractive stock outperforms the unattractive one.

This strategy can be implemented by using ETFs with two indexes. For example, suppose an investor is not sure whether the U.S. stock market will trend higher or lower over the next few months, but in either case this investor believes that financial stocks look more attractive than consumer discretionary stocks. An investor could buy an ETF that offers exposure to the financial sector, such as the Financial Select Sector SPDR (Ticker symbol: XLF), and sell short the same amount of shares of the Consumer Discretionary SPDR (Ticker symbol: XLY). By eliminating most of the influence of the stock market's overall direction, a long/short strategy greatly reduces volatility. This trade can be profitable to the extent that financial stocks outperform consumer discretionary stocks, and this outlook can be implemented at a fairly low level of cost and risk. The transparency of ETFs allows financial advisers and investors to monitor the results of the hedged trade easily, which is useful in deciding when the time has come to unwind the position.

• ALPHA HARVESTING •

Another hedging strategy that could be implemented using ETFs is alpha harvesting. In most stock portfolios, the market's overall direction (also referred to as beta) accounts for a large part of total return. In either up or down markets, beta is such a powerful force that it can dilute the value added by a financial adviser or fund manager in selecting specific sectors or stocks.

An alpha harvesting strategy aims to maximize the risk-adjusted return, or alpha, produced by successful management over full market cycles by hedging the impact of beta. To illustrate, let's compare the performance of two hypothetical portfolios, one being a long-only portfolio that allocates 100 percent of its assets to a portfolio of U.S. stocks. The other portfolio is an alpha generating portfolio, which has allocated 100 percent of its assets to a portfolio of U.S. stocks but also simultaneously sells short a stock index fund that is equal to 50 percent of the portfolio's value. The graph below compares the hypothetical performance of these two portfolios, assuming that the investment strategy successfully outperforms the market by 1 percent in both up and down markets.

Figure 7.3: Hypothetical Long-only versus Alpha Harvesting Strategy

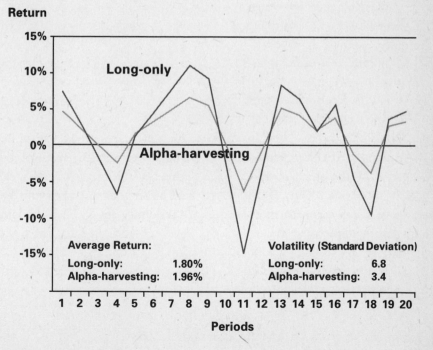

It's evident that the alpha harvesting strategy produces incrementally more return over the full holding period, while its volatility is just half as great as in the long-only portfolio. This example illustrates that since alpha measures risk-adjusted returns, alpha can be increased significantly not only by boosting returns but also by tempering the effect of the market's inherent volatility. Also note that borrowing—in order to sell shares short—was used, which is a way of leveraging the portfolio. It is commonly believed that leverage increases risk in a portfolio. While this is often true, in carefully structured alpha harvesting strategies, leverage used to sell ETFs short can reduce risk.

• MAINTAIN GREATER CONTROL OVER INVESTMENTS •

Like stocks, ETFs allow investors to exercise control over when and at what price they buy or sell shares. That's because they are able to place specific instructions in the form of limit or stop-loss orders. Limit orders are instructions as to the time and quantity of shares to be bought or sold. Stop-loss orders allow the sale or purchase of a stock once it rises above or falls below a certain price. Setting these trading guidelines allows investors to protect their gains or ensure that their losses don't exceed a certain level.

• WHO'S USING ETFS? •

It's hard to know exactly where all of the ETF assets are coming from. Unlike mutual funds, ETFs do not have extensive record-keeping that allows their sponsors to know who their investors are. That said, by looking at the volume of ETF trades it is possible to make assumptions as to whether money is flowing mainly from retail investors via smaller trades or from institutions through larger trades. Just a few years back it was commonly said that the majority of ETF assets were flowing in from institutions, including pension funds, hedge funds, portfolio managers, insurance funds, and other large companies. More recently, though, that pattern seems to have changed. Around the time this book was written about two thirds of ETF assets flowing into the iShares family of ETFs were coming from retail investors, generally through financial advisers buying ETFs on their clients' behalf. Half of all iShares ETF assets were estimated to be held by individuals. However, the majority of the trading volume in ETFs is still coming from institutional investors. According to Barclays, institutional trading (measured by daily share volume) makes up about 80 percent of ETF trading volume. Institutions tend to dominate trading volume because they are more active traders, with shorter holding periods.

• THE COMPETITION •

So, how do ETF assets compare to competing products? According to the Investment Company Institute's *2009 Fact Book*, all registered investment companies—which include mutual funds, ETFs, closed-end funds, and unit investment trusts—had total assets of just under $10.35 trillion at the end of 2008. The table below shows that ETFs accounted for $531 billion of that.

TABLE 7.6: ASSETS IN REGISTERED INVESTMENT COMPANIES

	MUTUAL FUNDS ($ BILLIONS)	CLOSED-END FUNDS ($ BILLIONS)	ETFS ($ BILLIONS)	UITS ($ BILLIONS)	TOTAL ($ BILLIONS)
1995	2,811	143	1	73	3,028
1996	3,526	147	2	72	3,747
1997	4,468	152	7	85	4,712
1998	5,525	156	16	94	5,791
1999	6,846	147	34	92	7,119
2000	6,965	143	66	74	7,248
2001	6,975	141	83	49	7,248
2002	6,390	159	102	36	6,687
2003	7,414	214	151	36	7,815
2004	8,107	254	228	37	8,626
2005	8,905	277	301	41	9,524
2006	10,397	298	423	50	11,167
2007	12,000	313	608	53	12,974
2008	9,601	188	531	29	10,349

SOURCE: INVESTMENT COMPANY INSTITUTE

When comparing total ETF assets with mutual fund assets, which accounted for a whopping $9.6 trillion, ETF assets are just a drop in the bucket. But compared with both closed-end funds and UITs, ETF assets were substantially higher. Closed-end funds ended 2008 with total assets of $188 billion, roughly a third of ETFs, while UITs had accumulated just $29 billion by year's end. It is also important to look at the growth of ETF assets compared with the other products to get a better sense of where they stand. Notice that while the growth in ETF assets has increased—and grown at a very fast clip in recent years—assets of both closed-end funds and UITs have zigzagged between 1995 and 2008, with UITs actually ending 2008 with $44 billion less in assets than they had in 1995 and closed-end funds having grown only $44 billion since then. It's also worth noting that the decline in ETF assets in the midst of the 2007–2008 credit crisis was substantially less than the decline in closed-end funds, UITs, and mutual funds.

In terms of the number of products on the market, ETFs are still at the low end. At the end of 2008 there were a total of 16,262 investment products, according to ICI, and ETFs accounted for 743 of those. This compares with 8,889 mutual funds, 646 closed-end funds, and 5,984 UITs. The following table tracks the product growth between 1995 and 2008 for each.

TABLE 7.7: NUMBER OF INVESTMENT COMPANIES (1995–2008)

	MUTUAL FUNDS	CLOSED-END FUNDS	ETFS	UITS	TOTAL
1995	5,761	500	2	12,979	19,242
1996	6,293	498	19	11,764	18,574
1997	6,778	488	19	11,593	18,878
1998	7,489	493	29	10,966	18,977
1999	8,003	512	30	10,414	18,959
2000	8,370	482	80	10,072	19,004
2001	8,519	492	102	9,295	18,408
2002	8,512	545	113	8,303	17,473
2003	8,427	584	119	7,233	16,363
2004	8,419	619	152	6,499	15,689
2005	8,451	635	204	6,019	15,309

	MUTUAL FUNDS	CLOSED-END FUNDS	ETFS	UITS	TOTAL
2006	8,723	647	359	5,907	15,636
2007	8,749	664	629	6,030	16,072
2008	8,889	646	743	5,984	16,262

SOURCE: INVESTMENT COMPANY INSTITUTE

• THE MUTUAL FUND MECCA •

Clearly, mutual funds are by far the greatest competitor to ETFs. Looking at the gap in assets between the two products, the idea of ETF assets ever catching up may seem like an improbability. But keep in mind that the mutual fund industry also had slow beginnings. In fact, it took the mutual fund industry a lot longer to get to the point ETFs are at today. The first mutual fund was launched in 1924, and it wasn't until the 1980s, about sixty years later, that mutual funds accumulated the level of assets currently invested in ETFs.

The table below shows the cash flow into mutual funds between 1985 and 2000, as well as total mutual fund assets; mutual funds held less than $500 billion in total assets in 1985. It took until 1990 for mutual fund assets to rise to $1 trillion, and then it was during the next ten years that their assets really ramped up. By the end of 2000, assets had increased to almost $7 trillion, and by 2007 to $12 trillion—though in 2008 assets fell back to 2005–2006 levels due to the credit crisis. While it might take years for total ETF assets to catch up, their growth is expected to outpace mutual funds on a percentage basis over the next few years.

TABLE 7.8: NET NEW CASH FLOW TO MUTUAL FUNDS (1985–2000)

YEAR	TOTAL MUTUAL FUND ASSETS ($ BILLIONS)
1985	495
1986	716
1987	770
1988	810
1989	982
1990	1,065

YEAR	TOTAL MUTUAL FUND ASSETS ($ BILLIONS)
1991	1,393
1992	1,643
1993	2,070
1994	2,155
1995	2,811
1996	3,526
1997	4,468
1998	5,525
1999	6,846
2000	6,967

SOURCE: INVESTMENT COMPANY INSTITUTE

• ETFS ON NON-U.S. EXCHANGES •

While the focus of this book is on ETFs listed on U.S. exchanges, it is certainly worth noting the progress of ETFs listed abroad, as several markets, particularly in Europe, have continued to exhibit strong growth in this market. According to Morgan Stanley, through the end of 2007 the worldwide total for ETF assets was roughly $796 billion, an increase of nearly 41 percent over the previous year. Meanwhile, the number of worldwide primary ETF listings climbed to 1,171, a 64 percent increase from the prior year. Growth has been particularly strong in Europe, where assets rose more than 60 percent in 2006 and an additional 43 percent in 2007—and the latter was in line with ETF asset growth in the United States. European ETF assets as of the end of 2007 totaled $128 billion, or about 16 percent of the market worldwide. The number of primary ETF listings in Europe has been climbing also. By the end of 2007 there were 423 primary ETF listings in Europe, the majority of which were listed in Germany, France, Italy, the United Kingdom, and Switzerland. Many more ETFs are planned for the European market.

Japan's ETF market is running a distant second to the European ETF market, with about $34.2 billion in total assets. Contrary to the strong growth in the U.S. and European markets, the growth of ETF assets in Japan ticked down between 2006 and 2007. In terms of the number of products, as of the end of 2007 Japan had only fifteen primary ETF listings. Canada, meanwhile, has just under $18 billion in total ETF assets, divided among forty-six ETFs.

• CHAPTER SUMMARY •

▶ While the first ETF was launched in 1993, it wasn't until 2000 that more products started being launched at a steady pace. In 2006 there was a major surge in new ETFs, and this growth wave continued through 2007 and beyond. As of September 2008, there were eight hundred exchange-traded products trading in the United States.

▶ Most of the ETFs that came to market early on were from Barclays and State Street, but in the past few years the market has been flooded with new entrants. More ETF providers are expected to enter the market as time goes on. Barclays continues to dominate the ETF space in terms of the number of products and amount of assets.

▶ The ETF market remains very concentrated among a small number of players. In terms of assets, the top five ETF companies account for the vast majority of ETF assets. When it comes to ETFs on the market, the top five players are responsible for about five hundred ETFs.

▶ ETFs can serve different functions inside a portfolio, making them appealing tools to both retail investors and financial professionals. Many retail investors use ETFs to construct a broad-based portfolio. Others opt for a core-and-explore portfolio, which entails using one or two broad ETFs as the core holding for the majority of the portfolio, and then using more narrow ETFs, individual securities, or actively managed funds to add weighting to other areas of it.

▶ ETFs are also commonly used as a way to increase exposure to certain areas of the market that previously had been difficult for retail investors to access. These areas include commodities and currencies, and strategies such as leveraging or shorting.

▶ Tax strategies, cash management, and pairs trades commonly are done using ETFs. To reduce taxes, investors can sell securities that have embedded losses and buy an ETF that offers similar exposure. ETFs can be used as a place to put excess cash or for pairs trades, which include buying a stock and shorting its sector ETF, or vice versa.

► ETFs have experienced strong and steady growth in assets, particularly over the past few years. But despite the number of new ETFs on the market and the ability to consistently attract new money from investors, ETF assets remain fairly concentrated in a few categories. In addition, assets are concentrated among a small number of ETF providers and a few popular products.

► Compared with the mutual fund industry, which has more than $10 trillion in assets, the ETF industry is still relatively nascent. However, over the next few years, the relative size of these two industries is expected to change: ETF asset growth is expected to outpace mutual fund asset growth on a percentage basis.

► While small compared with the United States, international ETFs also have experienced strong growth, especially in Europe.

8

Creating an Asset Allocation

While diversification and product selection are essential in creating a well-allocated portfolio, it is also important to ensure that a portfolio remains within a comfortable range of risk. Risk tolerance can vary widely from investor to investor. Some are willing to take significantly greater risks on the bet that they eventually will be rewarded with higher returns. Meanwhile, other investors are less tolerant of big swings in their portfolios and instead are willing to forgo the possibility of higher returns in order to maintain steadier, less volatile performance. Because tolerance of volatility can vary dramatically from one investor to another, understanding where they lie on that spectrum is key to creating a well-diversified portfolio that will suit each one's individual investing needs. This chapter explores methods for measuring an investor's tolerance for risk. It also explains how to use these methods, whether for putting together a simple asset allocation or, as a convenient alternative, choosing a prepackaged fund that implements various asset allocations based on varying levels of risk. This chapter also will explore the theory behind asset allocation, as well as the impact that a carefully conceived allocation may have on the performance of a portfolio over time.

• ACCOUNTING FOR RISK •

Many investors use the phrases "asset allocation" and "diversification" interchangeably, but they're not the same thing. A true asset allocation strategy takes into account an investor's tolerance for risk when diversifying a portfolio. This is a necessary step in helping investors meet their long-term goals. Portfolios that are created to provide the best possible returns for a given level of risk are referred to as "strategically allocated portfolios." In measuring risk tolerance, investors often are assigned to one of three categories: conservative, aggressive, or moderate (also referred to as balanced). Conservative investors generally don't want to take much risk. They tend to have portfolios that are heavier in bonds and cash, since those are often safer, less volatile investments than stocks. On the opposite end of the spectrum are aggressive investors, ones who are willing to weather ups and downs in their portfolios. Aggressive investors generally have the majority of their assets in stocks, which are more risky than bonds or cash. They also may participate in fairly volatile or cyclical asset classes such as oil, commodities, or real estate. Those in the middle category, which is composed of balanced or moderate investors, are willing to tolerate some risk but aren't interested in stomaching major swings in portfolio performance. These investors generally split their assets more evenly among stocks, bonds, and cash.

Risk tolerance is largely a personal preference. But age is also a major factor. Younger investors are more likely to be more aggressive. They have a longer time frame to accumulate assets, so they can tolerate more volatility earlier in life in the hopes of achieving better long-term returns. If they do experience a big loss, they have more time to make it up. Aggressive investors often have between 70 percent and 100 percent of their portfolio invested in stocks. For older investors, especially those who are already in retirement, this mix may be too risky. These investors do not have as much ability to accumulate large amounts of capital. They often become more conservative in protecting what they have, and their main financial goal may be to preserve their money so that some will last the rest of their lives. Because most bonds pay a fixed rate of interest, they are widely used by conservative investors and often represent more than half of such investors' portfolios.

• DEVELOPING AN ASSET ALLOCATION STRATEGY •

Determining an investor's type can require an evaluation of many factors including (but certainly not limited to) age, investment experience, tolerance for risk, income, savings, liabilities, and future objectives. Having a clear understanding of these matters is a good first step in developing a plan that can put the investor on the right path to meeting his or her goals. A common way to gather this information is through an investor questionnaire. These types of questionnaires can be found online on various company Web sites and are a great tool to get investors thinking about their goals and risk tolerance. However, keep in mind that they are just general guides. Also, because companies use different methodologies to determine appropriate asset allocations, it is likely that recommended allocations may differ from site to site. The following are a few examples of Web sites that offer free online questionnaires:

- Vanguard Group: personal.vanguard.com
- MetLife: metlife.com
- TIAA-CREF: ais4.tiaa-cref.org
- The Hartford: thehartford.com
- Oppenheimer Funds: oppenheimerfunds.com

The following sample questionnaire includes many common questions that could be used to help investors understand their tolerance for risk, current financial situation, and long-term goals, prior to developing a customized asset allocation. These questions should be considered before creating an asset allocation.

• SAMPLE INVESTOR QUESTIONNAIRE •

1. What is your current age?
    a. Under 35
    b. 35–45
    c. 46–55
    d. 56–70
    e. Over 70

2. When do you plan to withdraw money from this investment?
   a. Within 5 years
   b. In 5–10 years
   c. In 10–15 years
   d. In 15–20 years
   e. In over 20 years

3. What is the current value of your investment portfolio? (Stocks, bonds, mutual funds, cash, 401(k), IRA, etc.)
   a. Less than $50,000
   b. $50,000–100,000
   c. $100,000–250,000
   d. $250,000–500,000
   e. $500,000+

INVESTMENT EXPERIENCE

4. I own and/or have investment experience with:
   a. Cash, CDs, money markets
   b. Bonds
   c. Mutual funds
   d. ETFs
   e. Equities
   f. All of the above

5. A basic principle of investing is that the higher the return you seek, the more risk you face. Which of the following statements best describes your investment goal?
   a. I want to maximize growth by obtaining the highest total return on my investment.
   b. I want to obtain above average growth.
   c. I want to obtain moderate growth.
   d. I want stable returns while preserving most of my original investment.
   e. I want to avoid loss of my initial investment value.

VOLATILITY

6. The value of most investments fluctuates from year to year as well as over the short term. How would you feel if an investment you

had committed to for ten years lost 20 percent of its value during the first year?

    a. I would be extremely concerned and would sell my investment.

    b. I would be concerned and might consider selling my investment.

    c. I would be concerned, but I would not consider selling my investment.

    d. I would not be overly concerned given my long-term investment philosophy.

VARIATION

7. The graphs below show the possible outcomes of investment in three hypothetical portfolios over a period of twenty years, with each bar representing performance over one year. (*The maximum gain or loss on an investment is impossible to predict. The ranges shown in the graphs are hypothetical, not historical.*) Which portfolio best represents your realistic investing goal?

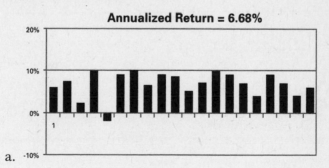

a.

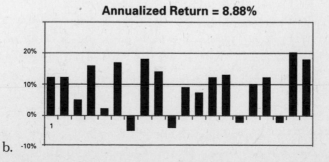

b.

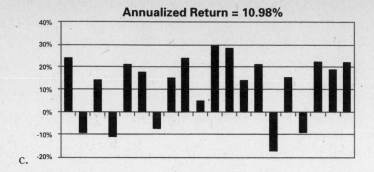

c.

8. If the stock market increased by 15 percent in one year while the value of your portfolio (invested primarily in bonds and cash) increased by 4 percent in the same year, how would you react?

   a. I would not change my portfolio.
   b. I would add some stocks to my portfolio, but they would make up no more than 50 percent of my account.
   c. I would replace the entire bond and cash portions of my portfolio with stocks.

• PUTTING TOGETHER A WELL-ALLOCATED PORTFOLIO •

Whether you are a financial adviser or an individual investor, this type of questionnaire can be used to help focus an appropriate asset allocation strategy. To illustrate, let's use as an example a fifty-year-old investor who is planning to retire in fifteen years, at age sixty-five. This investor plans to maintain the same steady stream of income until he retires. The money that he has been saving will need to last him through his retirement years. He considers himself to be a moderately experienced, long-term investor. From time to time, he does take modest risks. But he also tends to grow anxious whenever there is a meaningful drop in his portfolio. Occasionally, when the market appears volatile or risky, he will sell some of his riskier investments and move into safer ones. Because this investor still has several years before retiring, he can tolerate some risk. However, because he worries whenever his portfolio experiences poor performance, and may even sell riskier investments when that happens, he clearly does not like taking on heavy risk.

Based on information like this, a financial adviser might determine that this investor is probably a good candidate for a more moderate, or balanced, portfolio. Portfolios that fall under this category generally have from 40 percent to 60 percent of their assets invested in stocks and 40 percent to 60 percent in bonds. Risk also can be spread out in the stock portion of the portfolio by including U.S. stocks of varying sizes, such as large caps, midcaps, and small caps, as well as international stocks. The bond portion also can be diversified to spread out risk. For example, allocations to Treasury bonds, U.S. government agency bonds, corporate bonds with various quality ratings, and bonds of different maturities can be included.

The figures on page 158 show an example of a moderate portfolio's asset allocation. The top chart indicates how this portfolio is divided broadly between core asset classes, with 40 percent placed in equities and 60 percent in fixed income. In this instance, using ETFs such as the Spyder and the iShares MSCI EAFE to make up the U.S. and international equity portions, respectively, and the iShares Lehman Aggregate ETF to comprise the fixed income portfolio would be good options, as they provide broad-based exposure to equities and fixed income for a low cost. The bottom chart shows how the portfolio could be suballocated among different investments within each major asset class. In this example, the equity portion of the portfolio is divided between large caps and international equities, which have the greatest weights, and then mid- and small caps, which each make up a smaller percentage. The fixed income portion of the portfolio has investments in short- and long-term government bonds as well as corporate bonds and Treasury Inflation-Protected Securities (TIPS). Included in this example are popular examples of ETFs that could be used to create this portfolio.

This is only one example of how a portfolio can be allocated. The number of different investments included in a portfolio can vary based on the level of diversification being sought and the amount of complexity the investor can handle. The investor could choose to diversify the portfolio further, by including additional categories to vary risk. On the equity side, this could mean adding allocations to value and growth stocks, microcap stocks, and investments in specific economic sectors (e.g., health care) or global country markets (Japan). For the fixed income portion, government and corporate bonds of other durations could be added or, if the investor is interested in taking on more risk, high-yield bonds. Investments in alternative asset classes, such as currencies or commodities, also could be added.

Once the decisions have been made about which categories should be

Figure 8.1: Sample Asset Allocation of a Moderate Portfolio

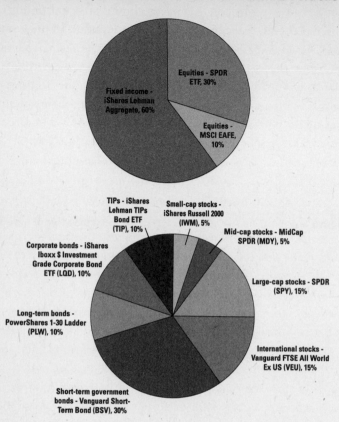

included in the portfolio, decisions should be made about how to divide the assets among those categories. The objective of this step is to match the investor's personal risk and return profile with the risk and return levels that each category offers. This is often done by looking at historical data to evaluate the past performance of certain securities or categories, as well as their historical levels of risk as measured by statistical tools such as standard deviation. (Risk tools will be discussed later in this book.) In the sample portfolio above, large caps and international equities account for a large percentage of the portfolio. In a portfolio designed for a higher risk profile, the allocation to small and midcaps might be larger than the allocation to large caps.

Now, let's look at examples of a conservative and an aggressive portfolio, using the same core asset classes and investment categories to show

how those allocations would change to target more or less risk, starting with a conservative portfolio. Generally, conservative portfolios have less than 40 percent of their allocation invested in equities. In this example, 20 percent will be allocated to equities and 80 percent to fixed income. The first chart below shows the division between ETFs representing core asset classes; the second shows details by specific investments. In many conservative portfolios, investors are interested in generating investment income that can maintain purchasing power against inflation. For that reason, this allocation includes a 30 percent investment in TIPS, a type of Treasury security that is especially well suited for inflation hedging.

Figure 8.2: Sample Asset Allocation of a Conservative Portfolio

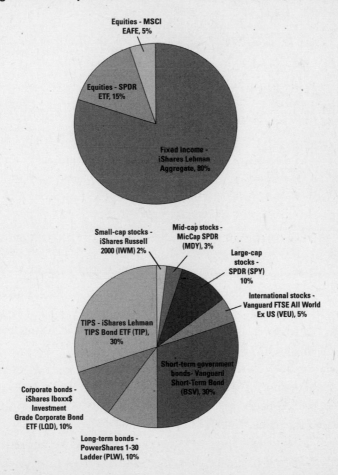

An aggressive portfolio generally will have between 70 percent and 100 percent of assets invested in equities. The example below uses a portfolio that has an 80 percent allocation to equities and 20 percent to fixed income. The first chart below shows the broad allocation among core asset classes. The second represents the specific breakdown by category.

Figure 8.3: Sample Asset Allocation of an Aggressive Portfolio

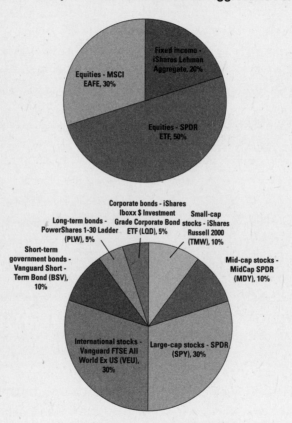

• CORRELATION OF ASSETS •

Another key to developing a risk-adjusted portfolio is understanding correlation, or how different asset classes and investments perform in relation to one another—i.e., do they tend to respond similarly to catalysts or do they tend more in opposite directions? The correlation coefficient is the statistical measurement used to determine this relationship between any two investments, indexes, or asset classes. The correlation coefficient ranges from 1 to −1, with 1 being a perfect positive correlation and −1 representing a perfect negative correlation. If two investments have a correlation of 1 that means they are moving in perfect sync with each other—when one rises, the other rises. A correlation of 0 (zero) indicates that two investments have a random relationship in their performance. Correlations should be considered broadly, by measuring the correlation of different asset classes. To maximize diversification, correlations between specific investments within the broader asset classes, such as the correlations between individual stocks, should also be considered.

Many times investors assume they are well diversified just because they own many different securities in their portfolio, but that's not the case. The real diversification is driven by how closely correlated pairs of securities inside a portfolio are. If they are correlated highly, the risk-reducing benefits of diversification may not be achieved, because investments may respond to conditions or events in the same way. On the other hand, if the portfolio has less correlated investments, while some are tumbling others may be rising, or at least holding value. As a result, risk is spread out. As a general rule, the lower the correlation between investments, the more diversification benefit a portfolio will have. There are a variety of online tools available to measure correlations, which allow different ticker symbols to be input so investors can see how pairs of investments are correlated. State Street Global Advisors, for instance, has a free correlation tracker on its Web site: ssgafunds.com/resources/correlation_tracker. html. This tool lets the investor enter the ticker of any stock and view other securities that have high or low correlations to it. Tickers can also be entered for two, three, or four securities and their correlations can be plotted.

The correlations between investments aren't set in stone. In many cases they can vary greatly. The following chart shows the rolling five-year correlations among stocks and bonds from June 1984 to January 2007. Each data point represents a look back at relationships in the monthly performance between the two asset classes over a five-year (sixty-month) period. It's evident how correlations were positive for several years, reaching as high as 0.5. However, around 2002 they turned negative, falling below −0.4.

Of all the major asset classes that are commonly used in diversified portfolios, only a few have consistently produced very low or negative

**Figure 8.4: Rolling Five-Year Correlation Among
Stocks and Bonds (1984–2007)**

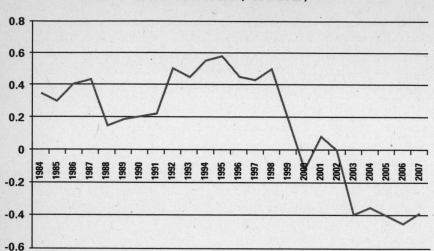

— Correlation

correlations with U.S. stocks: oil futures, precious metals, global currencies, and diversified commodities. However, three other asset classes have
produced fairly low correlations with equities, usually in the range of 0 to
0.5. They are high-grade U.S. bonds, Japanese stocks, and REITs.

• REBALANCING •

While having an asset allocation strategy in place will put an investor on
the right path to his/her long-term financial goals, it is as important to
maintain that allocation over time. For instance, suppose the investor has
a fairly balanced portfolio that has 60 percent of assets invested in stocks
and 40 percent invested in bonds. But then there is a major run-up in the
stock market that causes the equity allocation in a portfolio to rise from 60
percent to 75 percent. This change, produced by market action, has now
substantially increased the portfolio's overall level of risk. To avoid this,
there needs to be a system in place to make sure that if the target allocations change due to market action, they will be adjusted back to the target
mix. That system is known as "rebalancing," and it is one of the most
important features of a strategically allocated portfolio.

Rebalancing can be a useful feature for any strategic asset allocation strategy. It basically entails pruning back certain positions that have appreciated beyond their target allocation. It is what well-known mutual fund manager Peter Lynch frequently refers to as "cutting the flowers and watering the weeds." Rebalancing can be accomplished in two basic ways: automatically or with discretion.

Automatic rebalancing does not require human judgment. It can be done according to a set schedule (e.g., monthly, quarterly, semiannually, or annually) or whenever a given asset class drifts a specified amount away from its target (e.g., 5 percent above or below the guideline). For example, if a portfolio has a target of 60 percent in equity, and its automatic rebalancing trigger is 5 percentage points, it would be rebalanced if the equity portion falls below 55 percent or rises above 65 percent. On the other hand, discretionary rebalancing occurs based on the discretion of an investor, financial adviser, or portfolio manager and can be done in a way that minimizes transaction costs and tax implications. It also can take into account the reinvestment of income paid out by the portfolio, or the inclusion of new investment assets.

Determining when a rebalance will be triggered is only one component. There must also be a system in place to dictate what will happen inside the portfolio when a rebalance takes place. For example, when a rebalance is triggered, the portfolio could go back to its initial allocation. Another alternative may be to have the portfolio rebalance only partially. For instance, perhaps the portfolio will be rebalanced 50 percent of the way back. In the example above, in which equities increase from a 60 percent target and hit a 65 percent threshold, a partial rebalancing would bring the equity portion back halfway to the target, or 62.5 percent. This may be advantageous, as it allows the portfolio to participate somewhat in the market activity.

There are a few things to keep in mind in evaluating rebalancing methods. Many rebalancing events require selling shares that have appreciated, and this may result in a capital gain. Investors must pay income taxes on those gains, and under current law the tax is at ordinary income rates if the shares sold were held for less than one year. Tax consequences are not an issue when rebalancing is done in a tax-deferred portfolio, such as a 401(k) or Individual Retirement Account (IRA). However, investors may still incur costs or other fees on rebalancing transactions. (Discretionary rebalances can attempt to manage this.)

Rebalancing has several benefits. As mentioned above, if one part of the portfolio increases or decreases beyond its target, this can alter the level of risk in the portfolio. Rebalancing will then bring allocations back in line with their initial targets and ensure that the portfolio stays within the investor's target risk level. Rebalancing also can have an impact on performance, either positive or negative, over time.

To illustrate, let's look at two hypothetical portfolios between 1995 and 2007. Suppose that both started out with $1 million allocated 60 percent to stocks and 40 percent to bonds. The first of these portfolios was never rebalanced. The second portfolio was rebalanced automatically using a 100 percent threshold, meaning that when a rebalance was triggered, allocations went all the way back to the original targets. A rebalance was triggered when the equity allocation either fell below 55 percent or rose above 65 percent. Figure 8.5 on page 165 shows the difference in the equity allocation between the two portfolios. Notice how the equity portion of the unrebalanced portfolio spiked to nearly 80 percent around 2000. The equity portion of the rebalanced portfolio, meanwhile, fluctuated a bit but remained in a fairly tight range, between about 55 percent and 65 percent.

Now let's look at the impact that rebalancing had on the performance of these portfolios. Figure 8.6 shows that the unrebalanced portfolio outperformed the rebalanced portfolio starting in about 2000, when the stock market was doing well. But not long after that point, when the market began to decline, this pattern changed. Around 2003 the rebalanced portfolio began to outperform the unrebalanced portfolio. And by 2007, the rebalanced portfolio had increased to $3.43 million, compared with the unrebalanced portfolio, which had increased to $3.38 million—representing a $50,000 difference. (This hypothetical comparison does not take into account any extra tax or transaction costs incurred in rebalancing.) In addition to generating returns that are $50,000 higher, the rebalanced portfolio is also maintaining a somewhat lower volatility than the unrebalanced portfolio.

When stock markets are heading up, rebalancing may not seem attractive, as it could mean you miss out on some of the big gains. However, rebalancing can help to avoid being overexposed to specific high-performance market sectors at the peak of a bull market. Keep in mind that the positive or negative impact of rebalancing can vary depending on its frequency and the specific parameters that are set.

Figure 8.5: Variation in Equity Allocation Between Unrebalanced and Rebalanced Portfolios

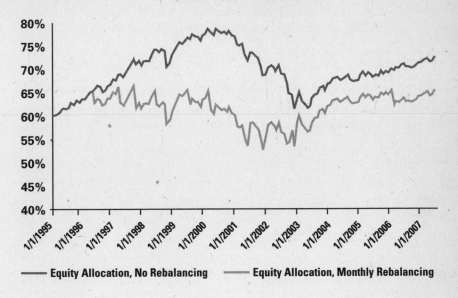

Equity Allocation, No Rebalancing   Equity Allocation, Monthly Rebalancing

Figure 8.6: Performance of Unrebalanced versus Rebalanced Portfolio

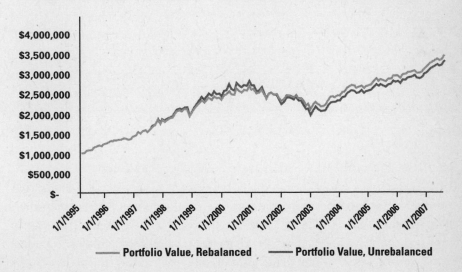

Portfolio Value, Rebalanced   Portfolio Value, Unrebalanced

• THE THINKING BEHIND ASSET ALLOCATION •

The roots of asset allocation are found in modern portfolio theory, or MPT, which was introduced in 1952 by economist Harry Markowitz. MPT models the trade-off between taking risks in a portfolio and the expected returns that are generated. One general idea advanced by modern portfolio theory is that rational investors will want to hold portfolios with the greatest expected return for any given level of risk. Markowitz referred to these as "efficient portfolios." All efficient portfolios can be plotted on what is known as the "efficient frontier." The horizontal axis measures the historic risk of the portfolio and the vertical axis measures historic returns.

Figure 8.7: Illustration of Efficient Frontier

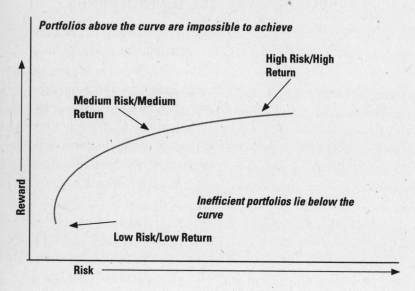

In the lower left segment of the efficient frontier would be a portfolio that is expected to produce the best return possible (based on historic results) by an investor who is only willing to assume the least amount of risk. As the investor's appetite for risk increases, the opportunities to generate better returns also increase. In the top right segment of the curve would be a portfolio that represents the best possible expected returns that can be achieved by assuming the highest level of risk. In theory, investors should not want to own any portfolios that lie below the efficient frontier, because they could instead choose another portfolio that offers higher expected returns at the same level of risk.

One method commonly used by financial professionals to distinguish efficient portfolios from inefficient ones is known as "mean variance analysis"—a mathematical technique that measures the expected returns of assets in a portfolio, the level of risk, and how different variables move together. Given a defined universe of investments or asset classes, this tool then can be used to identify the portfolios that optimize expected returns for each possible level of risk. In practice, this is done with powerful software programs that use optimization algorithms to identify these portfolios.

• STRATEGIC ASSET ALLOCATION FUNDS •

Investors know how important it is to save for retirement. But some just don't have the time, understanding, or willingness to manage their portfolios properly on their own. Others are not interested in using a financial professional. For either of these camps, strategic asset allocation funds are a viable alternative. These have a preset asset allocation in place. The main goal of these products is to provide investors with a simple way to generate long-term returns while only assuming as much risk as they are comfortable taking. These funds start out with a predetermined asset allocation called a "base policy mix." For instance, an aggressive fund might have a base policy mix that is 80 percent invested in equity and 20 percent invested in fixed income. The majority of asset allocation funds are currently mutual funds that invest in a combination of stocks and bonds. The ETF world also has launched various versions of such funds already and continues to do so. On the mutual fund side, strategic allocation funds are based on an investment model but are often actively managed. On the ETF side, strategic allocation funds generally pursue similar models, but they are usually implemented through passive index funds that seek to track a benchmark index. Strategic allocation funds also rebalance in order to maintain their allocations over time, though the way they rebalance can vary from product to product.

There are two primary types of asset allocation funds. One type is risk-based, often referred to as target-risk or lifestyle funds. The other is target-date funds, which also are known as life-cycle funds.

Target-risk Funds

Target-risk funds generally are allocated between stocks and bonds, and they are positioned for consumers in one of two ways. The first is according to the type of risk level they are targeting, which is why these products generally have labels such as conservative, moderate, balanced, or aggressive. Risk-based funds also can be identified according to their equity/fixed income mix. For example, a fund labeled a "60/40 fund" would keep 60 percent of assets in equities and 40 percent in fixed income. With risk-based funds, the asset allocation that is in place when the investor buys the fund generally remains the same throughout the life span of the fund. That means an aggressive fund that has an 80 percent allocation to equities and a 20 percent allocation to fixed income will maintain that allocation regardless of how much time passes.

One example of a target-risk ETF is the PowerShares Autonomic Balanced Growth NFA Global Asset Portfolio (Ticker symbol: PAO). This ETF is based on the New Frontier Global Dynamic Balanced Growth Index, which is an index of ETFs. The index targets an allocation of 75 percent equities and 25 percent taxable fixed income. The index is rebalanced quarterly, though in cases of high market volatility it could be rebalanced on a monthly basis. This portfolio invests in more than thirty ETFs in a variety of asset classes. The figure below shows how the investments are broadly allocated; the table shows the ETFs that comprise the top ten holdings of the portfolio.

Figure 8.8: Allocation of PowerShares Autonomic Balanced Growth NFA Global Asset Portfolio

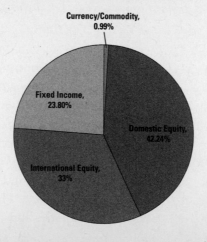

Currency/Commodity, 0.99%

Fixed Income, 23.80%

Domestic Equity, 42.24%

International Equity, 33%

TABLE 8.1: TOP TEN HOLDINGS

ETF	WEIGHT IN PORTFOLIO (%)
PowerShares Dynamic Large Cap Value Portfolio	9.27
PowerShares Dynamic Large Cap Growth Portfolio	7.27
PowerShares Emerging Markets Sovereign Debt Portfolio	5.03
Vanguard Emerging Markets ETF	4.68
Vanguard European ETF	4.59
iShares MSCI Japan Index Fund	4.52
iShares iBOXX $ InvesTop Investment Grade Bond ETF	4.51
PowerShares Dynamic Mid-Cap Growth Portfolio	4.46
PowerShares Dynamic Large Cap Portfolio	4.42
Vanguard Europe Pacific ETF	4.41
Total	53.16

SOURCE: POWERSHARES

Target-date Funds

Target-date investment products take risk-based allocation a step further. These funds also start out with a base policy mix, which is the initial allocation of the fund. But instead of maintaining a static allocation, these funds become more conservative over time as an investor's time horizon shortens. Target-date funds are based on a specific future date, often the year at which an investor expects to retire. For instance, an investor expecting to retire in 2040 would buy a 2040 target-date fund. Target-date funds generally are offered in increments of five or ten years. So a fund company might offer a family of target-date funds that includes a 2015 fund, a 2020 fund, a 2025 fund, and so on. As the target date approaches, the portfolio automatically adjusts its asset allocation to become more conservative.

Let's look at an example of a 2025 target-date portfolio to illustrate. If this portfolio were purchased in 2000, the investor would have twenty-five years until retirement. As a result, when this portfolio was bought it would be aggressive, with the majority of assets invested in equities. Figure 8.9 illustrates a typical asset allocation upon purchase. The top chart shows that this portfolio is 90 percent invested in equities and 10 percent invested in fixed income. The bottom chart illustrates the more specific breakdown of this portfolio. Because there is substantial time until retirement, the investor purchasing this portfolio can afford to take substantial risk. That is why the allocation in this example is even more aggressive than the aggressive portfolio discussed earlier.

Figure 8.9: Sample Asset Allocation of a 2025 Target-date Portfolio

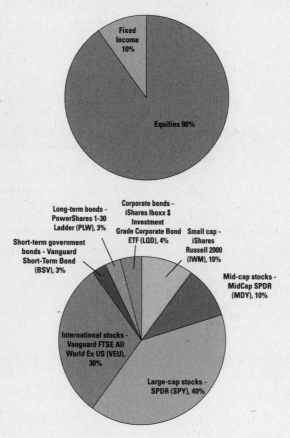

Target-date portfolios follow a predetermined path that dictates how the asset allocation will change gradually over time. The path that the fund follows as it makes changes inside the portfolio is known as the "glide path." It basically dictates when the fund will reduce its stock percentage and by how much. The following figure illustrates one glide path, showing how the allocation to equities decreases as retirement approaches. The decrease even continues after retirement for several years and then eventually levels off. The majority of the allocation from that point forth is generally invested in fixed income, though usually a modest equity allocation is maintained, perhaps 10 to 20 percent of total assets.

Figure 8.10: Example of a Target-date Fund Glide Path

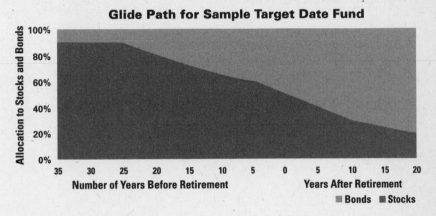

Glide Path for Sample Target Date Fund

It is evident how the glide path looks from an age perspective. The following table illustrates how the age of an investor corresponds to the glide path of a target-date fund.

TABLE 8.2: CHANGING ALLOCATION OF TARGET-DATE FUND ACCORDING TO INVESTOR'S AGE

	Before Retirement							Retirement	After Retirement			
Years	35	30	25	20	15	10	5	0	5	10	15	20
Stocks	90%	90%	90%	80%	72%	65%	60%	50%	40%	30%	25%	20%
Bonds	10%	10%	10%	20%	28%	35%	40%	50%	60%	70%	75%	80%
Age	Under 30	35	40	45	50	55	60	65	70	75	80	85

Note that twenty-five to thirty-five years prior to retirement this portfolio would have 90 percent invested in equities and 10 percent invested in bonds. (Many portfolios also would include a position in cash that might gradually increase over time as well.) As time passes and the investor has twenty years to go until retirement, the portfolio will change. The equity allocation would be reduced to 80 percent and the bond allocation would be increased to 20 percent. After another five years go by, with fifteen years left to go until the target date, 72 percent would be allocated to equities and 28 percent to nonequities. With ten years left until the target date, the portfolio would be adjusted to 65 percent stocks and 35 percent bonds; with five years to go the allocation would adjust to 60/40, still in favor of stocks, and once the target date is reached the portfolio would be divided evenly, 50/50.

This reduction in equity and corresponding increase in fixed income would continue at a measured pace for twenty years after the target date is reached. Ultimately, the portfolio would be allocated 20 percent in equity and 80 percent in fixed income. Having 20 percent exposure to equity allows the portfolio to remain diversified, which is necessary to make sure it continues to generate high enough returns so the investor's money would not run out. It also might provide opportunities for better returns than could be achieved by holding only fixed income.

Target-date ETFs

While the majority of target-date or life-cycle funds are mutual funds, several target-date ETFs have been introduced already, and more are expected to launch in the future. The first family of target-date ETFs to be launched was the TDX Independence ETFs, which were a product of TD Ameritrade and XShares. They currently offer five such ETFs. The TDX Independence In-Target ETF (Ticker symbol: TDX), which is the most conservative of the ETFs, is designed for people close to retirement. They also offer the TDX Independence 2010 ETF (Ticker symbol: TDD), the TDX Independence 2020 ETF (Ticker symbol: TDH), the TDX Independence 2030 ETF (Ticker symbol: TDN), and the TDX Independence 2040 ETF (Ticker symbol: TDV), each of which shifts its equity and fixed income exposures in conjunction with its target date.

The TDX Independence 2030 ETF offers a good illustration of how this ETF shifts its allocation over time. Unlike the PowerShares target-risk ETF described above, this one does not invest in other ETFs but in individual stocks of all international stocks, domestic stocks, and fixed income instead. At its inception the ETF is moderately aggressive, with about 22 percent in international equities, 66 percent in domestic equities, and 12 percent in fixed income. As it moves along the glide path the ETF gradually adjusts its exposure, so that by the time the target date is reached in 2030, the fund will have just 10 percent allocated to equities. Five years past the target date, the ETF will increase its risk to match that of the Lipper Conservative Funds Index, which currently allocates about 33 percent to equities.

The iShares family also has a series of target-date ETFs that range from very short-term funds through ones targeting the year 2040. Let's look at their 2015 target-date fund to give another example of these products. This fund is geared toward investors with a shorter span until retirement, and therefore begins with a fairly conservative allocation of about 43 percent invested in fixed income, 43 percent in domestic equity, 12 percent in international equity, and a small percentage allocated to domestic real estate and individual securities. The allocation as of September 2008 is shown below.

Figure 8.11: iShares 2015 Target-date Fund

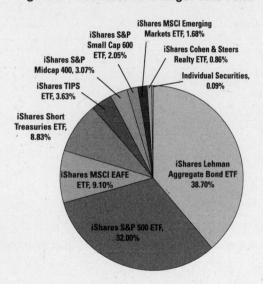

• FUTURE GROWTH OF STRATEGIC ALLOCATION FUNDS •

Both risk-based (lifestyle funds) and target-date (life-cycle funds) have become very popular in recent years, particularly in defined-contribution retirement plans such as 401(k)s. Most of this growth is due to the convenience that they offer. Strategic asset allocation funds take a major burden off investors by providing them with a choice of portfolios that are allocated based on different levels of risk. Target-date funds go an extra step, making the asset allocation process even easier by adjusting the allocation over time. Investors don't have to worry about changing their asset allocations or switching into a new fund as they get older and their risk tolerance changes. Target-date funds essentially provide investors with one-stop shopping for their retirement savings needs. In the figure below it's evident how both risk-based and target-date funds have seen a surge in asset growth between 1998 and 2007. Notice that with life-cycle funds (target-date funds) the majority of assets come from defined-contribution plans, such as 401(k)s.

Figure 8.12: Breakdown of Total Assets in Life-Cycle Funds

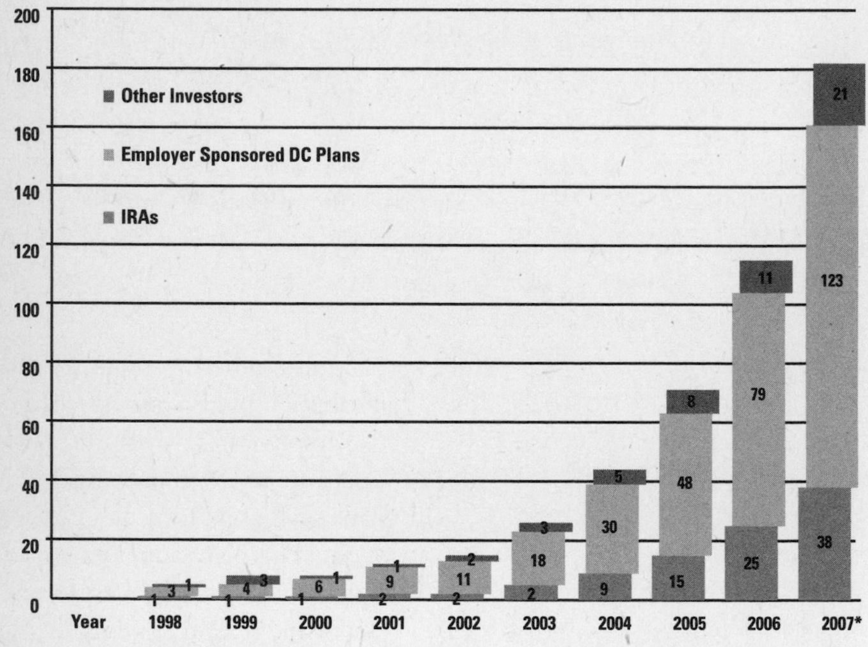

SOURCE: INVESTMENT COMPANY INSTITUTE

*2007 data is preliminary

Life-cycle and lifestyle funds are likely to continue growing at a rapid pace in the future as investors and financial professionals continue to embrace them. Part of that growth is also expected to come as a result of the Pension Protection Act that was signed into law in 2006. The act greatly strengthened the U.S. pension system, which many felt to be out

Figure 8.13: Breakdown of Total Assets in Lifestyle Funds

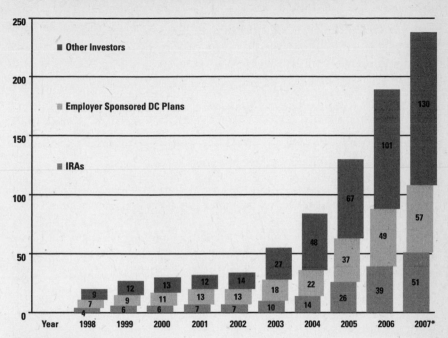

SOURCE: INVESTMENT COMPANY INSTITUTE

*2007 data is preliminary

of date and in need of major reform. But it also aimed to make it easier for people to participate in defined-contribution plans such as 401(k)s and to do so in a more effective way. For example, one provision of the act increases the incentives for retirement plan sponsors to automatically enroll employees in participant-directed plans such as 401(k)s. If employees do not want to participate, they may opt out. This provision is expected to increase substantially the number of employees enrolled in these plans, raising total retirement assets as a result. Part of the reason risk-based and target-date funds may become more popular is that these funds meet the needs of investors in retirement plans. As a result, a sizable portion of the assets that flow into retirement plans will be captured by these funds.

There is another provision of the act that is also driving the use of target-date funds. If employees are enrolled in a participant-directed plan but do not actively choose a specific fund, they are assigned to a default option that the plan sponsor has preselected. Historically, many plans have opted to use money market funds or stable value funds as default options, because they are low risk. But these choices also generate relatively low returns, which means they have more limited potential for long-term asset accumulation. That's why the Pension Protection Act encourages retirement plan sponsors to make the default option an investment with more potential for long-term accumulation. Since risk-based and target-date funds are designed to be risk-adjusted, long-term investing products, the expectation is that many plan sponsors will consider switching to these funds as their default option. According to surveys, this trend is under way, and target-date funds have become the leading default investment choice among participant-directed plans.

• IMPACT OF ASSET ALLOCATION •

Several authoritative studies have helped identify the impact that asset allocation has on the long-term performance of portfolios. Gary Brinson, Randolph Hood, and Gilbert Beebower conducted what were perhaps the best-known studies on this subject. The trio, often referred to as BHB, conducted their first study, titled "Determinants of Portfolio Performance," in 1986, and an updated one, which resulted in similar findings, in 1991. They examined several large pension plans to see how much of an impact asset allocation had on the variations in total returns each quarter. In these studies they evaluated several factors, including each pension plan's objectives and their constraints and requirements.

The first study found that asset allocation decisions accounted for 93.6 percent of the variations in portfolio returns over time. The results of the second study were similar and confirming: Asset allocation drove 91.5 percent of the variations in returns. These studies have been used widely to convey the impact of asset allocation. However, they also have spurred a lot of debate over exactly how much asset allocation affects performance. That's because while there was no question that asset allocation has a significant impact on variations of returns, it does not address the actual impact on performance. That is why, in 2000, another study was conducted that looked to clarify this issue. This study, conducted by Roger G. Ibbotson, a Yale professor and chairman of Ibbotson Associates, and Paul D. Kaplan, vice president and chief economist of Ibbotson Associates, asked the question: "Does asset allocation policy explain 40, 90, or 100 percent of performance?" It looked at monthly returns for balanced mutual funds over a ten-year period and the quarterly returns of pension funds over a five-year period. It addressed three separate points: the impact of asset allocation on the variability of returns over time; how much asset allocation policy explained the difference between the performances of funds; and finally, what portion of the return amount can be attributed to policy return. The analysis showed that asset allocation explained about 90 percent of the variability of a fund's returns over time. That conclusion was similar to the BHB study. But it also found that asset allocation explained only about 40 percent of the variation of returns *among* funds, and that on average across funds, asset allocation policy explained about 100 percent of the level of returns. Various other studies also have sought to determine the specific impact of asset allocation on returns, and there is still debate over its exact impact. However, most financial professionals agree that having an asset allocation strategy in place is an effective method for spreading risk and achieving more consistent returns.

• LOOKING IN THE REARVIEW MIRROR •

There is a drawback to strategically allocated portfolios. While they are able to successfully manage risk over the long term, they aren't forward-looking. Instead, they often look at past data produced by different asset classes, such as performance and volatility, to forecast how they will perform in the future.

Anyone who has ever been in the market for a mutual fund or other financial product should be familiar with this disclaimer: Past performance is not necessarily an indication of future returns. Even if a portfolio has had exceptional returns for a decade, that doesn't mean it will continue to do so. A perfect example took place in 2006. Bill Miller, the well-known portfolio manager of the Legg Mason Value Trust mutual fund, had been one of the elite few managers able to consistently beat the market. For fifteen years straight his fund topped the returns of the S&P 500 Index. In 2006, though, his streak ended. Not only did the fund underperform the S&P 500, but it underperformed by 9.9 percentage points. In 2007, Miller's performance relative to the index was even worse, trailing it by 12.2 percent, and in 2008, through July 31, the fund lagged the S&P by 16.6 percentage points. The lesson is, even though many people rely on historical data to predict the future, there is no guaranteeing that the results will be the same, or even close.

Mean variance optimizers work by forecasting returns, correlations, and standard deviations of different asset classes in creating portfolios. Many have expressed concern over this, including William J. Bernstein, a financial theorist and author of the book *The Intelligent Asset Allocator*. In an article for EfficientFrontier.com in April 1997, Bernstein explained that mean variance optimization, or MVO, is flawed because of its reliance on past data to make future estimations.

Bernstein wrote, "Since the required input returns, [standard deviations], and correlations are known with precision only in retrospect, mean variance optimization is worthless as a predictor of *future* optimal portfolios. This is because it is impossible to predict with anywhere near the required accuracy the returns, SDs, and correlations."

In the September 1999 issue of *The Journal of Financial Planning*, John Rekenthaler, research director for Morningstar, also took issue with using this method to create portfolios. He wrote, "The odds of correctly predicting the future returns, deviations, and correlations for several asset classes are well below those of winning $20 million from Ed McMahon. Which means that by definition, the efficient frontier isn't."

Another issue with strategically allocated portfolios is that they are relatively static. As mentioned earlier, with risk-based portfolios the targeted level of risk never changes, so the asset allocation never changes. Even as an investor's risk tolerance shifts over time, these portfolios are locked into the same level of risk. Target-date portfolios eliminate this issue somewhat by automatically becoming more conservative over time. However, these funds are still relatively static. They only make strategic changes once a year (at most) and the changes that they make to the portfolio are predetermined by the glide path.

• CHAPTER SUMMARY •

▶ Knowing an investor's risk tolerance is essential to developing an asset allocation strategy. Based on that level of risk, the portfolio should be diversified accordingly.

▶ The level of risk assumed in a portfolio depends on numerous factors, including personal preferences, age, current financial status, and long-term financial goals. A questionnaire is a helpful way for investors and financial professionals to uncover the answers to these questions and to determine how much risk is appropriate.

► One of the first steps in creating an asset allocation is deciding how broadly the portfolio should be allocated between equity and fixed income. The next step is to determine how to further divide those allocations among different types of investments.

► Understanding the correlations between investment of asset class pairs is key to establishing a well-diversified portfolio. The correlations measure how assets perform in relation to one another. The lower the correlation between asset pairs in a portfolio, the more diversification benefit they offer.

► Modern portfolio theory is responsible for much of the thinking behind strategic asset allocation. One idea behind modern portfolio theory is that portfolios should produce optimum returns for a given level of expected risk. By increasing risk, investors can pursue higher expected returns.

► Rebalancing is used to bring an asset allocation back in line if it moves away from its targets due to market action. This can be done either according to a set schedule or when an allocation to a specific asset class moves too far from its target.

► In recent years strategic asset allocation funds have boomed in popularity as many investors have looked to these funds as convenient "one decision" asset allocation programs. These funds begin with a set allocation that is based on a certain tolerance for risk. Target-based funds maintain that same risk level while target-date funds shift to become more conservative over time, as investors age and get closer to retirement.

► Target-date funds have a predetermined path that dictates when the portfolio will adjust allocations. Even after a target-date portfolio reaches its target date, it makes sense to maintain some exposure to equities. This adds diversification without causing a big increase in the portfolio's level of risk.

► While mutual funds still account for the majority of target-date and target-risk funds, there are now several ETF options available and others are on the way. Some of these ETFs invest in a variety of individual securities to accomplish this, while others invest in a range of other ETFs.

► Strategic asset allocation funds have seen strong growth and are expected to continue gathering substantial assets in the future, as more investors become aware of their many benefits, particularly as an option inside retirement plans.

► It's a widely held belief that asset allocation has a major impact on performance. Most financial professionals agree it has a greater impact than selecting individual securities or timing the market. Exactly how much of an impact asset allocation has on performance has been debated heavily.

► Strategic asset allocation is an effective way to balance long-term risk and returns. However, in many cases strategically allocated portfolios rely only on past data to forecast the future. They are also relatively passive portfolios, so they do not respond to changes in the market or economy in order to improve their returns, or to add alpha.

9

Adding Alpha

While creating a sound asset allocation is the key to delivering the risk-adjusted returns that are needed over the long term, when this is done passively—i.e., the portfolio is not adjusted based on major trends and changes in the overall market—there is limited potential to generate alpha—the returns that are generated above a certain benchmark after adjusting for risk. With people living longer and needing to save more money for retirement, adding alpha is more important than ever. This chapter will take asset allocation a step further by looking at how ETFs can be used to add alpha to portfolios and exploring the importance of adding even small amounts of alpha to a portfolio—and how that can compound over time.

There are two ways investors can consider adding alpha to their portfolios using ETFs. One is to construct a portfolio of ETFs that seek to produce returns that are better than the overall market; some of these "enhanced" or "intelligent" ETFs, including the methodology behind these products and how they work, will be discussed. Second, this chapter will examine incorporating a tactical strategy to improve portfolio returns, taking into account new developments in the market and ways to shift assets to take advantage of emerging trends, opportunities, and anomalies as they arise.

• IT'S ALL ABOUT ALPHA •

Almost everyone wishes they could generate higher returns in their portfolios, and now, more than ever, adding alpha before and during retirement is important. Recent statistics from the U.S. Census Bureau illustrate why. In 1967 the average life expectancy was 70.5 years. By 2015 life expectancy is expected to be 79 years. To most people, living longer would seem to be a good thing. However, for anyone who hasn't saved enough to live comfortably in retirement, those years can be less rewarding. Unfortunately, a large portion of the population isn't saving enough for the future, and many don't even know it. According to the Employee Benefit Research Institute's 2009 Retirement Confidence Survey, 54 percent of Americans say they are either somewhat confident or very confident that they will have enough money to live comfortably in retirement. That would be fine, except for the fact that they have not saved nearly enough—or anything at all, for that matter. In fact, the study also showed that 31 percent of workers who have not even saved for retirement still feel very or somewhat confident that they will be able to retire comfortably. Of those who have saved, 40 percent of all workers report having saved less than $10,000, and what's even scarier, 30 percent of the people over age 55 who were surveyed have saved less than $10,000 (excluding their homes and defined-benefit pension plans).

Part of the problem is that Americans may not know how much they should be saving for retirement. According to the study, only 44 percent of people have calculated roughly how much they likely will need in retirement and how much money they should save to meet their goals. To make matters worse, those who do attempt to gauge their postretirement financial needs may be underestimating how much money they will need to live comfortably—in fact, 47 percent of the people surveyed believe they will need less than $500,000 in retirement savings. To put this in some perspective, according to the Center for Research Retirement, an individual planning to retire in 2010 will have to pay more than $100,000 in out-of-pocket health-care expenses, and that increases to $188,000 for those planning to retire in 2030.

The following table illustrates the expectations of retirement savings among workers.

TABLE 9.1: WORKERS' ASSUMPTIONS ABOUT SAVINGS NEEDED FOR RETIREMENT

TOTAL RETIREMENT SAVINGS	WORKERS (%)
Under $250,000	28
$250,000–$499,999	19
$500,000–$999,999	23
$1 million–$1.9 million	11
$2 million or more	6
Don't know/don't remember	13

SOURCE: EMPLOYEE BENEFIT RESEARCH INSTITUTE AND MATHEW GREENWALD & ASSOCIATES, "2006 RETIREMENT CONFIDENCE SURVEY."

Generating alpha before and during retirement is important. And the good news is that doing it is not as hard as it seems. That's because returns are compounded over time, so depending on how long the investor has until retirement, boosting returns by even a little bit can amount to a lot by the time he or she reaches that point. In fact, to illustrate, suppose that a person begins saving at age thirty. She makes an initial investment of $10,000. For simplicity's sake, assume she has a constant annual return of 5 percent. After twenty years, her savings will have grown to more than $26,000, after thirty years to more than $43,000, and by the time she is seventy years old her savings will have accumulated to more than $70,000. Using the same example in another scenario, assume this same person had annual returns of 6 percent—just one percentage point higher. By the time she reaches age seventy, the savings will have grown to more than $102,000—that's more than a $30,000 difference. The tables below illustrate the dramatic difference in returns of someone with a $10,000 investment and annual earnings of 5 percent, 6 percent, and 8 percent over a period of forty years.

TABLE 9.2: TOTAL RETURNS FOR INVESTOR EARNING 5 PERCENT ANNUAL RETURNS

	ANNUAL RETURNS	TOTAL RETURN
Year 1	5%	$ 10,500.00
Year 5	5%	$ 12,762.82

	ANNUAL RETURNS	TOTAL RETURN
Year 10	5%	$ 16,288.95
Year 20	5%	$ 26,532.98
Year 30	5%	$ 43,219.42
Year 40	5%	**$ 70,399.89**

**TABLE 9.3: TOTAL RETURNS FOR INVESTOR EARNING
6 PERCENT ANNUAL RETURNS**

	ANNUAL RETURNS	TOTAL RETURN
Year 1	6%	$ 10,600.00
Year 5	6%	$ 13,382.26
Year 10	6%	$ 17,908.48
Year 20	6%	$ 32,071.35
Year 30	6%	$ 57,434.91
Year 40	6%	**$ 102,857.18**

**TABLE 9.4: TOTAL RETURNS FOR INVESTOR EARNING
8 PERCENT ANNUAL RETURNS**

	ANNUAL RETURNS	TOTAL RETURN
Year 1	8%	$ 10,800.00
Year 5	8%	$ 14,693.28
Year 10	8%	$ 21,589.25
Year 20	8%	$ 46,609.57
Year 30	8%	$ 100,626.57
Year 40	8%	**$ 217,245.21**

It is evident that even a small increase in returns could have a major impact on this investor's savings. Of course, this can be done by socking away more money on a regular basis. However, when that is not an option, the solution is to increase returns either by including products inside the portfolio that generate superior returns or by overlaying the portfolio with a strategy that will allow the investor to improve performance by taking advantage of market developments. In the example above, if the investor was able to add 1 percent to their preretirement savings it would increase their savings to more than $1 million. And what's more, those extra savings would help the nest egg last until beyond age ninety-five.

• ENHANCED ETFS •

So, how can an investor use ETFs to add alpha to a portfolio? One way is to simply buy products that offer better risk-adjusted returns than traditional indexes, and this is the premise behind enhanced, or intelligent, ETFs. These products are based on next-generation indexes that are composed of securities chosen for their investment performance or risk-control merits. These ETFs were mentioned earlier in the book. Now let's take a closer look at how they differ from traditional indexes and ETFs.

One objective of a traditional ETF is to provide exposure to a certain segment of the market by tracking closely to a passive index. These can be indexes that provide exposure to the broad U.S. stock market, a group of stocks of a certain size, stocks of a particular sector or industry, or stocks from a certain country or region. They provide a way to tap broadly into a particular area of the market. But what if the investor is looking for more than that? Instead of just having a broad sampling, what if he/she would rather own the best stocks within that area? That is where intelligent indexes come in. The Intellidexes were one of the first indexes to make a name for themselves doing this. These indexes choose securities based on factors that go beyond size or market value. They use a quantitative process to evaluate the securities within a given universe and then select those that have the best chance of appreciating or outperforming on a risk-adjusted basis. If the quantitative model is successful, it can have the potential to outperform a corresponding, passive index. These indexes were the basis for the first two intelligent ETFs, both of which were launched by PowerShares in 2003, the Dynamic Market Intellidex ETF (Ticker symbol: PWC) and the Dynamic OTC Intellidex Index (Ticker symbol: PWO). Following a high level of investor acceptance of these initial intelligent ETFs, a larger series based on these indexes was launched.

Similar to other broad market ETFs, the Dynamic Market Intellidex ETF chooses from a pool of two thousand of the largest U.S. stocks (based on market capitalization) that trade or are quoted on the American Stock Exchange, the New York Stock Exchange, or the NASDAQ. However, unlike most traditional indexes, this index does not simply choose the largest stocks from that pool. Instead, the universe of stocks first is divided into ten sectors, and then within those sectors stocks are divided according to their size. The stocks are ranked according to a quantitative screen that evaluates more than two dozen criteria, such as fundamental growth, timeliness, valuation, and risk. Within each sector a predetermined number of stocks then are selected from each size category. Those stocks make up the one hundred stocks that are represented in the index. The screening process not only selects the stocks with the greatest potential but also weeds out stocks that are overvalued and present higher risk.

The second intelligent ETF from PowerShares that was based on a quantitatively driven Intellidex was the Dynamic OTC Intellidex Index ETF. To create the index, one thousand of the largest U.S. stocks that are quoted on the NASDAQ are evaluated. That universe of stocks is divided into nine economic sectors, then divided according to size, and ranked. The top one hundred stocks are included in the intelligent index, with a certain number chosen from each category. In the Intellidexes, once the securities are selected, their weight in the index is determined using a modified equal weighting methodology rather than according to their market capitalization, as is commonly done. With modified equal dollar weighting, each security represents a predetermined weight that is based on the relative market cap of the underlying securities. In this case, this is done to distribute exposure more uniformly among more companies, avoiding overweighting stocks that are overvalued already and underweighting stocks that are undervalued. These indexes also rebalance quarterly.

The introduction of intelligent indexes added an active element to ETFs that had never before existed. While ETFs based on these indexes are still passive investments, because they are pinned to an index and lack a human's active management, by incorporating a quantitative screen intelligent indexes provide investors with the opportunity to capture alpha—excess risk-adjusted return above the market average. In addition, because a strict, rules-based quantitative analysis is used to choose stocks for the index, it keeps the human emotion that can be present in actively managed funds out of the process.

• FUNDAMENTAL ETFS •

Another category of ETFs that seeks to produce returns above traditional passive indexes are those that are based on indexes that choose and weigh stocks according to fundamental factors. ETFs based on these indexes are similar to those based on the Intellidexes, as the idea is typically to find stocks of the largest or strongest companies as well as to add a bit of active management to the process. However, with fundamentally weighted indexes the focus is on how much of a weight the stocks have within the index. Securities with the best fundamental profile receive the greatest weight in the index. These indexes aim to provide a better risk/reward profile than traditional market cap weighted indexes. They also are considered by some to be less volatile.

A fundamental index selects and weighs components based on a combination of fundamental factors such as dividends, earnings, and sales. Some ETFs similarly use one with a combination of factors, while others rely on a single criterion, such as dividends or earnings. The first fundamental ETF was the PowerShares FTSE RAFI 1000 ETF (Ticker symbol: PRF), which selects one thousand stocks with a rules-based model that includes sales, cash flow, book value, and dividends. The performance of the FTSE RAFI 1000 has provided an early test of how well fundamental indexes can perform versus traditional market cap weighted benchmarks. In the table below, actual performance since 2005 is supplemented with hypothetical back-test data showing how the index hypothetically would have performed over the past ten years.

TABLE 9.5: PERFORMANCE COMPARISON (FOR PERIODS ENDING FEBRUARY 28, 2008)

INDEX	1 YEAR (%)	3 YEARS ANNUALIZED (%)	5 YEARS ANNUALIZED (%)	10 YEARS ANNUALIZED (%)
FTSE RAFI	−8.66	6.20	13.96	7.10
S&P 500	−5.08	5.84	11.32	3.50
Russell 1000	−5.40	6.19	11.86	3.83

SOURCE: POWERSHARES

Based on this data it appears that fundamental indexes occupy a middle ground between market cap weight and equal weight indexes. They tend to track somewhat closer to market cap weight index performance over time while avoiding those indexes' large cap bias and vulnerability to momentum-driven markets.

One benefit of fundamental indexing is that it can help in tempering portfolio risk, especially during momentum-driven markets. By selecting and weighting components based on company data and periodically rebalancing the index to reflect new data, fundamental indexes should have a lower price-to-earnings ratio and less volatility than market cap weighted indexes. Performance data also suggest that fundamental indexes may tend to overweight value stocks and underweight growth stocks relative to comparable market cap weighted indexes.

However, there are critics of fundamental weighting, specifically those who adhere to the efficient market theory. Generally speaking, efficient market theories say that markets are, in general, fairly valued. Proponents of these theories believe that all pertinent information about securities in the market is known to investors and has been acted on in a rational and expected way. Therefore, according to efficient market theorists, the value of the overall market is a good reflection of the value of the underlying securities. As a result, it is difficult, if not impossible, to create a portfolio that will over the long term perform better than a passive index that provides broad exposure to the market. In addition, some critics have taken issue with the level of turnover within some fundamentally weighted indexes. The belief here is that the turnover of securities inside the portfolio will be higher than in traditional cap weighted indexes. The actual level of turnover will, however, depend on the particular index and how often it rebalances.

• TACTICAL STRATEGIES •

Whereas using ETFs that generate alpha is one way to seek higher returns in a portfolio, another increasingly common strategy trend is to use ETFs within a portfolio that is being tactically managed to constantly adjust the asset allocation in order to maximize returns. Tactical models are longer-term investment tools that are used to exploit emerging trends in the market. Most tactical strategies begin by using a computer-generated quantitative model—often referred to as a "black box." These models generally look at several different factors that could influence the direction of different asset classes, including overall economic indicators such as inflation and more fundamental or technical characteristics of certain asset classes. Tactical models evaluate all of these factors and use them to determine when to adjust the allocation of a portfolio and by how much. Tactical models work by generating either positive or negative signals for each represented asset class. Generally, a positive signal means that the weight of the asset class should be increased and a negative signal means that the weight of the asset class should be decreased. The changes that are made to the strategic allocation are referred to as tactical, or dynamic, shifts. Depending on how the model is set up, these shifts can be made broadly by overweighting or underweighting the core asset classes, equities, and fixed income. Or they can be done on a more granular level. In the case of equities, this could mean increasing or decreasing the allocation to certain equity categories, such as large caps, small caps, or international stocks. In fixed income investing, tactical shifts might be made between groups of securities based on their different maturities or credit quality, or other factors. For instance, a shift might be made between short-term and long-term government bonds.

Applying a tactical model to a portfolio of ETFs can be a particularly effective strategy. This is due in large part to the trading flexibility found with ETFs. For example, when a tactical model generates a negative signal, indicating that a shift out of a certain asset class should be made, ETFs provide a way to do this quickly, easily, and relatively cost-effectively. ETFs are also transparent, which makes it easy to see what is inside and avoid the unintentional overlap of securities. Because so many ETF options are available, investors can add exposure easily to any area of the market. Most tactical models evaluate a combination of factors in order to generate a signal. Below is a list of some of the constituents that are commonly used in tactical models.

Macroeconomic Factors

Macroeconomic factors are those that have a far-reaching impact on the overall economy. It is a category that is often included in tactical models because these factors can have major impacts on the directions of different asset classes, especially equities. As a result, looking at different macroeconomic factors is helpful in developing a positive or negative signal for equities versus fixed income.

A variety of macroeconomic factors can be considered. One of the most commonly used is monetary policy, in particular, determining the direction of interest rates, as this can be a good indicator of where value might be found within the market. When interest rates are on the rise, bond performance generally suffers and stocks tend to do well. When interest rates are declining, generally the opposite holds true, although certain areas of the stock market respond differently to interest rate changes. The greatest impact that interest rates generally have on the market is often when unexpected increases or decreases occur. That is why being able to accurately forecast the direction of interest rates can be highly advantageous.

A 2005 article written by Federal Reserve chairman Ben Bernanke and Kenneth Kuttner, an Oberlin College professor and former assistant vice president in the research departments of the Federal Reserve banks of New York and Chicago, highlights the impact that unexpected changes in monetary policy have on the stock market. Briefly, the study found "a relatively strong and consistent response of the stock market to unexpected monetary policy actions, using Federal funds futures data to gauge policy expectations." An unexpected hike of 25 basis points (0.25 percent) could cause stock prices to rise about 1 percent, according to the findings. The study also determined that the reactions to unexpected changes differed across industries, "with the high-tech and telecommunication sectors exhibiting a response half again as large as that of the broad market indices. Other sectors, such as energy and utilities, seem not to be significantly affected by monetary policy."

Yields and Valuation

Some tactical models compare earnings yields or dividend yields with bond yields to help determine the attractiveness of equities versus fixed income. The earnings yield is the ratio of earnings per share produced by an equity (or group of equities) divided by the current trading price per share. Earnings yield, which is expressed as a percentage, is the inverse of the price-to-earnings ratio. Dividend yield is another metric that can be used in a tactical model. It is measured using the annual dividend paid per share of a security divided by the current (or recent) price per share.

Looking at the spreads between either earnings or dividend yields and bond yields can be an effective way to gauge broadly the attractiveness of equities versus fixed income. For instance, the earnings yield of the S&P 500 might be compared with the yield for the ten-year Treasury bond. An investor also can look at the difference in yields between high-rated and low-rated corporate bonds, which is called the credit spread, as well as the overall direction of the yield curve, as that can be helpful in providing an outlook on future changes in interest rates and economic growth. If the yield curve is high or heading up, that generally means that fixed income instruments could give equities a run for their money.

Momentum

The momentum of the market is a technical indicator that could be used to help determine the outlook for different asset classes. Momentum is measured by looking at shorter-term factors such as the performance of securities and volume. This can provide a sense of the strength or weakness of a security, a group of securities, or the overall market. Momentum can be evaluated in several ways; for example, whether it is occurring on a long-term or short-term basis and how constant or short-lived it is. In general, though, momentum is a shorter-term indicator, so it should be approached with caution. Other than by highly sophisticated traders, momentum should not be used to make frequent, short-term trades.

Market Sentiment

Market sentiment—how investors currently feel about the overall market—can be a useful factor to consider inside a tactical model, as it can have an impact on investor behavior and therefore on the performance of stocks and bonds. If investors think stocks are heading higher, then investment sentiment on the stock market is positive. On the flip side, if investors perceive stocks are heading lower, then sentiment is negative. One way to get a sense of investor sentiment is by looking at a market volatility indicator. The Chicago Board Options Exchange Volatility Index, or VIX, is an index that measures market volatility based on stock options activity. Higher values imply that investor uncertainty is high and lower values imply uncertainty is lower. This is usually an inverse indicator for investors, because when uncertainty is low, equities are considered to be a better value.

Risk

Risk metrics can be used inside a tactical model to control the volatility of the portfolio. Tactical models can use several measures to assess risk factors, such as standard deviations or value at risk (VaR); the latter uses statistical analysis to forecast worst-case-loss scenarios for a portfolio over a certain period of time. The commonly used Monte Carlo simulation, which estimates future performance returns by looking at outcomes for numerous hypothetical scenarios, is one method for calculating VaR. Measuring the rate of change of risk also can help determine the overall direction of equities. That's because there is often a relationship between recent changes in risk and the future performance of equities.

• NO TWO TACTICAL MODELS ARE THE SAME •

Most tactical asset allocation models begin by using a quantitative, statistical, and numbers-based model to generate signals that determine whether to shift the strategic portfolio. But the way that tactical models operate can vary dramatically. For instance, there are many different metrics and combinations of these metrics that tactical models can take into account to create a signal. Then, there are various ways to implement those signals. For example, if a tactical model looks at several criteria and generates a positive signal indicating, for instance, that the allocation to large cap stocks should be increased, how much should the allocation be altered? Or, if the model generates a negative signal for large cap stocks, should the allocation from that area be moved into another investment in the portfolio, spread out among all other investments, or be put into a neutral investment such as cash or short-term bonds?

Also, some tactical models use a framework that is completely quantitative. In this case, regardless of how the tactical model is set up, a quantitative, rules-based approach should be obeyed absolutely in order to provide solid and consistent investing discipline. But not all tactical models adhere strictly to a completely quantitative process. Instead, they rely on "investment committees" to interpret signals and decide whether or not to act on the signal and to what extent. Allowing tactical shifts to be made this way is common. But it can also be problematic. Not sticking to a strict policy when making shifts can jeopardize the investment discipline of the portfolio, creating confusion as well as inconsistencies. Also, allowing decisions to be made by people can lead to emotional and psychologically driven trades, such as buying high and selling low. Committee oversight even can lead to incorrect trades if the signals are misinterpreted. Any of these problems can make the portfolio more volatile, produce inconsistent returns, and increase the chances that the portfolio will underperform its stated benchmark.

People often are influenced by outside factors that can have a big impact on their investment behavior. The emerging field of behavioral finance addresses some of the mental and emotional issues that can affect people's investment decisions. Behavioral finance seeks to understand the reasoning behind investor behavior and how those behaviors affect the market. Behavioral finance addresses the decisions that investors make that are not rational but are instead based on psychological and emotional reactions. The following are some of the more common emotional and psychologically driven investing behaviors.

Fear of Loss. This is one of the most common emotion-driven investing responses. It is based on the idea that the fear of losing money outweighs the prospect of making money. This is also referred to as loss-aversion.

Following the Pack. This entails mimicking the behavior of others, such as when investors pour a lot of money into a hot sector. This was the case with technology in the late 1990s, when investors threw money at technology stocks, causing the sector to inflate greatly and create the tech bubble. This type of behavior is often referred to as herding or chasing the hot dot.

Acting on Misinformation. Investors act on misinformation when they make investment decisions based on information that is either irrelevant or doesn't tell the full story. This might mean, for instance, that an investor will decide to sell an investment after hearing a negative news report without gathering more information that could help him make a fully informed decision.

Mental Accounting. This happens when investors mentally divide up their assets into separate and distinct pieces as opposed to viewing them as a whole. For instance, this could mean viewing a retirement account, a college savings account, and a taxable account as separate entities, leading the investor to make decisions that affect each piece instead of the overall financial picture.

Fear of Change. When investors remain tied to an investment even if it is no longer a good investment simply because they are afraid that the investment will appreciate after they sell it, their investment behavior is being dictated by their fear of change.

Overconfidence. Investors experience overconfidence when they are overly optimistic about their ability to spot an opportunity. Often these investors believe their stock-picking skills to be superior to those of others.

• MAKING A SHIFT •

For investors who are interested in tactically managed ETF portfolios, several options are currently available, with more expected to be rolled out in the future. But before choosing any one model, investors should make sure they are aware of exactly how it functions. It's important to know which asset classes and ETFs the model is investing in, how it generates signals, the philosophy for making shifts for the portfolio, and of course the all-in costs of the model.

Let's provide an example of how a tactical model can work. Before the model makes any changes to the strategically allocated portfolio, it is in its neutral position. From that position, shifts can be made. To illustrate, we'll use a tactical model based on the moderate portfolio, which, in its neutral position, is 40 percent invested in equities and 60 percent invested in fixed income. Figure 9.1 shows the general and specific allocations of investments.

For this example, suppose that the tactical model is allowed to shift the allocation to any asset classes by 20 percent above or 20 percent below its neutral position. This means that if the model produces a positive signal for international equities, which account for 15 percent of the portfolio, the model may increase the allocation up to 18 percent (the original 15 percent allocation plus 20 percent of that). On the other hand, if the signal is negative, indicating that there should be a decrease in the allocation, it may be reduced to 12 percent (the original 15 percent minus 20 percent of that).

Let's suppose that the model produces positive signals for each of the equity investments. Figure 9.2 shows how a shift would translate broadly to the portfolio. The portfolio is in its neutral position (top), before the shifts have been made. The chart below it shows the portfolio after the signals generated by the tactical model were applied. In this instance, let's say the model generated a positive signal for equities, causing the portfolio to increase its equity allocation by 20 percent, or from 40 percent to 48 percent. Meanwhile, the allocation to fixed income experienced a proportional decline, bringing that allocation to 52 percent. It is evident how this

Figure 9.1: Asset Allocation of a Moderate Portfolio Before a Tactical Shift

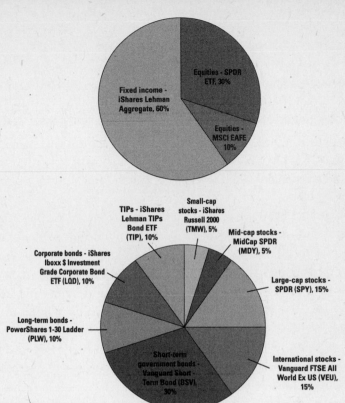

shift could apply to the individual investments inside the portfolio. Notice that the general breakdown of the investments looks fairly similar in both portfolios. However, they have shifted slightly in order to increase the allocation to the equity classes and decrease the allocation to fixed income by a corresponding amount.

In addition to shifting weights of the portfolios based on positive or negative signals, tactical portfolios, like the strategic portfolios, also should be monitored and rebalanced to ensure they are in line with the target tactical allocation. A rebalance can take place according to a set schedule, such as monthly or quarterly. Or it can be triggered if any asset class moves more than a certain percentage from its target.

**Figure 9.2: Asset Allocation of a Moderate Portfolio
After a Tactical Shift**

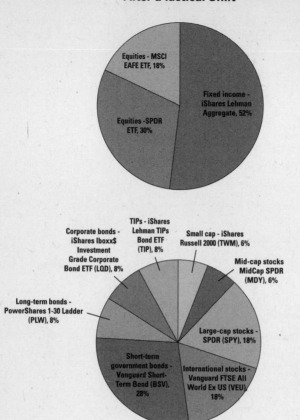

• **ROTATING AROUND SECTORS** •

In addition to using a strategy to make timely adjustments to a broadly
allocated portfolio, in order to pursue higher risk-adjusted returns an investor can execute a similar strategy that focuses on more specific segments
of the market, such as sectors and countries. A sector-based portfolio can
be constructed by adjusting exposure to varied sectors of the market based
on their outlooks, in order to take advantage of the particular sectors that
are in favor at any given time, while a portfolio that adjusts its exposures
among countries that are expected to have the best performing markets
could have a similar impact. Sector portfolios usually aren't designed as

core holdings. However, when an investor's goal is to add an extra layer of diversification, sector and country rotation strategies can be valuable.

Because of changes that occur regularly in the economy, the market is always going through cycles, during which time certain areas are in favor while others are not. This means that at any particular point in the cycle there are generally some sectors that are outperforming or, at least, performing better than their peers. One often touted sector rotation strategy is the Stovall Rotation strategy created by Standard and Poor's chief investment strategist Sam Stovall. This strategy is centered on the premise that at any given time the market is undergoing one of four stages—early recession, full recession, early recovery, and late recovery. At any given stage certain sectors are going to be in favor. For instance, during an early recession companies in the services sector, utilities, and cyclical and transportation stocks generally are expected to perform better. Once the country is engaged in a full recession, as indicated by falling gross domestic product, falling interest rates, and falling consumer sentiment, the sectors that tend to perform well include cyclical and transportation stocks as well as industrials and technology. Once an early recovery ensues, industrials, energy, and basic materials are expected to be in favor, while the later stages of the recovery bring with them strong performance for energy, staples, and service companies.

However, there are varied ways that sector rotation portfolios can function. Some are more seasonal in nature, for instance, tending toward retail and consumer discretionary stocks near the holidays or travel and transportation stocks during the summer months. Another method that has often proven successful is a quantitative-based model in which each sector is evaluated continuously to determine when the portfolio shifts its allocation into and away from each sector when market dynamics change.

ETFs are particularly adaptive tools for sector rotations. Because they themselves trade like stocks, it is quick and easy to purchase or sell shares of a sector ETF when it's necessary to rotate into or out of a stock. They also provide extensive diversification to sectors of the market, as many sector ETFs represent upward of fifty stocks in their given sector. It is also very cost-effective to get this heightened level of diversification, as the expense ratios are often as low as 0.20 percent, and with the advent of online and discount brokers, commission costs to trade are often very low. With the constant expansion of the ETF market, investors also have numerous options. In any given sector there are often more than a dozen options to choose from, allowing investors to pick an ETF that best suits their individual needs.

Sector rotation portfolios can divide the market in varied ways. For instance, well-known broad market indexes such as the S&P 500 Index and the Dow Jones U.S. Total Market Index can be divided into ten sectors. For illustration purposes, let's look at the ten sectors that make up the Dow Jones U.S. indexes. Each of these sectors is tracked by an ETF, which makes it easy to invest in specific sectors without overlapping other securities. The following is a list of those ten ETFs, and a brief description of what they track:

1. **iShares Dow Jones U.S. Basic Material Sector ETF:** Tracks companies in the U.S. basic materials sector, including those in the chemicals, forestry, paper, industrial metals, and mining industries.

2. **iShares Dow Jones U.S. Energy ETF:** Tracks companies in the U.S. energy sector, including oil and gas producers and oil equipment, services, and distribution companies.

3. **iShares Dow Jones U.S. Industrials Index:** Tracks companies in the U.S. industrials sector, including construction and materials, aerospace and defense, electronic and electrical equipment, and industrial engineering companies.

4. **iShares Dow Jones U.S. Consumer Goods Index:** Tracks companies in the U.S. consumer goods sector, including companies involved with automobiles and parts, beverage and food producers, household goods, and leisure goods.

5. **iShares Dow Jones U.S. Health Care Index:** Tracks companies in the U.S. health care sector, including companies involved in health care equipment and services, pharmaceuticals, and biotechnology.

6. **iShares Dow Jones U.S. Consumer Services Index:** Tracks companies in the U.S. consumer services sector, including companies involved in food and drug retailing, general retailers, media, and travel and leisure.

7. **iShares Dow Jones U.S. Telecommunications Index:** Tracks companies in the U.S. telecommunications sector, including companies involved with fixed-line telecommunications and mobile telecommunications.

8. **iShares Dow Jones U.S. Utilities Index:** Tracks companies in the U.S. utilities sector, including companies involved with electricity and gas, water, and multiutilities.

9. **iShares Dow Jones U.S. Financials Index:** Tracks companies in the U.S. financials sector, including companies involved in banking and insurance other than life insurance, life insurance, real estate, and general finance.

10. **iShares Dow Jones U.S. Technology Index:** Tracks companies in the U.S. technology sector, including companies involved with software and computer services, and technology hardware and equipment.

A sector rotation portfolio can be designed to follow varied models or strategies. For instance, a model can assign specific allocations to each sector that vary by differing degrees depending on the changing market dynamics and fundamentals of the sector; alternatively, a model could assign each of the sectors an equal weight in the portfolio, and if the model generates a negative signal for a sector, the portfolio can move entirely out of that sector and reallocate those assets evenly among the remaining sectors for which the model remains positive, or it can reallocate those assets to a sector-neutral investment such as cash or fixed income. The latter two options are illustrated by the two figures that follow.

Let's assume that the portfolio is divided equally among ten iShares sector ETFs. When all sectors are positive the portfolio is distributed evenly, with 10 percent invested in each sector. When a negative signal is generated for a particular sector, the 10 percent that was allocated to that sector is redistributed to other sectors of the portfolio. For this example, let's say that the portfolio turned negative on three sectors: financials, energy, and consumer services, due to deteriorating sector fundamentals and changing market conditions. It is evident in Figure 9.3 how the portfolio would

Figure 9.3: Allocation of Sector Rotation Before and After Shift

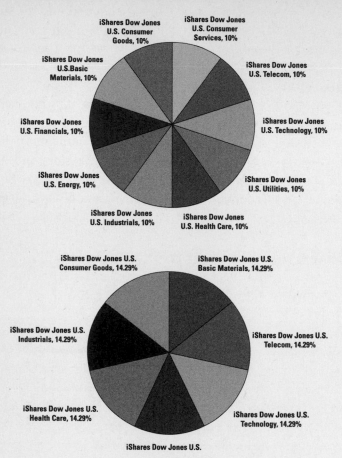

look, first when it is positive on each of the sectors and then how it is redistributed after a shift is made away from those three sectors.

As an alternative, another way to structure a sector rotation portfolio is to include an allocation to fixed income, such as short-term Treasuries, when the portfolio turns negative on certain sectors. To illustrate how shifts can be made in a sector rotation portfolio, the iShares Lehman Short Treasury Bond ETF, which tracks the performance of Treasuries with one to twelve months remaining until maturity, will be used. In this portfolio, let's suppose that when in a neutral position all ten sectors are weighted equally. So, if the model turns positive on all of the sectors, it will be 100 percent invested in equities. If the model turns negative on, say, three of the sectors, it will rotate out of those sectors and into the short-term Treasury ETF. As a result, the portfolio would be 70 percent in equities and 30 percent in fixed income. If it becomes positive again on a given sector, the model will rotate back into that sector and out of the Treasury ETF.

In the graph below, it is evident how the portfolio turned negative on the three sectors mentioned on page 200. As a result, the model rotated out of those sectors and into fixed income. The resulting portfolio was 70 percent invested in equities, through seven different sectors, and 30 percent invested in short-term Treasuries. The iShares Short Treasury Bond Fund (SHV), which has an average duration of 0.35 years, is one option that can be used to allocate the fixed income portion of the portfolio.

Figure 9.4: Sample Sector Rotation Portfolio After Shift

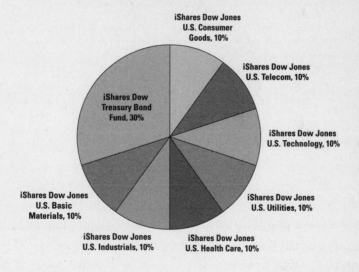

Another alternative to use inside a sector rotation portfolio is to vary the allocations to different sectors by different percentages based on positive and negative signals. For instance, when a portfolio begins to turn negative on a sector, instead of reducing the allocation to zero, an option is to lower it by, say, 25 percent, in order to maintain some exposure to that sector. For a final example, let's say the portfolio was negative on the same three sectors mentioned earlier. Below is how the portfolio would look after the shift was made.

Figure 9.5: Sample Sector Rotation Portfolio After Shift

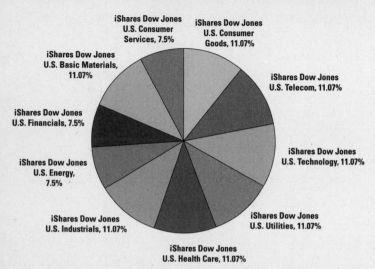

Performance

A sector rotation portfolio can provide an effective way to add alpha to a portfolio. The following table shows the performance of the ten sectors that make up the S&P 500 Index as well as the performance of the S&P 500 Composite Index. The shaded areas are the years in which the sector outperformed the S&P 500. For each year, between four and seven sectors outperformed the S&P 500. If a sector rotation model had been able to rotate into the best performing sectors, it could have improved performance greatly. For example, let's focus on 2005. That year, four sectors—energy, health care, utilities, and financials—outperformed the index. Another four sectors underperformed the S&P 500 but were still in positive territory. The remaining two sectors had negative returns. A sector rotation portfolio could have benefited by rotating out of those two sectors and into a sector-neutral investment, such as fixed income or T-bills, or by reallocating those assets into other sectors.

TABLE 9.6: PERFORMANCE OF TEN S&P 500 SECTORS VERSUS THE S&P 500 INDEX

	1997 (%)	1998 (%)	1999 (%)	2000 (%)	2001 (%)	2002 (%)	2003 (%)	2004 (%)	2005 (%)	2006 (%)
S&P 500 Energy	25.28	0.62	18.72	15.68	-10.39	-11.13	25.63	31.54	31.37	24.21
S&P 500 Materials	8.42	-6.18	25.25	-15.72	3.48	-5.45	38.19	13.20	4.42	18.63
S&P 500 Industrials	27.04	10.88	21.50	5.88	-5.74	-26.34	32.19	18.03	2.32	13.29
S&P 500 Consumer Discretionary	34.35	41.14	25.17	-20.00	2.78	-23.82	37.41	13.24	-6.36	18.64
S&P 500 Health Care	43.73	43.88	-10.66	37.05	-11.95	-18.82	15.06	1.68	6.46	7.53
S&P 500 Consumer Staples	32.89	15.76	-15.09	16.78	-6.40	-4.26	11.57	8.16	3.58	14.36
S&P 500 Telecommunications	41.24	52.38	19.14	-38.81	-12.25	-34.11	7.08	19.86	-5.63	36.80
S&P 500 Utilities	24.65	14.83	-9.18	57.18	-30.44	-29.99	26.26	24.28	16.84	20.99
S&P 500 Financials	48.15	11.43	4.11	25.70	-8.95	-14.64	31.03	10.89	6.47	19.19
S&P 500 Information Technology	28.54	78.14	78.74	-40.90	-25.87	-37.41	47.23	2.56	0.99	8.42
S&P 500 Composite Index	33.36	28.58	21.04	-9.10	-11.89	-22.10	28.68	10.88	4.91	15.80

SOURCE: STANDARD & POORS

• SECTOR ROTATION ETFS •

There are a few ETFs currently on the market that offer sector or industry rotation strategies, and more are likely to come in the future, as they provide a simple and cost-effective way to utilize this strategy. One such ETF is the Claymore/Zacks Sector Rotation Strategy (Ticker symbol: XRO). This ETF, which has an expense ratio of 0.60 percent, rotates its weightings among nine sectors that are represented in the Zacks Sector Rotation Index. This index chooses sectors of the market believed to have superior risk-return profiles and then chooses from within those sectors one hundred of the highest ranking stocks. The index is a modified equal dollar weighted index and is rebalanced quarterly. The chart below shows how the ETF was allocated as of October 2008.

Figure 9.6: Sector Allocation of Claymore/Zacks Sector Rotation Strategy (Ticker symbol: XRO)

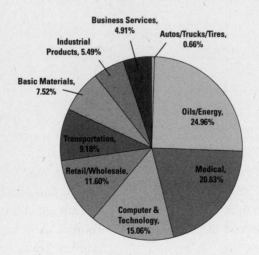

Another ETF option in this category is the PowerShares Value Line Industry Rotation Portfolio (Ticker symbol: PYH). This ETF, which has an expense cap of 0.60 percent, is based on the Value Line Industry Rotation Index, which is made up of roughly seventy-five stocks. This index ranks all of the industries in its universe according to their industry timeliness, and then within that it selects the highest ranking stocks from fifty of the highest rated industries. The index is equal dollar weighted and is rebalanced quarterly. The graph below shows the asset allocation of this portfolio as of December 2008.

Figure 9.7: Allocation of PowerShares Value Line Industry Rotation Portfolio (Ticker symbol: PYH)

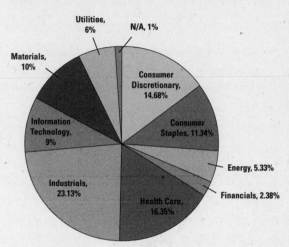

• COUNTRY ROTATION •

In addition to narrowing in on different sectors of the U.S. market, portfolios also can generate alpha by using ETFs to rotate between countries to respond to developments in the global financial markets. The first chapter talked about the performance of international markets and how they often move in different directions from the U.S. market. Including a country rotation portfolio can be a good way to take advantage of developments in international markets and pursue higher returns. A country rotation portfolio works by moving assets in and out of countries outside the United States based on the outlook for each country. At different times, foreign countries will have stronger investment potential for a variety of reasons, while others may have weaker potential.

Some country rotation portfolios utilize tactical models to analyze the countries' potential to determine which equity markets have the best chance of outperforming those of the United States at a given time. They then invest in those countries that are believed to have stronger equity market performance potential and steer clear of countries with weaker equity market outlooks. Country rotation models can include a variety of country groupings.

ETFs are also effective tools for implementing a country rotation model, because they provide exposure to an array of countries and regions and also diversify investments within each. Currently, about one hundred U.S.-listed ETFs provide exposure to markets outside the United States. Because ETFs trade like stocks, buying and selling shares generally is quick and convenient. This is a big benefit inside a country rotation portfolio, because when a signal is generated, ETFs allow the portfolio to move in or out of a country easily. In addition, international ETFs, particularly those that represent more liquid markets, are generally very cost-effective and have relatively low expense ratios—often significantly lower than comparable actively managed international mutual funds—and spreads are often narrow; again, this is especially true for more liquid markets.

As in the sector rotation portfolio, there are various ways to divide the international market in order to construct a country rotation portfolio. To illustrate, let's look at countries in the MSCI EAFE Index. This index tracks the following twenty-one countries: Australia, Austria, Belgium, Canada, Denmark, Finland, France, Germany, Hong Kong, Ireland, Italy, Japan, the Netherlands, New Zealand, Norway, Portugal, Singapore, Spain, Sweden, Switzerland, and the United Kingdom. Three variations of country rotation portfolios will be explored to illustrate how tactical shifts in the portfolio allocation can be made when a signal is generated. In the first, let's assume that when the portfolio is positive on all of the countries within the MSCI EAFE Index, it is equally distributed among these countries. In the first example, when a negative signal is generated for ten of these countries, the portfolio shifts that weight to the remaining eleven. Figure 9.8 shows the initial allocation of the portfolio when it is positive on all of the countries and then after a tactical shift is made that turns it negative on ten of them, eliminating their exposure in the portfolio.

For another option, when the portfolio generates a negative signal, instead of redistributing the weight the iShares Lehman Short Treasury Bond ETF could be substituted. In Figure 9.9, let's again assume the model turned negative on the same ten countries within the portfolio. That would result in a portfolio that is allocated roughly 47.64 percent to fixed income,

Figure 9.8: Country Rotation Portfolio Before and After Shift

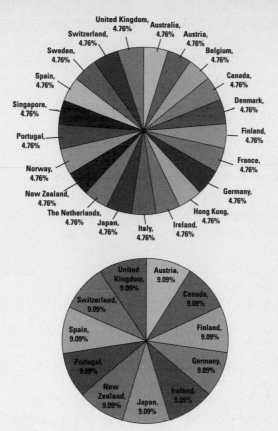

with the rest divided evenly among the remaining eleven countries. This allocation is visible in Figure 9.9.

As a final example, instead of eliminating the allocation to a specific country if a negative signal is generated, it could be adjusted by a certain percentage so as to maintain some exposure, particularly if there is an unexpected development that causes the outlook to change. For this example assume that when the portfolio is negative on a country, the allocation is reduced by 20 percent and redistributed equally to the other countries. The resulting reallocation is visible in Figure 9.10.

Figure 9.9: Country Rotation Portfolio After Shift

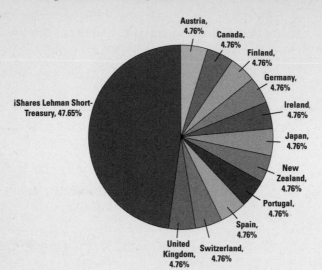

Figure 9.10: Country Rotation Portfolio After Shift

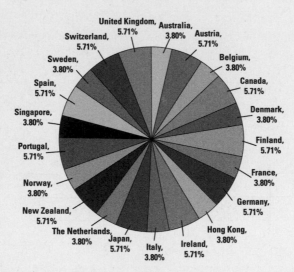

Performance

The following table shows how a country rotation portfolio can be used to pursue additional returns in a portfolio. Using the MSCI EAFE as a benchmark, it is clear how individual countries outperformed the MSCI

EAFE over various periods of time. Over the one-year period ended December 12, 2008, four countries outperformed the MSCI index; over a three-year period, ten countries outperformed; and over both a five-year and a ten-year period, five countries outperformed (as indicated by the shaded boxes). Also note that the outperforming countries varied considerably over these time periods. A successful portfolio rotation could have allowed the investor to capitalize on these shifts to minimize losses or generate alpha. Canada, which is not included in the MSCI EAFE, is also included.

TABLE 9.7: PERFORMANCE OF INDIVIDUAL COUNTRIES IN MSCI EAFE INDEX VERSUS THE INDEX

COUNTRY	1 YEAR (%)	3 YEAR (%)	5 YEAR (%)	10 YEAR (%)
Australia	−59.49	−12.04	0.14	3.27
Austria	−70.92	−26.27	−2.94	0.13
Belgium	−69.10	−26.27	−9.04	−8.53
Canada	−48.17	−9.18	3.67	6.74
Denmark	−50.82	−4.17	7.07	5.47
Finland	−59.47	−8.22	−2.03	0.67
France	−48.48	−8.36	0.39	0.25
Germany	−51.25	−4.43	2.40	−0.72
Hong Kong	−52.94	−6.40	0.44	1.19
Ireland	−72.86	−30.99	−14.25	−10.46
Italy	−55.78	−15.56	−5.15	−3.51
Japan	−37.70	−12.51	−0.63	−1.10
The Netherlands	−52.62	−10.31	−1.54	−3.51
New Zealand	−60.39	−22.04	−9.61	−2.00
Norway	−68.02	−17.24	1.46	4.79
Portugal	−58.03	−8.28	−1.72	−4.43
Singapore	−52.19	−4.34	2.97	3.23
Spain	−48.62	−1.95	5.05	1.93
Sweden	−54.65	−12.49	−0.02	0.95

COUNTRY	1 YEAR (%)	3 YEAR (%)	5 YEAR (%)	10 YEAR (%)
Switzerland	−39.45	−6.92	2.23	−0.06
United Kingdom	−52.49	−13.49	−3.7	−3.74
EAFE (plus Canada)	−49.33	−10.81	−0.52	−0.87

SOURCE: MSCI BARRA

• COUNTRY ROTATION ETF •

As of December 2008 there was only one country rotation ETF on the market, the Claymore/Zacks Country Rotation ETF (Ticker symbol: CRO), which has an expense ratio cap of 0.75 percent and tracks the performance of the Zacks Country Rotation Index. This index includes more than two hundred securities from various international companies that are based in countries whose economies have high income levels, strong legal protection, and sophisticated stock exchanges. The index includes stocks of companies represented in the MSCI EAFE Index, with the inclusion of Canada and the exclusion of Greece. The ETF generally invests at least 90 percent of its assets in common stocks and ADRs. The graph below shows the allocation of the ETF at the end of September 2008, when almost 100 percent of its assets were divided among ten countries.

Figure 9.11: Allocation of Claymore/Zacks Country Rotation ETF (Ticker symbol: CRO)

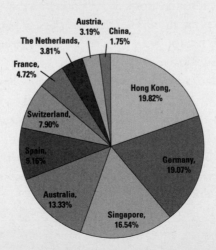

• CHAPTER SUMMARY •

► Alpha is outperformance of a benchmark on a risk-adjusted basis. As people are living longer and need more money to carry them through retirement, adding alpha to a portfolio is becoming increasingly important.

► One way to pursue alpha in a portfolio is to purchase enhanced, or intelligent, ETFs that seek better returns than traditional indexes. Intelligent indexes use quantitative models to select a portfolio of securities with the potential to outperform.

► ETFs based on fundamentally weighted indexes also could add alpha to a portfolio. Fundamentally weighted indexes weigh stocks according to factors such as earnings, dividend payouts, revenue, employees, or book value.

► Tactical asset allocation models seek to add alpha by producing returns above a strategically allocated portfolio. These models work by shifting the allocations of a strategic portfolio to take advantage of opportunities in the market.

► Tactical models can rely on a number of factors when creating a signal. Some of these are macroeconomic, such as rising or falling interest rates. No two tactical models are exactly the same.

► When employing a tactical model, it is important to maintain a disciplined approach. This will lead to more consistent, long-term results and reduce the possibility of emotion-driven or incorrect trades.

► One reason quantitative models work is because they eliminate human emotion from the stock selection process.

► Tactical models are not limited to portfolios of broad asset classes. They also can be applied to portfolios that provide more precise exposure to specific areas of the market.

► Sector rotation and country rotation are two types of portfolios that can benefit greatly from a tactical trading model.

► A sector rotation portfolio divides the market into varied sectors and shifts the weights of those sectors depending on developments and trends in the market. ETFs are useful tools for implementing sector rotation portfolios, as they provide exposure to different areas of the market.

► Because certain sectors perform differently under varied circumstances, being able to move in and out of sectors, as opposed to being 100 percent invested in all sectors at all times, can help to pursue alpha.

▶ A country rotation portfolio shifts assets among countries depending on the economic, political, and market conditions affecting each country. Because of the varying performances of countries from year to year, a country rotation model can be an effective way to invest in those that are trending up and rotate out of those that are trending down. This is another effective way to pursue alpha.

▶ ETFs are also great tools for country rotation portfolios, as they provide access to a variety of international markets plus diversification within each country, all at a relatively low cost to the investor.

10

The Next Phase for ETFs

In recent years ETFs have been one of the fastest growing financial products, and that trend is not expected to change going forward. But where will the growth come from? One of the most likely sources of new assets is the retirement market, an area that ETFs have been slow to penetrate. This is largely because of the way ETFs trade, which makes them incompatible with many of the trading platforms used in the defined-contribution retirement plan market today. However, a few companies have been working to overcome these issues, and their creative solutions likely will make ETFs more readily available to investors through workplace retirement plans. Future growth in ETF assets also is expected to come as a result of innovations on the product side, as ETF providers continue to expand their menus of investment options. One product innovation in particular that has everyone in the industry buzzing is active ETFs. Active ETFs, which essentially bring active management to ETFs, had arrived only recently on the scene at the time this book was written. In the future, though, these products have the potential to make ETFs appealing to an even wider audience. This chapter will explore avenues of growth for the ETF industry that are likely to spur significant growth over the next few years.

• WHAT'S NEXT •

By the end of 2008, U.S. ETF assets had reached just over $530 billion (a decline from more than $600 billion in 2007 due to the financial crisis). By 2011, some experts forecast that those assets will rise to more than $1 trillion within the United States, and $2 trillion worldwide. Most agree this is achievable if the economy is able to regain its footing in 2009. In addition, a continued torrid pace of growth will depend on other variables, such as whether or not ETFs gain more acceptance inside U.S. defined-contribution retirement plans. These plans include 401(k)s, which are retirement savings plans for employees of corporations; 403b plans, which are for employees of public education institutions and nonprofit organizations; and 457 plans, which are offered by employers within the public sector, such as government employers. Theoretically, ETFs are a great fit for these plans. In many cases they offer lower fees than many of the mutual funds that are currently available to participants in these plans. Their fee structure is more transparent, and performance is often more consistent over time.

• THE PROBLEM •

So why is this market still dominated by mutual funds while ETFs are gaining ground only very slowly? The main reason involves the way retirement plans work and the platforms that they run on. With defined-contribution plans such as 401(k)s, participants defer a certain percentage of each paycheck into the plan. Technically, the plan sponsor collects each deferral and passes it on to the plan custodian periodically, perhaps monthly. Therefore, assets constantly are flowing into the plan, and they are allocated to various investments according to participants' instructions. This type of investing works well with mutual funds primarily because most mutual fund shares used by defined-contribution retirement plans are no-load, meaning there is no sales charge for periodic investments of small amounts per participant.

ETFs don't function quite the same way. Because ETFs trade like stocks, shares are bought and sold through brokers. That means that each time an ETF trade is placed (buy or sell), there is a commission. Even though most ETFs generally have low expense ratios, if a commission must be paid each time a trade is made, the costs can really add up. In addition, ETFs can be traded at any time throughout the trading day. This makes keeping records of ETF data much more difficult than with mutual funds, which are set up to trade just once a day.

Additionally, unlike mutual funds, ETFs can be bought only in whole shares. So, if a retirement plan has fifty dollars to invest on behalf of a participant, and the ETF is trading at twelve dollars, the plan can't purchase an even number of shares. Most retirement plan administrative platforms have not devised a way to allow participants to purchase ETF shares.

• THE SOLUTION •

The good news is that there are ways to overcome these issues. Actually, there are several potential solutions, but just a few are expected to make the most headway in putting ETFs inside these plans. One solution is packaging. This basically means putting ETFs inside another product that is able to function on the trading platforms used by 401(k)s and other defined-contribution plans. For example, ETFs can be purchased and held by mutual funds. Instead of having a mutual fund of individual stocks or bonds, creating mutual funds that invest entirely in ETFs overcomes the administrative problems of trading ETFs such as the record keeping, and issues with fractional shares. In addition, packaging allows plan participants to take advantage of many other benefits of ETFs, such as increased diversification.

Creating risk-based and target-date funds of ETFs may make mutual funds of ETFs an even better fit for the retirement market, and some companies have started doing this already. The idea is to have a mutual fund invested in a combination of ETFs in order to create conservative, moderate, and aggressive risk-based portfolios as well as target-date portfolios that become more conservative over time. While most actively managed equity mutual funds charge between 1.2 percent and 1.5 percent, ETFs packaged inside mutual funds may achieve considerably lower total costs while offering more consistent returns than many actively managed mutual funds. Combining ETFs inside mutual funds also solves the issue of purchasing fractional shares.

In addition to mutual fund–based ideas, some companies have started offering ETFs within other structures, such as collective trusts, that also mesh well with defined-contribution plan platforms. Collective trusts are similar to mutual funds, but they are offered primarily to institutional investment accounts, including defined-benefit retirement plans. As with mutual funds, putting ETFs inside collective trusts could solve many of the problems with trading ETFs. One drawback to collective trusts has been that they are not always valued daily, as mutual funds and ETFs are.

In addition to packaging, another solution that some companies have been exploring is to create new trading record-keeping platforms that can accommodate ETFs. These platforms generally work by bundling ETF trades together before making purchases in order to reduce brokerage costs. These platforms also generally allow the record-keeping system to assign fractional shares of ETFs to individual participant accounts.

Yet another concept is to offer a self-directed brokerage account as one investment choice in a retirement plan menu. This potentially opens to each plan participant access to thousands of individual stocks, bonds, and ETFs. Typically the participant directly bears all trading costs and transaction charges in a self-directed brokerage account, and the cost barrier has been a major reason these accounts have not yet become more popular. Another reason is that some plan sponsors fear that participants will make poor choices when they have such broad access to investments.

• IMPACT ON ASSETS •

If ETFs are embraced by retirement plans on a wider scale, it could be a huge boon to the ETF industry. Just look at the impact that the retirement plan market has had on mutual fund assets. According to the Investment Company Institute, as of the end of 2007 the U.S. retirement market had accumulated $17.6 trillion in total assets, which is equal to roughly 40 percent of all U.S. household financial assets. In all, in 2007, mutual funds managed 26 percent of those assets. The following chart shows that retirement market assets in mutual funds have continued to increase from $2.5 trillion in 2000 to $4.6 trillion in 2007. It's worth noting that the increase in mutual fund assets is largely due to the increase of total retirement assets, as mutual funds don't appear to be taking market share from other investments.

**Figure 10.1: Mutual Fund Assets in
Retirement Market (in $ trillions)**

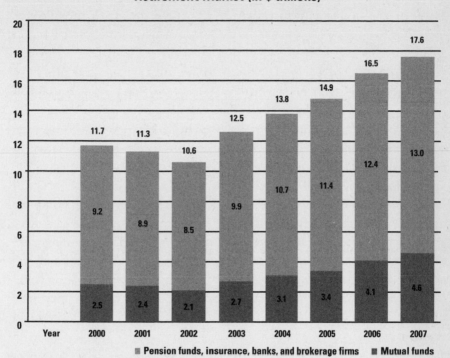

SOURCES: INVESTMENT COMPANY INSTITUTE, FEDERAL RESERVE BOARD, NATIONAL ASSOCIATION OF GOVERNMENT
DEFINED CONTRIBUTION ADMINISTRATORS, AMERICAN COUNCIL OF LIFE INSURERS, AND INTERNAL REVENUE SERVICE
STATISTICS OF INCOME DIVISION

The majority of retirement assets in mutual funds come from IRAs and employer-sponsored defined-contribution plans. In fact, mutual funds manage more than 50 percent of defined-contribution plan assets and 47 percent of IRA assets. The following table shows the consistent growth of mutual fund assets in both of these venues. In employer-sponsored defined-contribution plans, mutual fund assets increased from $135 billion in 1991 to $1.547 trillion in 2008. Meanwhile, mutual fund assets in IRAs rose from $185 billion in 1991 to $1.598 trillion in 2007.

TABLE 10.1: MUTUAL FUND ASSETS IN RETIREMENT ACCOUNTS

	TOTAL MUTUAL FUND RETIREMENT ASSETS ($ BILLIONS)	EMPLOYER-SPONSORED DEFINED-CONTRIBUTION PLAN MUTUAL FUND ASSETS[1] ($ BILLIONS)	IRA MUTUAL FUND ASSETS ($ BILLIONS)
1991	320	135	185
1992	416	184	233
1993	578	263	315
1994	661	320	342
1995	918	445	474
1996	1,174	579	595
1997	1,548	768	780
1998	1,959	978	981
1999	2,551	1,274	1,277
2000	2,497	1,249	1,249
2001	2,355	1,179	1,176
2002	2,084	1,040	1,044
2003	2,674	1,347	1,327
2004	3,090	1,569	1,521
2005	3,460	1,760	1,700
2006	4,111	2,083	2,028
2007	4,613	2,390	2,304
2008	3,145	1,547	1,598

[1] Defined-contribution plans include 401(k), 403(b), 457, and Keogh plans, and other defined-contribution plans without 401(k) features.

SOURCES: INVESTMENT COMPANY INSTITUTE, FEDERAL RESERVE BOARD, AND U.S. DEPARTMENT OF LABOR

Based on the sheer size of the retirement market, the many ideas that are making ETFs more readily available through that channel are likely to spur industry growth. As discussed earlier, the retirement plan market could grow even faster in the future because of the Pension Protection Act that was enacted in 2006. This law made it more attractive for plan sponsors to enroll employees in defined-contribution plans automatically, and this is expected to cause a major increase in the number of people investing in these plans and therefore in total retirement assets. Because of the ever-increasing awareness of the benefits of ETFs, there's a good chance that an increasing part of the assets flowing into defined-contribution plans will be captured by ETFs. This is specifically true for risk-based and target-date funds of ETFs, which are emerging as the most popular default investment choices in automatic enrollment plans.

• OTHER PACKAGING WITH ETFS •

While the defined-contribution market represents a great potential opportunity for the ETF market, it isn't the only growth prospect. Packaging ETFs in several other ways also can spur greater investor interest by making ETFs available through a number of different channels. Many of these ideas are still new, though they are expected to gain steam as more investors and financial professionals become aware of them and better understand their benefits. The following are some of the products that are expected to increase usage of ETFs:

- ► Separately managed accounts (SMA) and wrap accounts
- ► Unified managed accounts (UMA)
- ► Insurance products
- ► Unit investment trusts (UIT)
- ► Closed-end funds
- ► 529 college savings plans

• SEPARATELY MANAGED ACCOUNTS AND WRAPS •

SMAs of ETFs were some of the first products that were used to package ETFs. SMAs are individual investment portfolios, which are similar in some ways to mutual funds. Both are managed by a professional money manager; however, unlike mutual funds in which the investors' money is pooled together and each investor is given only shares in a whole, SMA investors directly own the underlying securities. This allows these accounts to be more customizable and offer more tax control. For example, in an SMA a security could be sold if the investor already had a big position in it elsewhere. In addition, for tax purposes the investor could direct the SMA manager to sell specific securities at a loss at the end of the year to reduce taxable income. While mutual funds aim for broad appeal among investors in all tiers of affluence, SMAs generally focus on high net worth investors. Often the minimum investment required in an SMA is fifty thousand dollars or more. The table below compares major differences between SMAs and mutual funds.

TABLE 10.2: SEPARATELY MANAGED ACCOUNTS (SMA) VERSUS MUTUAL FUNDS

	SEPARATELY MANAGED ACCOUNT (SMA)	MUTUAL FUND
Ownership	Individual securities or funds are owned by the investor.	Assets are pooled and commingled; investor owns a share.
Minimum Investment	$50,000–$100,000 per account is typical.	$100–$2,000 minimum investment per fund
Funding	Can use existing stocks, bonds, and/or cash	Cash
Tax Efficiency	Established cost basis for each security	Cost basis may include embedded capital gains realized before the investor joined the fund.
Portfolio Holdings	Investor can request security exclusions.	Sole discretion of portfolio manager
Level of Service	A consultative process; individualized service	Varies by financial professional
Fees	Typically, the fee is a percentage of the assets under management.	Sales charges and other fees may apply.

Wrap accounts are portfolios that combine several different financial products and charge one combined fee to the investor (usually including any brokerage charges to buy or sell investments). Wraps can be prepackaged solutions—including turnkey asset allocation programs—or more tailored investments. For instance, an adviser can pick specific mutual funds from a universe of funds available to construct the wrap. Typically, wrap accounts invest in some combination of mutual funds and individual stocks and bonds. However, ETFs also can work well as investment choices in wraps, as well as SMAs. By combining the benefits inherent in

ETFs with the advantages of either SMAs or wraps, investors can participate in portfolios that are highly diversified, flexible, and more tax efficient.

As ETFs become more prevalent inside these products, SMAs and wraps also represent a good growth opportunity for ETFs, as the markets for these products have been growing steadily.

• UNIFIED MANAGED ACCOUNTS •

Unified managed accounts are in many ways the next generation of SMAs. The purpose of the UMA is to provide investors with a way to more holistically manage their assets. Within these accounts or platforms, investors are able to combine several types of investments and even accounts, for instance a household cash account and a retirement account, under one administrative umbrella. Those assets then can be managed as one big pie instead of as individual pieces. There has been growing excitement about UMAs in the investment community, although in terms of development they are still in their infancy. Although some companies have introduced branded UMA products, the industry is still working toward a consensus definition of what constitutes a UMA. As discussed in earlier chapters, ETFs can have a variety of roles in a portfolio, such as acting as a core holding, rounding out a portfolio, tapping into certain segments of the market, or providing strategic tax benefits. Inside UMAs, ETFs potentially can serve a variety of such functions.

• INSURANCE PRODUCTS •

ETFs first began creeping into certain insurance products a few years ago. Recently, they have begun to catch on as insurance product providers are beginning to understand the benefits that they offer. This has been most notable so far in variable insurance products, including annuities and life insurance. Variable annuities (VAs) are hybrid insurance contracts and investment securities, and they help investors accumulate money in managed portfolios on a tax-deferred basis. They are very popular during an investor's retirement savings accumulation phase because special features that they offer have the potential to guarantee income for the life of one or more annuitants, which eliminates the fear that many people have of running out of money during their retirement years.

Most variable annuities include a variety of investment options. Recently, one popular option has been strategic asset allocation products such as risk-based or target-date portfolios. In fact, in some variable annuity products, product manufacturers have seen more than 70 percent of new asset flows going into these portfolios.

Another popular insurance product in which ETFs have growth opportunities is variable universal life (VUL) insurance policies. These products offer life insurance features and a cash value that can be allocated among investment choices. One of the main selling points for these products is the flexibility that they offer to policyholders. For instance, holders can decide how they want to invest cash value and how much they will pay in premiums at any given time. There is potential for the cash value of the policy to decline if the investments inside the policy decline.

ETFs can work very well in VAs or VULs. That's mainly because they assist in alleviating two of the main concerns that consumers of these products generally have: high costs and complexity. In addition, ETFs actually add a third benefit, which is that they offer the potential of more consistent long-term performance. Let's address each of these benefits in more detail.

Lower Costs. By adding specific ETFs as investment options within a variable annuity or variable universal life product, insurance companies actually can hedge the long-term liability risks associated with product guarantees more efficiently, and this cost savings can flow down to the consumer.

Complexity. One of the biggest concerns that financial advisers and consumers have in purchasing insurance products is their complexity. However, the next generation of VA and VUL products could include funds of ETFs as investment options designed to simplify some of the products' complexity.

Consistent Performance. This is one of the biggest benefits of including ETFs inside insurance products. The fact that ETFs often produce more consistent long-term returns than actively managed mutual funds has been discussed already. Performance can be even more consistent when an investment manager uses a tactical model to manage a portfolio of ETFs to enhance a portfolio's risk-return balance.

As more VAs and VULs turn to ETFs as investment options, ETFs will have opportunities to accumulate assets. According to the National Association of Variable Annuities, or NAVA, as of the third quarter of 2007, nearly $1.5 trillion was held in U.S. variable annuity assets, compared with slightly less than $1.3 trillion in assets one year before. Meanwhile, total variable annuity sales for the third quarter were $46.2 billion, a 24.9 percent increase from the third quarter of 2006.

• CLOSED-END FUNDS •

As of this writing, ETFs had not really taken off inside closed-end funds, though it seems to be only a matter of time before they do. Closed-end funds were mentioned earlier in the book, but to recount, these are funds that issue a fixed number of shares that are traded on an exchange. While some people group closed-end funds with ETFs, they actually have very different structures. With closed-end funds, a fixed number of shares are issued, and the price that the shares trade at is determined by the supply and demand in the market, not necessarily just the value of their underlying assets. As a result, a closed-end fund may trade above or below its net asset value (at a premium or a discount). This is different from ETFs, which are able to create and redeem new shares constantly, which allows them to keep their shares trading close to or at their underlying value.

There are various reasons it makes sense to use ETFs inside closed-end funds; for example, their greater transparency, liquidity, lower management fees, and other benefits. It's hard to say exactly how much opportunity there is for ETFs inside closed-end funds. As is evident in the following chart, closed-end fund assets remained in a fairly tight range between 1995 and 2002. However, more recently they have started to become popular again within the financial product distribution community. Since 2003, there has been a steady uptrend in their assets, which ended 2007 with $315 billion.

• 529 COLLEGE SAVINGS PLANS •

These 529 college savings plans have become popular investment vehicles for parents saving for a child's future college funding needs—particularly as the cost of attending college has been increasing an average of 4 percent to 5 percent each year. The cost for in-state students to attend a public

Figure 10.2: Closed-end Fund Assets (billions of dollars, year-end, 1995–2007)

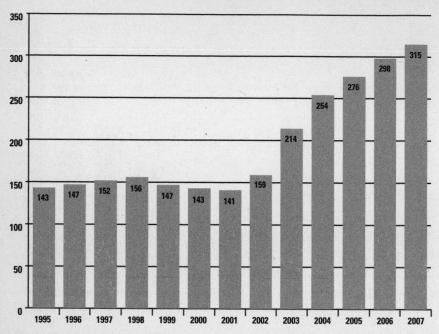

SOURCE: INVESTMENT COMPANY INSTITUTE

college for the 2008–2009 school year was around $18,000; for out-of-state students that price jumps to more than $29,000; and for private schools the cost is more than $37,000. The 529 plans are tax-advantaged plans sponsored by states, state agencies, or educational institutions. They come in two forms: (1) a prepaid plan that allows investors to buy credits at certain colleges to be used for tuition; and (2) college savings plans that use managed investment accounts to plan for college. The latter is where the opportunity for ETFs exists. These plans also have been experiencing strong growth. As is evident in the following chart, in 2007 these plans had accumulated $112.5 billion in assets, compared to just $200 million in 1998.

Most college savings plans provide several investment options. Currently, the bulk of the ones available to 529 investors are strategically managed asset allocation models, which utilize actively managed funds, just like the insurance and 401(k) worlds. However, because of the ability to

Figure 10.3: 529 College Savings Plan Assets (in billions)

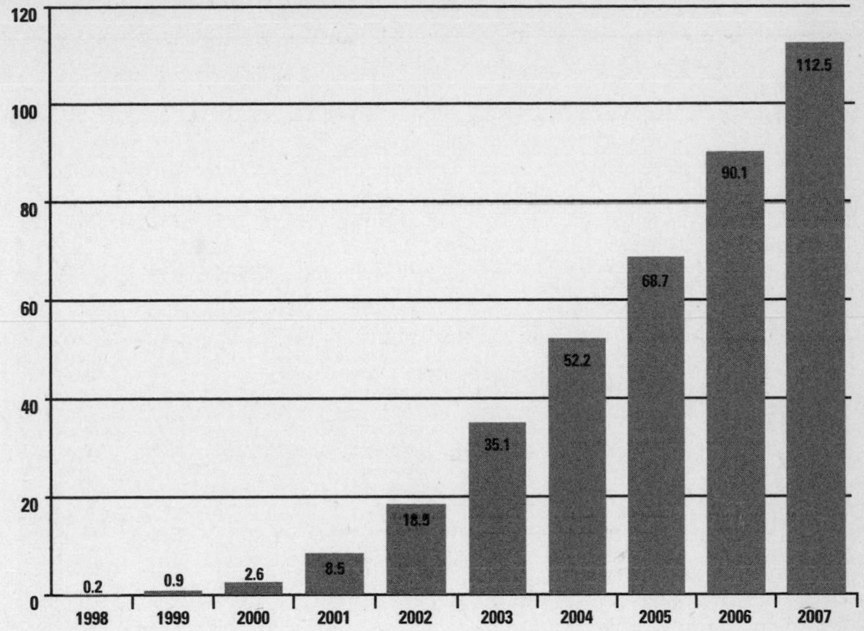

SOURCE: INVESTMENT COMPANY INSTITUTE

decrease costs and improve performance, portfolios of ETFs could make great options for these plans.

• NEW PRODUCT STREAM •

Hundreds of new ETFs in a variety of styles and formats are likely to make their way into the market over the next few years and could help attract assets. The expectation is that these new products will continue to drift away from the broad-based ETF of the early days. Like many of the ETFs that have been launched recently, the majority that are expected to be rolled out will be focused on specific niches of the market. They are also likely to be more focused on the fixed income ETF space, alternative asset classes like commodities and currencies, strategies such as leverage and inverse ETFs, and more active management.

There's also a good chance that these products will start coming out at a quicker pace than before, in part because of efficiencies in getting filings approved at the SEC. In the past, filing was a slow process, mainly because of the need to receive exemptive relief from certain SEC rules before coming to market. However, in 2006 the SEC announced interest in finding ways to streamline the approval process. Already the process to move more traditional, plain vanilla ETFs to market has become much faster.

• CHAPTER SUMMARY •

▶ Because of their many benefits, including transparency and low costs, ETFs are a great fit for the defined-contribution retirement plan market. If ETFs are able to gain wide acceptance in these plans, total ETF assets could soar.

▶ The 401(k) platforms are tailor-made for mutual funds because of how they trade. The technology of these platforms makes trading ETFs costly and difficult, which has largely prevented ETFs from gaining access to these plans on a wide scale.

▶ One way to overcome this issue is by creating mutual funds of ETFs. Because these are portfolios of ETFs, they have many of the benefits of ETFs and can trade easily on 401(k) platforms.

▶ Packaging ETFs in other wrappers, such as inside insurance products, also will help asset growth, making ETFs more accessible to investors through different channels.

▶ Developments on the product side also could contribute to ETF asset growth going forward. The introduction of an active ETF could prompt many big mutual fund companies to begin offering ETFs. Also, the continued rollout of ETFs that track different niches of the market could help attract assets.

Appendix

Complete List of U.S.-Listed ETFs as of June 2009

ETF	SYMBOL
CLAYMORE	
Claymore S&P Global Water	CGW
Claymore U.S. Capital Markets Bond ETF	UBD
Claymore U.S. Capital Markets Micro-Term Fixed Income ETF	ULQ
Claymore U.S.-1—The Capital Markets Index ETF	UEM
Claymore/Alphashares China	TAO
Claymore/AlphaShares China Small Cap Index ETF	HAO
Claymore/BBD High Income Index ETF	LVL
Claymore/BNY BRIC ETF	EEB
Claymore/BNY Mellon Frontier Markets ETF	FRN
Claymore/Clear Global Exchanges Brokers and Asset Managers Index	EXB
Claymore/Clear Global Timber	CUT
Claymore/Clear Spin-Off ETF	CSD
Claymore/Delta Global Shipping Index ETF	SEA
Claymore/Great Companies LCG ETF	XGC

ETF	SYMBOL
Claymore/MAC Global Solar Energy Index ETF	TAN
Claymore/Morningstar Information Super Sector Index ETF	MZN
Claymore/Morningstar Manufacturing Super Sector Index ETF	MZG
Claymore/Morningstar Services Super Sector Index ETF	MZO
Claymore/NYSE Arca Airline ETF	FAA
Claymore/Ocean Tomo Growth ETF	OTR
Claymore/Ocean Tomo Patent ETF	OTP
Claymore/Robb Report Global Luxury Index ETF	ROB
Claymore/Robeco Developed Intl ETF	EEN
Claymore/Sabrient Defensive Equity Index ETF	DEF
Claymore/Sabrient Insider ETF	NFO
Claymore/Sabrient Stealth ETF	STH
Claymore/SWM Canadian Energy Income Index ETF	ENY
Claymore/Zacks Dividend Rotation ETF	IRO
Claymore/Zacks International Multi-Asset Income Index ETF	HGI
Claymore/Zacks Mid-Cap Core ETF	CZA
Claymore/Zacks Multi-Asset Income Index ETF	CVY
Claymore/Zacks Sector Rotation ETF	XRO
DIREXION	
Direxion Daily 10-Yr Treasury Bear 3x Shares	TYO
Direxion Daily 10-Yr Treasury Bull 3x Shares	TYD
Direxion Daily 30-Yr Treasury Bear 3x Shares	TMV
Direxion Daily 30-Yr Treasury Bull 3x Shares	TMF
Direxion Developed Markets Bear 3x Shares	DPK
Direxion Developed Markets Bull 3x Shares	DZK
Direxion Emerging Markets Bear 3x Shares	EDZ
Direxion Emerging Markets Bull 3x Shares	EDC
Direxion Energy Bear 3x Shares	ERY
Direxion Energy Bull 3x Shares	ERX

ETF	SYMBOL
Direxion Financial Bear 3x Shares	FAZ
Direxion Financial Bull 3x Shares	FAS
Direxion Large Cap Bear 3x Shares	BGZ
Direxion Large Cap Bull 3x Shares	BGU
Direxion Mid Cap Bear 3x Shares	MWN
Direxion Mid Cap Bull 3x Shares	MWJ
Direxion Small Cap Bear 3x Shares	TZA
Direxion Small Cap Bull 3x Shares	TNA
Direxion Technology Bear 3x Shares	TYP
Direxion Technology Bull 3x Shares	TYH
DEUTSCHE BANK	
PowerShares Deutsche Bank Agriculture Fund	DBA
PowerShares Deutsche Bank Base Metals Fund	DBB
PowerShares Deutsche Bank Commodity Index Trac	DBC
PowerShares Deutsche Bank Energy Fund	DBE
PowerShares Deutsche Bank G10 Currency Harvest	DBV
PowerShares Deutsche Bank Gold Fund	DGL
PowerShares Deutsche Bank Oil Fund	DBO
PowerShares Deutsche Bank Precious Metals Fund	DBP
PowerShares Deutsche Bank Silver Fund	DBS
PowerShares Deutsche Bank USD Index Bearish	UDN
PowerShares Deutsche Bank USD Index Bullish	UUP
FIDELITY	
Fidelity Nasdaq Composite Index Tracking Stock	ONEQ
FIRST TRUST	
First Trust Amex Biotech Index Fund	FBT
First Trust Cons. Discret. AlphaDEX	FXD
First Trust Cons. Staples AlphaDEX	FXG
First Trust DB Strategic Value ETF	FDV

ETF	SYMBOL
First Trust DJ Global Select Dividend	FGD
First Trust DJ Internet Index Fund	FDN
First Trust DJ Select MicroCap ETF	FDM
First Trust Dow Jones STOXX Select Dividend 30 Index Fund	FDD
First Trust Energy AlphaDEX Fund	FXN
First Trust Financials AlphaDEX	FXO
First Trust FTSE EPRA/NAREIT Global Real Estate Index Fund	FFR
First Trust Health Care AlphaDEX	FXH
First Trust Industrials AlphaDEX	FXR
First Trust IPOX-100 Index Fund	FPX
First Trust ISE Chindia	FNI
First Trust ISE Global Wind Energy ETF	FAN
First Trust ISE Water Index Fund	FIW
First Trust ISE-Revere Natural Gas	FCG
First Trust Large Cap Core AlphaDEX	FEX
First Trust Large Cap Growth Opportunities AlphaDEX Fund	FTC
First Trust Large Cap Value Opportunities AlphaDEX Fund	FTA
First Trust Materials AlphaDEX Fund	FXZ
First Trust Mid Cap Core AlphaDEX	FNX
First Trust Morningstar ETF	FDL
First Trust Multi Cap Value AlphaDEX Fund	FAB
First Trust Multi CG AlphaDEX	FAD
First Trust NASDAQ Clean Edge U.S. Liquid Series Index Fund	QCLN
First Trust NASDAQ-100 Equal Weighted Index Fund	QQEW
First Trust NASDAQ-100 Ex-Technology Sector Index Fund	QQXT
First Trust NASDAQ-100-Technology Sector Index Fund	QTEC
First Trust S&P REIT Index Fund	FRI
First Trust Small Cap Core AlphaDEX	FYX
First Trust Technology AlphaDEX	FXL
First Trust Utilities AlphaDEX Fund	FXU

ETF	SYMBOL
First Trust Value Line 100 Fund	FVL
First Trust VL Dividend	FVD
First Trust VL Equity Allocation	FVI
GLOBAL X FUNDS	
Global X/InterBolsa FTSE Colombia 20 ETF	GXG
GREENHAVEN	
GreenHaven Continuous Commodity Index Fund	GCC
MERRILL LYNCH	
HOLDRS B2B Internet	BHH
HOLDRS Biotech	BBH
HOLDRS Broadband	BDH
HOLDRS Europe 2001	EKH
HOLDRS Internet	HHH
HOLDRS Internet Architecture	IAH
HOLDRS Internet Infrastructure	IIH
HOLDRS Market 2000+	MKH
HOLDRS Merrill Lynch Market Oil Service	OIH
HOLDRS Merrill Lynch Pharmaceutical	PPH
HOLDRS Merrill Lynch Regional Bank	RKH
HOLDRS Merrill Lynch Retail	RTH
HOLDRS Merrill Lynch Semiconductor	SMH
HOLDRS Merrill Lynch Software	SWH
HOLDRS Merrill Lynch Telecom	TTH
HOLDRS Merrill Lynch Utilities	UTH
HOLDRS Merrill Lynch Wireless	WMH
HOLDRS TeleBras	TBH
BARCLAYS	
iShares Cohen & Steers Realty Major	ICF
iShares COMEX Gold Trust	IAU
iShares Dow Jones EPAC Select Dividend	IDV

ETF	SYMBOL
iShares Dow Jones Select Dividend Index Fund	DVY
iShares Dow Jones Transportation Average Index Fund	IYT
iShares Dow Jones U.S. Aerospace & Defense Index Fund	ITA
iShares Dow Jones U.S. Basic Materials Index	IYM
iShares Dow Jones U.S. Broker-Dealers Index Fund	IAI
iShares Dow Jones U.S. Consumer Goods Index Fund	IYK
iShares Dow Jones U.S. Consumer Index Fund	IYC
iShares Dow Jones U.S. Energy Sector Fund	IYE
iShares Dow Jones U.S. Financial Sector Index Fund	IYF
iShares Dow Jones U.S. Financial Services Index Fund	IYG
iShares Dow Jones U.S. Health Care Index Fund	IYH
iShares Dow Jones U.S. Health Care Providers Index Fund	IHF
iShares Dow Jones U.S. Home Construction Index Fund	ITB
iShares Dow Jones U.S. Industrial Sector Index Fund	IYJ
iShares Dow Jones U.S. Insurance Index Fund	IAK
iShares Dow Jones U.S. Medical Devices Index Fund	IHI
iShares Dow Jones U.S. Oil & Gas Exploration & Production Index Fund	IEO
iShares Dow Jones U.S. Oil Equipment & Services Index Fund	IEZ
iShares Dow Jones U.S. Pharmaceutical Index Fund	IHE
iShares Dow Jones U.S. Real Estate Index Fund	IYR
iShares Dow Jones U.S. Regional Banks Index Fund	IAT
iShares Dow Jones U.S. Technology Index Fund	IYW
iShares Dow Jones U.S. Telecommunications Index Fund	IYZ
iShares Dow Jones U.S. Total Market Index Fund	IYY
iShares Dow Jones U.S. Utilities Index Fund	IDU
iShares FTSE China (HK Listed) Index Fund	FCHI
iShares FTSE Developed Small Cap ex–North America Index Fund	IFSM
iShares FTSE EPRA/NAREIT Asia Index Fund	IFAS
iShares FTSE EPRA/NAREIT Europe Index Fund	IFEU

ETF	SYMBOL
iShares FTSE EPRA/NAREIT Global Real Estate ex-U.S. Index Fund	IFGL
iShares FTSE EPRA/NAREIT North America Index Fund	IFNA
iShares FTSE NAREIT Industrial/Office Index Fund	FIO
iShares FTSE NAREIT Mortgage REITs Index Fund	REM
iShares FTSE NAREIT Real Estate 50 Index Fund	FTY
iShares FTSE NAREIT Residential Index Fund	REZ
iShares FTSE NAREIT Retail Index Fund	RTL
iShares FTSE/Xinhua China 25 Index Fund	FXI
iShares Goldman Sachs Natural Resources Index Fund	IGE
iShares Goldman Sachs Network Index Fund	IGN
iShares Goldman Sachs Semiconductor Index Fund	IGW
IShares Goldman Sachs Software Index Fund	IGV
iShares Goldman Sachs Technology Index Fund	IGM
iShares GS $ InvesTopTM Corporate Bond Fund	LQD
iShares GSCI Commodity-Indexed Trust Fund	GSG
iShares iBoxx $ HY Corp Bond Fund	HYG
iShares JP Morgan Em Bond Fd	EMB
iShares KLD 400 Social Index Fund	DSI
iShares KLD Select Social Index Fund	KLD
iShares Latin America 40 Index Fund	ILF
iShares Lehman 10–20 Year Treasury Bond Fund	TLH
iShares Lehman 1–3 Year Credit Bond Fund	CSJ
iShares Lehman 1–3 Year Treasury Bond Fund	SHY
iShares Lehman 20 Year Treasury Bond Fund	TLT
iShares Lehman 3–7 Year Treasury Bond Fund	IEI
iShares Lehman 7–10 Year Treasury Bond Fund	IEF
iShares Lehman Aggregate	AGG
iShares Lehman Credit Bond Fund	CFT
iShares Lehman Government/Credit Bond Fund	GBF

ETF	SYMBOL
iShares Lehman Intermediate Credit Bond Fund	CIU
iShares Lehman Intermediate Government/Credit Bond Fund	GVI
iShares Lehman MBS Fixed-Rate Bond	MBB
iShares Lehman Short Treasury Bond Fund	SHV
iShares Lehman TIPS Bond Fund	TIP
iShares Morningstar Large Core Index Fund	JKD
iShares Morningstar Large Growth Index Fund	JKE
iShares Morningstar Large Value Index Fund	JKF
iShares Morningstar Mid Core Index Fund	JKG
iShares Morningstar Mid Growth Index Fund	JKH
iShares Morningstar Mid Value Index Fund	JKI
iShares Morningstar Small Core Index Fund	JKJ
iShares Morningstar Small Growth Index Fund	JKK
iShares Morningstar Small Value Index Fund	JKL
iShares MSCI ACWI (All Country World Index) Index Fund	ACWI
iShares MSCI ACWI ex US Index Fund	ACWX
iShares MSCI All Country Asia ex Japan Index Fund	AAXJ
iShares MSCI All Peru Capped Index Fund	EPU
iShares MSCI Australia Index Fund	EWA
iShares MSCI Austria Index Fund	EWO
iShares MSCI Belgium Index Fund	EWK
iShares MSCI Brazil Index Fund	EWZ
iShares MSCI BRIC Index Fund	BKF
iShares MSCI Canada Index Fund	EWC
iShares MSCI Chile Index Fund	ECH
iShares MSCI EAFE Index Fund	EFA
iShares MSCI EAFE Small Cap	SCZ
iShares MSCI Emerging Index Fund	EEM
iShares MSCI EMU Index Fund	EZU

ETF	SYMBOL
iShares MSCI France Index Fund	EWQ
iShares MSCI Germany Index Fund	EWG
iShares MSCI Growth Index Fund	EFG
iShares MSCI Hong Kong Index Fund	EWH
iShares MSCI Israel Capped Investable Market Index Fund	EIS
iShares MSCI Italy Index Fund	EWI
iShares MSCI Japan Index Fund	EWJ
iShares MSCI Japan Sm Cap	SCJ
iShares MSCI Kokusai	TOK
iShares MSCI Malaysia Index Fund	EWM
iShares MSCI Mexico Index Fund	EWW
iShares MSCI Netherlands Index Fund	EWN
iShares MSCI Pacific Ex-Japan Index Fund	EPP
iShares MSCI Singapore Index Fund	EWS
iShares MSCI South Africa Index Fund	EZA
iShares MSCI South Korea Index Fund	EWY
iShares MSCI Spain Index Fund	EWP
iShares MSCI Sweden Index Fund	EWD
iShares MSCI Switzerland Index Fund	EWL
iShares MSCI Taiwan Index Fund	EWT
iShares MSCI Thailand Investable Market Index Fund	THD
iShares MSCI Turkey Investable Market Index Fund	TUR
iShares MSCI United Kingdom Index Fund	EWU
iShares MSCI Value Index Fund	EFV
iShares Nasdaq Biotechnology	IBB
iShares NYSE 100 Index Fund	NY
iShares NYSE Composite Index Fund	NYC
iShares Russell 1000	IWB
iShares Russell 1000 Growth	IWF

ETF	SYMBOL
iShares Russell 1000 Value	IWD
iShares Russell 2000	IWM
iShares Russell 2000 Growth	IWO
iShares Russell 2000 Value	IWN
iShares Russell 3000	IWV
iShares Russell 3000 Growth	IWZ
iShares Russell 3000 Value	IWW
iShares Russell Microcap Index Fund	IWC
iShares Russell Midcap Growth Index	IWP
iShares Russell Midcap Index Fund	IWR
iShares Russell Midcap Value Index	IWS
iShares S&P 100 Index Fund	OEF
iShares S&P 1500 Index Fund	ISI
iShares S&P 500 Growth Index Fund	IVW
iShares S&P 500 Index Fund	IVV
iShares S&P 500 Value Index Fund	IVE
iShares S&P Asia 50	AIA
iShares S&P Cali Muni Bond	CMF
iShares S&P Europe 350 Index Fund	IEV
iShares S&P Global 100 Index Fund	IOO
iShares S&P Global Clean Energy Index Fund	ICLN
iShares S&P Global Consumer Discretionary Sector Index Fund	RXI
iShares S&P Global Consumer Staples Sector Index Fund	KXI
iShares S&P Global Energy Index Fund	IXC
iShares S&P Global Financial Index Fund	IXG
iShares S&P Global Healthcare Index Fund	IXJ
iShares S&P Global Industrials Sector Index Fund	EXI
iShares S&P Global Infrastructure	IGF
iShares S&P Global Materials Sector Index Fund	MXI

ETF	SYMBOL
iShares S&P Global Nuclear Energy Index Fund	NUCL
iShares S&P Global Technology Index Fund	IXN
iShares S&P Global Telecommunications Index Fund	IXP
iShares S&P Global Timber & Forestry Index Fund	WOOD
iShares S&P Global Utilities Sector Index Fund	JXI
iShares S&P MidCap 400 Growth Index Fund	IJK
iShares S&P MidCap 400 Index Fund	IJH
iShares S&P MidCap 400 Value Index Fund	IJJ
iShares S&P National Municipal Bond Fund	MUB
iShares S&P NY Muni	NYF
iShares S&P SmallCap 600 Growth Index Fund	IJT
iShares S&P SmallCap 600 Index Fund	IJR
iShares S&P SmallCap 600 Value Index Fund	IJS
iShares S&P US Preferred Stock Fund	PFF
iShares S&P World ex-US Property	WPS
iShares S&P/Citigroup 1-3 Year International Treasury Bond Fund	SHY
iShares S&P/Citigroup International Treasury Fund	IGOV
iShares S&P/TOPIX 150 Index Fund	ITF
iShares Silver Trust	SLV
VANECK	
Market Vectors Coal ETF	KOL
Market Vectors Environment Index ETF Fund	EVX
Market Vectors Gaming ETF	BJK
Market Vectors Global Alternative Energy ETF	GEX
Market Vectors Gulf States Index ETF	MES
Market Vectors Hard Assets Producers ETF	HAP
Market Vectors High Yield Municipal Index ETF	HYD
Market Vectors Indonesia Index ETF	IDX
Market Vectors Pre-Refunded Municipal Index ETF	PRB

ETF	SYMBOL
Market Vectors Short Municipal Index ETF	SMB
Market Vectors Solar Energy ETF	KWT
Market Vectors Steel Index ETF Fund	SLX
Market Vectors TR Gold Miners	GDX
Market Vectors TR Russia ETF	RSX
Market Vectors–Africa Index ETF	AFK
Market Vectors–Agribusiness ETF	MOO
Market Vectors–Lehman Brothers AMT-Free Intermediate Muni	ITM
Market Vectors–Lehman Brothers AMT-Free Long Municipal Index	MLN
Market Vectors–Nuclear Energy ETF	NLR
POWERSHARES	
Diamonds	DIA
PowerShares 1-30 Treasury Ladder Portfolio	PLW
PowerShares Active AlphaQ Fund	PQY
PowerShares Active Low Duration Fund	PLK
PowerShares Active Mega Cap Fund	PMA
PowerShares Active Multi-Cap Fund	PQZ
PowerShares Active U.S. Real Estate Fund	PSR
PowerShares Aerospace & Defense	PPA
PowerShares Autonomic Balanced Growth NFA Global Asset Portfolio	PAO
PowerShares Autonomic Balanced NFA Global Asset Portfolio	PCA
PowerShares Autonomic Growth NFA Global Asset Portfolio	PTO
PowerShares BLDRS Asia 50 ADR Index Fund	ADRA
PowerShares BLDRS Developed Markets 100 ADR Index Fund	ADRD
PowerShares BLDRS Emerging Markets 50 ADR Index Fund	ADRE
PowerShares BLDRS Europe 100 ADR Index Fund	ADRU
PowerShares Buyback Achievers	PKW
PowerShares Cleantech Portfolio	PZD
PowerShares Dividend Achievers	PEY

ETF	SYMBOL
PowerShares Dividend Achievers	PFM
PowerShares DWA Developed Market Technical Leaders Portfolio	PIZ
PowerShares DWA Emerging Market Technical Leaders Portfolio	PIE
PowerShares DWA Technical Leaders Portfolio	PDP
PowerShares Dynamic Banking	PJB
PowerShares Dynamic Basic Materials	PYZ
PowerShares Dynamic Biotech & Genome	PBE
PowerShares Dynamic Build & Construction	PKB
PowerShares Dynamic Consumer Discretionary	PEZ
PowerShares Dynamic Consumer Staples	PSL
PowerShares Dynamic Developed International Opportunities Portfolio	PFA
PowerShares Dynamic Energy	PXI
PowerShares Dynamic Energy E&P	PXE
PowerShares Dynamic Financial	PFI
PowerShares Dynamic Food & Beverage	PBJ
PowerShares Dynamic Healthcare	PTH
PowerShares Dynamic Healthcare Serv	PTJ
PowerShares Dynamic Industrials	PRN
PowerShares Dynamic Insurance	PIC
PowerShares Dynamic Large Cap	PJF
PowerShares Dynamic LargeCap Growth	PWB
PowerShares Dynamic LargeCap Value	PWV
PowerShares Dynamic Leisure & Entertainment Portfolio	PEJ
PowerShares Dynamic MagniQuant	PIQ
PowerShares Dynamic Media	PBS
PowerShares Dynamic Mid Cap	PJG
PowerShares Dynamic Mid Cap Growth	PWJ
PowerShares Dynamic Mid Cap Value	PWP
PowerShares Dynamic Networking	PXQ

ETF	SYMBOL
PowerShares Dynamic Oil Services	PXJ
PowerShares Dynamic Pharmaceuticals	PJP
PowerShares Dynamic Retail	PMR
PowerShares Dynamic Semiconductors	PSI
PowerShares Dynamic Small Cap	PJM
PowerShares Dynamic Small Cap Value	PWY
PowerShares Dynamic SmallCap Growth	PWT
PowerShares Dynamic Software	PSJ
PowerShares Dynamic Technology	PTF
PowerShares Dynamic Telecom	PTE
PowerShares Dynamic Utilities	PUI
PowerShares Emerging Markets Sovereign Debt Portfolio	PCY
PowerShares Financial Preferred	PGF
PowerShares FTSE NASDAQ Small Cap Portfolio	PQSC
PowerShares FTSE RAFI Asia Pacific ex-Japan Portfolio	PAF
PowerShares FTSE RAFI Developed Markets ex-U.S. Portfolio	PXF
PowerShares FTSE RAFI Developed Markets ex-U.S. Small-Mid Portfolio	PDN
PowerShares FTSE RAFI Emerging Markets Portfolio	PXH
PowerShares FTSE RAFI Europe Portfolio	PEF
PowerShares FTSE RAFI Japan Portfolio	PJO
Powershares FTSE RAFI US 1000 Portfolio	PRF
PowerShares FTSE RAFI US 1500 Small-Mid Portfolio	PRFZ
PowerShares Global Agriculture Portfolio	PAGG
PowerShares Global Biotech Portfolio	PBTQ
PowerShares Global Clean Energy Portfolio	PBD
PowerShares Global Coal Portfolio	PKOL
PowerShares Global Emerging Markets Infrastructure Portfolio	PXR
PowerShares Global Gold and Precious Metals Portfolio	PSAU
PowerShares Global Nuclear Portfolio	PKN

ETF	SYMBOL
PowerShares Global Progressive Transportation Portfolio	PTRP
PowerShares Global Steel Portfolio	PSTL
PowerShares Global Water Portfolio	PIO
PowerShares Global Wind Energy Portfolio	PWND
PowerShares Golden Dragon Halter USX China Portfolio	PGJ
PowerShares High Yield Corporate Bond Portfolio	PHB
PowerShares India Portfolio	PIN
PowerShares Insured CA Municipal Bond Portfolio	PWZ
PowerShares Insured National Municipal Bond Portfolio	PZA
PowerShares Insured NY Municipal Bond Portfolio	PZT
PowerShares Intl Dividend Achievers	PID
PowerShares Listed Private Equity	PSP
PowerShares Lux Nanotech Portfollo	PXN
PowerShares MENA Frontier Countries Portfolio	PMNA
PowerShares Nasdaq Internet Portfolio	PNQI
PowerShares NASDAQ NextQ Portfolio	PNXQ
PowerShares NASDAQ-100 BuyWrite Portfolio	PQBW
PowerShares Preferred Portfolio	PGX
PowerShares Trust	Q
PowerShares S&P 500 BuyWrite Portfolio	PBP
PowerShares Value Line Industry Rotation Portfolio	PYH
PowerShares Value Line Timeliness	PIV
PowerShares VRDO Tax Free Weekly Portfolio	PVI
PowerShares Water Resource Portfolio	PHO
PowerShares WilderHill Clean Energy Portfolio	PBW
PowerShares WilderHill Progressive Energy Portfolio	PUW
PowerShares XTF: Dynamic Market Portfolio	PWC
PowerShares XTF: Dynamic OTC Portfolio	PWO
PowerShares Zacks Micro Cap	PZI

ETF	SYMBOL
PowerShares Zacks Small Cap	PZJ
ProShares Short Dow30	DOG
ProShares Short Financials	SEF
ProShares Short MidCap400	MYY
ProShares Short MSCI EAFE	EFZ
ProShares Short MSCI Emerging Markets	EUM
ProShares Short Oil & Gas	DDG
ProShares Short	PSQ
ProShares Short Russell2000	RWM
ProShares Short S&P500	SH
ProShares Short SmallCap600	SBB
ProShares Ultra Basic Materials	UYM
ProShares Ultra Consumer Goods	UGE
ProShares Ultra Consumer Services	UCC
ProShares Ultra DJ-AIG Commodity	UCD
ProShares Ultra DJ-AIG Crude Oil	UCO
ProShares Ultra Dow30	DDM
ProShares Ultra Euro	ULE
ProShares Ultra Financials	UYG
ProShares Ultra FTSE/Xinhua China 25	XPP
ProShares Ultra Gold	UGL
ProShares Ultra Health Care	RXL
ProShares Ultra Industrials	UXI
ProShares Ultra MidCap400	MVV
ProShares Ultra MSCI EAFE	EFO
ProShares Ultra MSCI Emerging Markets	EET
ProShares Ultra MSCI Japan	EZJ
ProShares Ultra Oil & Gas	DIG
ProShares Ultra	QLD

ETF	SYMBOL
ProShares Ultra Real Estate	URE
ProShares Ultra Russell MidCap Growth	UKW
ProShares Ultra Russell MidCap Value	UVU
ProShares Ultra Russell1000 Growth	UKF
ProShares Ultra Russell1000 Value	UVG
ProShares Ultra Russell2000	UWM
ProShares Ultra Russell2000 Growth	UKK
ProShares Ultra Russell2000 Value	UVT
ProShares Ultra S&P500	SSO
ProShares Ultra Semiconductors	USD
ProShares Ultra Silver	AGQ
ProShares Ultra SmallCap600	SAA
ProShares Ultra Technology	ROM
ProShares Ultra Telecommunications	LTL
ProShares Ultra Utilities	UPW
ProShares Ultra Yen	YCL
ProShares UltraShort Basic Materials	SMN
ProShares UltraShort Consumer Goods	SZK
ProShares UltraShort Consumer Services	SCC
ProShares UltraShort DJ-AIG Commodity	CMD
ProShares UltraShort DJ-AIG Crude Oil	SCO
ProShares UltraShort Dow30	DXD
ProShares UltraShort Euro	EUO
ProShares UltraShort Financials	SKF
ProShares Ultrashort FTSE/Xinhua China	FXP
ProShares UltraShort Gold	GLL
ProShares UltraShort Health Care	RXD
ProShares UltraShort Industrials	SIJ
ProShares UltraShort Lehman 20+ Year Treasury	TBT

ETF	SYMBOL
ProShares UltraShort Lehman 7-10 Year Treasury	PST
ProShares UltraShort MidCap400	MZZ
ProShares UltraShort MSCI EAFE	EFU
ProShares UltraShort MSCI Emerging Markets	EEV
ProShares UltraShort MSCI Japan	EWV
ProShares UltraShort Oil & Gas	DUG
ProShares UltraShort QQQ	QID
ProShares UltraShort Real Estate	SRS
ProShares UltraShort Russell MidCap Growth	SDK
ProShares UltraShort Russell MidCap Value	SJL
ProShares UltraShort Russell1000 Growth	SFK
ProShares UltraShort Russell1000 Value	SJF
ProShares UltraShort Russell2000	TWM
ProShares UltraShort Russell2000 Growth	SKK
ProShares UltraShort Russell2000 Value	SJH
ProShares UltraShort S&P500	SDS
ProShares UltraShort Semiconductors	SSG
ProShares UltraShort Silver	ZSL
ProShares UltraShort SmallCap600	SDD
ProShares UltraShort Technology	REW
ProShares UltraShort Telecommunications	TLL
ProShares UltraShort Utilities	SDP
ProShares UltraShort Yen	YCS
RYDEX	
Rydex 2x Russell 2000 ETF	RRY
Rydex 2x S&P 500 ETF	RSU
Rydex 2x S&P MidCap 400 ETF	RMM
Rydex 2x S&P Select Sector Energy ETF	REA
Rydex 2x S&P Select Sector Financial ETF	RFL

ETF	SYMBOL
Rydex 2x S&P Select Sector Health Care ETF	RHM
Rydex 2x S&P Select Sector Technology ETF	RTG
Rydex CurrencyShares Australian Dollar Trust	FXA
Rydex CurrencyShares British Pound Sterling Trust	FXB
Rydex CurrencyShares Canadian Dollar Trust	FXC
Rydex CurrencyShares Euro Currency Trust	FXE
Rydex CurrencyShares Japanese Yen Trust	FXY
Rydex CurrencyShares Mexican Peso Trust	FXM
Rydex CurrencyShares Swedish Krona Trust	FXS
Rydex CurrencyShares Swiss Franc Trust	FXF
Rydex ETF Trust	RSP
Rydex Inverse 2x Russell 2000 ETF	RRZ
Rydex Inverse 2x S&P 500 ETF	RSW
Rydex Inverse 2x S&P MidCap 400 ETF	RMS
Rydex Inverse 2x S&P Select Sector Energy ETF	REC
Rydex Inverse 2x S&P Select Sector Financial ETF	RFN
Rydex Inverse 2x S&P Select Sector Health Care ETF	RHO
Rydex Inverse 2x S&P Select Sector Technology ETF	RTW
Rydex Russell Top 50 ETF	XLG
Rydex S&P 500 Pure Growth ETF	RPG
Rydex S&P 500 Pure Value ETF	RPV
Rydex S&P Equal Weight Consumer Discretionary	RCD
Rydex S&P Equal Weight Consumer Staples ETF	RHS
Rydex S&P Equal Weight Energy ETF	RYE
Rydex S&P Equal Weight Financial ETF	RYF
Rydex S&P Equal Weight Health Care ETF	RYH
Rydex S&P Equal Weight Industrials ETF	RGI
Rydex S&P Equal Weight Materials ETF	RTM
Rydex S&P Equal Weight Technology ETF	RYT

ETF	SYMBOL
Rydex S&P Equal Weight Utilities ETF	RYU
Rydex S&P Midcap 400 Pure Growth	RFG
Rydex S&P Midcap 400 Pure Value	RFV
Rydex S&P Smallcap 600 Pure Growth	RZG
Rydex S&P Smallcap 600 Pure Value	RZV
STATE STREET	
SPDR Barclays Capital Convertible Bond ETF	CWB
SPDR Barclays Capital Intermediate Term Credit Bond ETF	ITR
SPDR Barclays Capital Long Term Credit Bond ETF	LWC
SPDR Barclays Capital Mortgage Backed Bond ETF	MBG
SPDR Barclays Capital Short Term International Treasury Bond ETF	BWZ
SPDR Barclays Capital TIPS ETF	IPE
SPDR DB International Government Inflation-Protected Bond ETF	WIP
SPDR DJ EURO STOXX 50 ETF	FEZ
SPDR DJ Global Titans ETF	DGT
SPDR DJ STOXX 50 ETF	FEU
SPDR DJ Wilshire Global Real Estate ETF	RWO
SPDR DJ Wilshire Intl Real Estate	RWX
SPDR DJ Wilshire Large Cap ETF	ELR
SPDR DJ Wilshire Large Cap Value ET	ELV
SPDR DJ Wilshire Lg Cap Growth	ELG
SPDR DJ Wilshire Mid Cap ETF	EMM
SPDR DJ Wilshire Mid Cap Growth ETF	EMG
SPDR DJ Wilshire Mid Cap Value ETF	EMV
SPDR DJ Wilshire REIT ETF	RWR
SPDR DJ Wilshire Small Cap ETF	DSC
SPDR DJ Wilshire Small Cap Growth	DSG
SPDR DJ Wilshire Small Cap Value	DSV
SPDR DJ Wilshire Total Market ETF	TMW

ETF	SYMBOL
SPDR FTSE/Macquarie GI 100 ETF	GII
SPDR Gold Trust	GLD
SPDR Homebuilders ETF	XHB
SPDR KBW Bank ETF	KBE
SPDR KBW Capital Markets ETF	KCE
SPDR KBW Insurance ETF	KIE
SPDR KBW Regional Banking ETF	KRE
SPDR Lehman 1–3 Month T-Bill ETF	BIL
SPDR Lehman Aggregate Bond ETF	LAG
SPDR Lehman California Municipal Bond ETF	CXA
SPDR Lehman High Yield Bond ETF	JNK
SPDR Lehman Intermediate Term Treasury ETF	ITE
SPDR Lehman International Treasury Bond	BWX
SPDR Lehman Long Term Treasury ETF	TLO
SPDR Lehman Municipal Bond	TFI
SPDR Lehman New York Municipal Bond ETF	INY
SPDR Lehman Short Term Municipal Bond ETF	SHM
SPDR MidCap Trust Series I	MDY
SPDR MS Technology	MTK
SPDR MSCI ACWI ex-US ETF	CWI
SPDR Russell/Nomura PRIME Japan ETF	JPP
SPDR Russell/Nomura Small Cap Japan	JSC
SPDR S&P 500	SPY
SPDR S&P Biotech ETF	XBI
SPDR S&P BRIC 40	BIK
SPDR S&P China ETF	GXC
SPDR S&P Dividend ETF	SDY
SPDR S&P Emerging Asia Pacific ETF	GMF
SPDR S&P Emerging Europe ETF	GUR

ETF	SYMBOL
SPDR S&P Emerging Latin America ETF	GML
SPDR S&P Emerging Markets ETF	GMM
SPDR S&P Emerging Markets Small Cap ETF	EWX
SPDR S&P International Consumer Discretionary Sector ETF	IPD
SPDR S&P International Consumer Staples Sector ETF	IPS
SPDR S&P International Dividend ETF	DWX
SPDR S&P International Energy Sector ETF	IPW
SPDR S&P International Financial Sector ETF	IPF
SPDR S&P International Health Care Sector ETF	IRY
SPDR S&P International Industrial Sector ETF	IPN
SPDR S&P International Materials Sector ETF	IRV
SPDR S&P International Mid Cap ETF	MDD
SPDR S&P International SmallCap ETF	GWX
SPDR S&P International Technology Sector ETF	IPK
SPDR S&P International Telecommunications Sector ETF	IST
SPDR S&P International Utilities Sector ETF	IPU
SPDR S&P Metals & Mining ETF	XME
SPDR S&P Middle East & Africa ETF	GAF
SPDR S&P Oil & Gas Equip & Service	XES
SPDR S&P Oil & Gas Explor & Product	XOP
SPDR S&P Pharmaceuticals ETF	XPH
SPDR S&P Retail ETF	XRT
SPDR S&P Semiconductor ETF	XSD
SPDR S&P World ex-US ETF	GWL
SPDR Select Sector Fund—Basic Industries	XLB
SPDR Select Sector Fund—Consumer Discretionary	XLY
SPDR Select Sector Fund—Consumer Staples	XLP
SPDR Select Sector Fund—Energy Select Sector	XLE
SPDR Select Sector Fund—Financial	XLF

ETF	SYMBOL
SPDR Select Sector Fund—Health Care	XLV
SPDR Select Sector Fund—Industrial	XLI
SPDR Select Sector Fund—Technology	XLK
SPDR Select Sector Fund—Utilities	XLU
UNITED STATES COMMODITY FUNDS	
United States 12 Month Oil	USL
United States Gasoline Fund LP	UGA
United States Heating Oil Fund LP	UHN
United States Natural Gas Fund LP	UNG
United States Oil Fund	USO
VANGUARD	
Vanguard Consumer Discretion ETF—DNQ	VCR
Vanguard Consumer Staples ETF—DNQ	VDC
Vanguard Div Appreciation ETF—DNQ	VIG
Vanguard Emerging Markets ETF	VWO
Vanguard Energy ETF	VDE
Vanguard Europe Pacific	VEA
Vanguard European ETF	VGK
Vanguard Extended Duration Treasury ETF	EDV
Vanguard Extended Market ETF—DNQ	VXF
Vanguard Financials ETF—DNQ	VFH
Vanguard FTSE All World Ex US ETF	VEU
Vanguard Growth ETF—DNQ	VUG
Vanguard Health Care ETF—DNQ	VHT
Vanguard High Dividend Yield ETF—DNQ	VYM
Vanguard Industrials ETF—DNQ	VIS
Vanguard Information Tech ETF—DNQ	VGT
Vanguard Intermediate-Term Bond ETF	BIV
Vanguard Large-Cap ETF—DNQ	VV

ETF	SYMBOL
Vanguard Long-Term Bond ETF	BLV
Vanguard Materials ETF—DNQ	VAW
Vanguard Mega Cap 300 ETF	MGC
Vanguard Mega Cap 300 Growth	MGK
Vanguard Mega Cap 300 Value	MGV
Vanguard Mid-Cap ETF—DNQ	VO
Vanguard Mid-Cap Growth ETF—DNQ	VOT
Vanguard Mid-Cap Value ETF—DNQ	VOE
Vanguard Pacific ETF	VPL
Vanguard REIT ETF—DNQ	VNQ
Vanguard Short-Term Bond ETF	BSV
Vanguard Small-Cap ETF—DNQ	VB
Vanguard Small-Cap Growth ETF—DNQ	VBK
Vanguard Small-Cap Value ETF—DNQ	VBR
Vanguard Telecom ETF—DNQ	VOX
Vanguard Total Bond Market ETF	BND
Vanguard Total Stock Market ETF—DNQ	VTI
Vanguard Utilities ETF—DNQ	VPU
Vanguard Value ETF—DNQ	VTV
WISDOMTREE	
WisdomTree DEFA Fund	DWM
WisdomTree DEFA High-Yielding Equity Fund	DTH
WisdomTree Dividend Top 100 Fund	DTN
WisdomTree Dreyfus Brazilian Real Fund	BZF
WisdomTree Dreyfus Chinese Yuan Fund	CYB
WisdomTree Dreyfus Emerging Currency Fund	CEW
WisdomTree Dreyfus Euro Fund	EU
WisdomTree Dreyfus Indian Rupee Fund	ICN
WisdomTree Dreyfus Japanese Yen Fund	JYF

ETF	SYMBOL
WisdomTree Dreyfus New Zealand Dollar Fund	BNZ
WisdomTree Dreyfus South African Rand Fund	SZR
WisdomTree Earnings 500 Fund	EPS
WisdomTree Earnings Top 100 Fund	EEZ
WisdomTree Emerging Market SmallCap Fund	DGS
WisdomTree Emerging Markets High-Yielding Fund	DEM
WisdomTree Europe High-Yielding Equity Fund	DEW
WisdomTree Europe SmallCap Dividend Fund	DFE
WisdomTree Europe Total Dividend Fund	DEB
WisdomTree High-Yielding Equity Fund	DHS
WisdomTree India Earnings Fund	EPI
WisdomTree International Basic Materials Sector Fund	DBN
WisdomTree International Communications Sector Fund	DGG
WisdomTree International Consumer Cyclical Sector Fund	DPC
WisdomTree International Consumer Non-Cyclical Sector Fund	DPN
WisdomTree International Dividend Top 100 Fund	DOO
WisdomTree International Energy Sector Funds	DKA
WisdomTree International Financial Sector Fund	DRF
WisdomTree International Health Care Sector Fund	DBR
WisdomTree International Industrial Sector Fund	DDI
WisdomTree International LargeCap Dividend Fund	DOL
WisdomTree International MidCap Dividend Fund	DIM
WisdomTree International Real Estate Fund	DRW
WisdomTree International SmallCap Fund	DLS
WisdomTree International Technology Sector Fund	DBT
WisdomTree International Utilities Sector Fund	DBU
WisdomTree Japan High-Yielding Equity Fund	DNL
WisdomTree Japan SmallCap Fund	DFJ
WisdomTree Japan Total Dividend Fund	DXJ

ETF	SYMBOL
WisdomTree LargeCap Dividend Fund	DLN
WisdomTree LargeCap Growth Fund	ROI
WisdomTree Low P/E Fund	EZY
WisdomTree MidCap Dividend Fund	DON
WisdomTree MidCap Earnings Fund	EZM
WisdomTree Middle East Dividend ETF	GULF
WisdomTree Pacific ex-Japan High-Yielding Equity Fund	DNH
WisdomTree Pacific ex-Japan Total Dividend Fund	DND
WisdomTree SmallCap Earnings Fund	EES
WisdomTree Total Dividend Fund	DTD
WisdomTree Total Earnings Fund	EXT
WisdomTree Trust SmallCap Dividend Fund	DES
WisdomTree U.S. Current Income Fund	USY
XSHARES	
AirShares EU Carbon Allowances Fund	ASO
XShares TDX Independence 2010 ETF	TDD
XShares TDX Independence 2020 ETF	TDH
XShares TDX Independence 2030 ETF	TDN
XShares TDX Independence 2040 ETF	TDV
XShares TDX Independence In-Target ETF	TDX

Glossary

% CHANGE—the percentage change of the last transaction from the previous closing price.

401(K)—a type of retirement savings plan set up by an employer that allows employees to set aside money for retirement on a pretax basis. Employers may match a percentage of the amount that employees defer into the plan. Contributions by both employees and employers, as well as investment earnings and interest, are not taxed until the funds are withdrawn. If the employee withdraws money before age 59½, he or she may be required to pay an early withdrawal penalty tax.

12B-1 FEES—These are fees that mutual funds charge to pay for distribution and marketing expenses. The fee is deducted from the fund's assets. The fee is charged periodically as a percentage of fund assets.

ACTIVE MANAGEMENT—a style of investing, usually pursued by a portfolio manager, in which securities are bought and sold in anticipation of changes in their value. Most active managers are charged with beating the performance of a specific index or benchmark on either an absolute or risk-adjusted basis.

ADMINISTRATOR—a firm that is responsible for assisting in reporting and communication with investors, retirement plan participants, or regulators.

AFTER-TAX RETURNS—the portion of investment return that remains after accounting for taxes. After-tax returns depend on the investor's personal tax bracket and therefore differ from investor to investor.

ALPHA—a manager's return relative to the return of a specified benchmark after adjusting for risk. If a mutual fund manager uses the S&P 500 Index as a benchmark, any returns that the manager generates above the index that are not explained by the fund's beta (volatility relative to the index) contribute to alpha. Note that alpha can be either positive, such as when the manager outperforms the index on a risk-adjusted basis, or negative, as when the manager underperforms.

ASSET ALLOCATION—the process of spreading an investment among various asset classes, such as stocks, bonds, and cash or cash equivalents, based on different levels of risk and a desire to diversify assets broadly across financial markets.

ASSET CLASS—investment categories that are used inside a portfolio. Bonds, U.S. stocks, real estate, precious metals, and cash are examples of widely used asset classes.

AUTHORIZED PARTICIPANT—an authorized participant is usually an institutional investor, specialist, or market maker who has signed a participant agreement with an ETF sponsor or distributor. Authorized participants are able to transact directly with the fund or trust on an in-kind basis to create or redeem ETF shares. If they want to create new ETF shares, they trade the underlying securities of an ETF to the sponsor and receive in return actual ETF shares. To redeem shares, they swap shares with the sponsor and receive a basket of individual securities that underlie the ETF.

AVERAGE DAILY VOLUME—the average number of ETF shares traded per day over any given period.

BASE POLICY MIX—the predetermined asset allocation of a strategically allocated fund. For instance, if a portfolio begins with an allocation that is invested 70 percent in stocks and 30 percent in bonds, that is the base policy mix.

BASIS POINT—a unit of measure equal to one one-hundredth of 1 percent, or .01 percent.

BEHAVIORAL FINANCE—an emerging field of study that is dedicated to understanding the psychology behind investor decisions and why the market moves in certain ways.

BENCHMARK—the target, often an index such as the S&P 500, which a fund manager is assigned to match or outperform.

BETA—the measure of an asset's volatility in relation to an index or investment. Beta measures systematic risk, a type of risk that cannot be eliminated by increasing diversification within the same asset class or universe.

BID/ASK RATIO—This is the ratio of the asking price of a security in relation to the bid price. At any given time the investor buys at the asking price and sells at the bid price, a transaction cost is generated equal to the spread between the two prices.

CAPITAL GAIN—When a capital asset is sold for a profit, the capital gain is the difference between the net sale price and the net cost (original basis). If an asset is sold below its cost, the difference is a capital loss.

CAPITAL GAINS DISTRIBUTION—distributions that are paid to mutual fund or ETF shareholders from the realized capital gains on the underlying securities. Capital gains distributions generally occur near the end of the calendar year or financial year, and they are taxable to fund shareholders.

CAPITAL GAINS TAX—the tax levied on profits from the sale of capital assets. Under current U.S. federal tax law, long-term capital gains are realized when an asset is held for at least twelve months. These are taxed differently from short-term capital gains, which are incurred on assets held for less than twelve months.

CAPITALIZATION-WEIGHTED INDEX—These are indexes that weigh according to their market cap, or the aggregate market value of all shares. In market cap–weighted ETFs the larger the market cap of a company is, the greater the weight its stock will have in the portfolio.

CLOSED-END FUNDS—registered investment companies that issue baskets of securities that can trade on an exchange. Closed-end funds issue a fixed number of shares. The shares of a closed-end fund often trade above or below the net asset value of its underlying securities.

COMMISSION—the fee paid to a broker to execute a trade, based on the number of shares, bonds, options, and/or their dollar value.

CONCENTRATION RISK—a measure of the level of diversification in an ETF. It uses the weights within the ETF of each constituent security as the basis for the measure. Concentration risk operates on the notion that the lower the weight of each constituent security and the more securities held, the greater diversification is. The general idea is that the more securities in an ETF portfolio the less exposure the investor has to unsystematic risk.

CORRELATION—a measurement of how two or more investments move in price or performance in relation to one another.

CORRELATION COEFFICIENT—the statistical measurement that is used to determine the correlation between investments or between an investment and an index. The correlation coefficient ranges from 1 to −1, with 1 being the highest possible correlation and −1 the lowest. If two investments have a correlation of 1, that means they are moving in lockstep. Investments with a correlation of −1 move in exactly the opposite direction.

COST BASIS—the original price of an asset; used to determine the asset's capital gain or loss at the time of sale.

CREATION UNITS—the smallest block of ETF shares that can be created or redeemed from the fund company. In equity ETFs, creation units usually consist of fifty thousand ETF shares. When authorized participants want to create ETF shares, they will exchange a portfolio of securities that underlie the ETF's holdings for ETF shares. Because of the creation units' large size, only market makers and institutions can afford to buy or sell them. All other investors can buy or sell ETF shares in any size lot at the market price on an exchange.

DIVERSIFICATION—the process of dividing assets between different investments with the goal of spreading risk.

DIVIDEND—a portion of a company's profit paid to common and preferred shareholders. A stock selling for ten dollars a share with an annual dividend of fifty cents a share is said to have a dividend yield of 5 percent.

DIVIDEND-WEIGHTED INDEX—an index that selects and weighs the securities in an index based on their dividend payouts. This is an alternative to the traditional market cap–weighting method.

DIVIDEND YIELD—the ratio of annual dividends paid by a stock, fund, or ETF divided by the current price.

DOLLAR COST AVERAGING—a method of purchasing securities by investing a fixed amount of money at set intervals. By purchasing more shares when the price is low and fewer shares when the price is high, a goal is to reduce average purchase cost over time.

DOW JONES INDUSTRIAL AVERAGE—one of the best-known U.S. indexes of stocks. It is a price-weighted average of thirty actively traded blue-chip stocks, widely considered to be a barometer of how shares of the largest U.S. companies and U.S. capital markets are performing.

EARNINGS-WEIGHTED INDEX—indexes that select and weigh stocks based on their earnings. This is one alternative to the traditional market cap–weighting method.

EARNINGS YIELD—a ratio of the annual earning of a stock or a fund's component stocks divided by the current price.

EXCHANGE-TRADED FUND—an investment product that combines features from both index funds and stocks. Like index funds, ETFs track indexes; however, like stocks, ETFs can be bought and sold through brokers and their shares are traded throughout the day on an exchange.

EXPENSE RATIO—a measure of a fund's expenses that is calculated by dividing management fees and expenses by average assets over a period of time. The expense ratio helps investors judge how effectively an ETF manager handles the operational issues of the underlying securities.

FIXED INCOME—one of the core asset classes. It includes assets that pay a fixed dollar amount, such as bonds.

FUND MANAGER—the person whose responsibility it is to oversee the allocation of a pool of money invested in a particular mutual fund. The fund manager is charged with investing the money in securities to achieve the best possible returns. The fund manager's goal is often to beat a stated benchmark. ETFs also have fund managers, but they usually are passive; i.e., they try to track a given index.

FUTURES CONTRACT—an agreement that allows investors to buy or sell a quantity of assets on a future date at a set price. Futures contracts often are used in commodities trading.

GLIDE PATH—the predetermined path that target-date funds follow, which dictates when and how they should change their asset allocation over time.

GOING SHORT—selling stock or ETF shares that an investor does not own by borrowing shares from a broker, under the assumption that the price will fall and shares then can be bought back cheaper, thus creating a trading profit. If the price of the security that's been sold short increases, the investor may at some point suffer a loss when that short is covered.

GROWTH STOCKS—stocks that have generally exhibited faster than average gains in earnings over several years.

HEDGE FUND—a fund that uses sophisticated investment strategies in the hope of generating high returns. Hedge funds generally require very high minimum investments and are only available to a limited number of investors.

INCEPTION DATE—the first day of trading for a mutual fund or ETF.

INDEX MUTUAL FUND—a passively managed mutual fund that invests only in the securities of a particular index in the exact ratio in which they occur in that index.

INDEXING—a passive investing strategy in which a portfolio of stocks is created to track the total return performance of an index of stocks.

INDIVIDUAL RETIREMENT ACCOUNT (IRA)—a tax-deferred account that allows annual contributions for each participant.

INTERNATIONAL DIVERSIFICATION—a strategy that attempts to reduce risk by investing in the securities of more than one country.

LARGE CAP—companies with large market capitalizations, generally greater than $10 billion.

LEGAL STRUCTURE—the way that an ETF is set up. There are three primary structures: unit investment trusts, open-end funds, and grantor trusts.

LEHMAN BROTHERS AGGREGATE BOND INDEX—a broad-based fixed income index that is composed of government, corporate mortgage-backed bonds, and asset-backed securities that are of investment-grade quality or better, have at least one year to maturity, and have an outstanding par value of at least $100 million.

LIMIT ORDER—an order to buy or sell a stated amount of a security at or better than a specified price.

LIQUID MARKET—a market that allows for the buying or selling of large quantities of an asset at any time and at low transaction costs.

LONG-TERM CAPITAL GAIN—a profit on the sale of a security or mutual fund share that has been held for more than one year.

MANAGEMENT FEES—In mutual funds and ETFs, this term refers to the money that an investment adviser charges investors for managing and administering a fund.

MARKET CAP—a public company's share price multiplied by the total number of shares outstanding.

MARKET CAP CLASSIFICATION—usually defined as microcap, small cap, midcap, large cap, and megacap securities. The boundaries are not standardized because market participants often define them differently.

MARKET IMPACT—a measure of the price impact of executing a hypothetical trade of fifty thousand ETF shares. Market impact serves as a proxy for how efficient it is to trade in and out of an ETF.

MARKET ORDER—an order to buy or sell a stated amount of a security at the most advantageous price obtainable immediately after the order is entered.

MATURITY—the average date at which bonds or other debt-related securities in an ETF make final payments.

MORGAN STANLEY CAPITAL INTERNATIONAL (MSCI) EMERGING MARKETS INDEX—a broad gauge of emerging markets that tracks twenty-six emerging market countries.

MORGAN STANLEY CAPITAL INTERNATIONAL EUROPE, AUSTRALASIA, AND FAR EAST (MSCI EAFE) INDEX—a broad gauge of the international equities market as it tracks stocks from European, Australasian, and Far Eastern markets.

MUTUAL FUND—pools of money that are managed by an investment adviser through an investment company structure.

NET ASSET VALUE—a calculation of a fund's value per share that subtracts liabilities from the total assets of the fund and then divides by the number of shares outstanding.

NET YIELD—the rate of return on a security minus purchase costs, commissions, or markups.

OPEN-END FUNDS—an investment structure used by mutual funds and some ETFs and authorized under the Securities and Exchange Commission Investment Company Act of 1940 ("the 40 Act").

PAPER GAIN (OR LOSS)—unrealized capital gains (or losses) on securities held in a portfolio based on a comparison of current market price to original cost.

PASSIVE MANAGEMENT—an investment style designed to mirror a benchmark's price or performance over time.

PLAN SPONSORS—the entities that establish pension plans, including private business entities acting on behalf of their employees; state and local entities operating on behalf of their employees; unions acting on behalf of their members; and individuals representing themselves.

PORTFOLIO DIVERSIFICATION—investing in different asset classes and in securities of many issuers in an attempt to reduce overall risk and to avoid damaging a portfolio's performance by the poor performance of a single security, industry, or country.

PORTFOLIO TRANSACTION COSTS—the expenses associated with buying and selling securities for a fund, including commissions, purchase and redemption fees, exchange fees, and other miscellaneous costs.

PORTFOLIO TURNOVER RATE—a ratio used by mutual funds and ETFs to measure trading activity. It is calculated as the total of all annual purchases or all annual sales divided by the average of portfolio assets. Higher turnover rates often are associated with higher management fees and expenses and possibly higher tax costs.

PRICE-TO-BOOK RATIO—a measure of valuation in a stock. Book value is the net worth of a company or its total assets.

PRICE-TO-EARNINGS RATIO—a common measure of valuation for stocks. For ETFs, the P/E is the weighted average P/E ratio of the stocks in the portfolio.

PRICE-WEIGHTED INDEX—an index that assigns a greater weight to higher-priced stocks by weighting all components based on their trading price.

PRIMARY EXCHANGE—the main exchange on which an ETF is listed.

PRIVATE EQUITY—an investment in a company or entity that is not public, meaning that it does not trade on a major stock exchange.

PROSPECTUS—a written disclosure document that is required to sell public, containing the essential facts that an investor needs to make an informed decision. Prospectuses are used by mutual funds and ETFs to describe fund objectives, risks, and other essential information.

QUALIFIED RETIREMENT PLAN—a retirement plan established by employers for their employees.

REALIZED PROFIT (LOSS)—a capital gain or loss on securities held in a portfolio, generated upon the sale of those securities.

REDEEM—to exchange fund shares for their monetary value in either cash or in-kind securities.

REINVESTMENT—use of investment income to buy additional securities. Many mutual funds and some ETFs offer the option of automatically reinvesting dividends and capital gains distributions.

REIT—Real Estate Investment Trust. REITs are companies, many of which are publicly traded, that invest in and operate various types of real estate or real estate–related assets such as apartments, office buildings, shopping centers, etc. REITs are a form of regulated investment company.

RETURN—the change in the value of a portfolio over a defined period divided by either the average or ending price.

RISK-AVERSE—a description of an investor who, when faced with alternative investments with the same expected return but different degrees of risk, generally prefers the one with the lower risk.

RISK-BASED FUNDS—funds that are divided among asset classes based on different levels of risk.

RISK TOLERANCE—an investor's ability or willingness to accept declines in the prices of investments while waiting for them to increase in value.

RUSSELL 1000 INDEX—an index that measures the performance of one thousand of the largest companies in the Russell 3000 Index, representing approximately 92 percent of the total market capitalization of the Russell 3000 Index.

RUSSELL 2000 INDEX—an index that measures the performance of two thousand of the smallest companies in the Russell 3000 Index, representing approximately 8 percent of the total market capitalization of the Russell 3000 Index.

RUSSELL 3000 INDEX—an index that measures the performance of three thousand publicly held U.S. companies based on total market capitalization, which represents approximately 98 percent of the investable U.S. market.

S&P 500 INDEX—Widely regarded as the standard for measuring large cap U.S. stock market performance, this popular index includes a representative sample of leading companies in leading industries. More than $750 billion of assets are indexed to the S&P 500.

S&P MID-CAP 400 INDEX—an index that measures the performance of the midsize company segment of the U.S. market. More than $25 billion is indexed to the S&P Mid-Cap 400.

SALES CHARGE—the fee charged by a mutual fund when shares are purchased, usually payable as a commission to a marketing agent, such as a financial adviser.

SECTOR ALLOCATION—a strategy for diversifying an investment among particular sectors of an economy, such as technology, utilities, consumer staples, health care, etc. Broad market index ETFs are diversified across industries, while sector ETFs concentrate on particular industries.

SEPARATELY MANAGED ACCOUNT (SMA)—an individual investment portfolio that is professionally managed, often to meet the customized needs of the investor. While mutual funds and ETFs aim broadly to reach many types of investors, SMAs generally target only the high net worth investors. Often the minimum investment required in an SMA is above fifty thousand dollars.

SHORT SALE—the practice of selling a security one does not currently own in the hope that it will decline in price. In order for an investor to sell a security short, he or she must have the ability to borrow it to make delivery to the buyer. When an investor purchases that security in order to close out that short position, that position is said to be covered.

STANDARD AND POOR'S DEPOSITARY RECEIPT ETF (SPDR)—This was the first ETF to be launched in 1993, and it remains a broad-based ETF that tracks the five hundred securities in the S&P 500.

STANDARD DEVIATION—a statistical measurement used to gauge the volatility of an asset or a portfolio. Standard deviation is considered a standard measure of investment risk.

STRATEGIC ASSET ALLOCATION—the process of dividing assets between asset classes and investments in order to create a portfolio that will deliver the best returns for a given level of risk.

TACTICAL ASSET ALLOCATION—a technique that is applied to a strategically allocated portfolio. It works by shifting around the weights of certain assets when opportunities in the market arise in order to enhance the returns of the portfolio.

TARGET-DATE FUNDS—funds in which the asset allocation changes over time to become more conservative. Target-date funds often are based on a date by which the investor expects to retire. As the target date approaches, the portfolio adjusts its asset allocation to become more conservative. The predetermined path that target-date funds follow, which dictates when and how the asset allocation changes, is known as the glide path.

TAX-LOSS HARVESTING—a way to minimize tax liability on investments at the end of the year by selling securities with embedded losses in order to reduce taxable income.

TRACKING ERROR—a measure of how closely each ETF tracks the performance of its stated benchmark. It is measured by taking the standard deviation of the daily total return difference between the ETF and the corresponding benchmark. Tracking error can be used to quantify how well an ETF manager is matching the benchmark. The lower the tracking error, the better the ETF manager is replicating the stated benchmark.

TRANSACTION FEE—a charge an intermediary, such as a broker-dealer or a bank, assesses for assisting in the sale or purchase of a security. These include commissions, markups, and markdowns.

TURNOVER RATE—a measure of a fund's trading activity during a particular period. Portfolios with high turnover rates incur higher transaction costs and are more likely to distribute capital gains, which are taxable in nonretirement accounts.

UNDERLYING INDEX—the stated benchmark of a given ETF. The ETF will try to match the performance of its underlying benchmark.

UNIT INVESTMENT TRUSTS (UIT)—one type of ETF structure. ETFs structured as UITs must fully replicate their benchmark indexes. Dividends may not be reinvested in funds with this legal structure, and lending of securities is not allowed.

VALUE STOCKS—stocks that represent good value in relation to their earnings or assets or have above-average dividend payouts.

VENTURE CAPITAL—an industry that invests in small start-up companies with future growth potential. Usually their investments provide capital to help the business run in the early stages, until they are able to develop revenues and growth momentum.

VOLATILITY—the degree of changes in price or performance in a security or fund. Volatility is often considered to be a measure of risk.

VOLUME—the number of shares traded in a given period.

WEIGHTING—the scheme used to weigh the constituent securities in an index or ETF. Common weighting schemes include market cap–weighted, equally weighted, and fundamentally weighted.

YIELD—the percentage return paid on a stock in the form of dividends, or the effective rate of interest paid on a bond or note.

YIELD TO MATURITY—a metric applied only to fixed income ETFs. The weighted yield to maturity provides an indication of an ETF's ability to generate income.

Disclosure

This book is designed to provide accurate and authoritative information concerning its subject matter, including exchange-traded funds, sometimes called "ETFs." The author is not providing legal, accounting, or other professional services. The principles discussed in this book do not constitute personalized investment advice. If legal advice or other expert assistance is required, the services of an appropriate professional adviser should be sought.

While the author feels that the investment information and strategies presented in this book are sound, and have been utilized by people and entities in the past, they are not guaranteed to produce particular results in the future. The author discusses a number of ETFs in this book, but a reference to an ETF is not to be treated as a recommendation for the purchase or sale of any particular ETF mentioned, and the reader should not assume that other investment companies that are not mentioned in the book are viewed either more or less favorably than the companies mentioned. In addition, the policies, practices, and portfolios of investment companies, including ETFs mentioned in this book, can change over time, so the reader should focus on the principles discussed in this book, not the specific funds mentioned.

The information provided in this book may contain for illustrative purposes some performance information regarding ETFs mentioned in this book. Given the changing nature of the portfolios of ETFs, there can be no assurance that such information remains accurate other than for historical purposes.

Index